CREATIVITY AT WORK

Creativity at Work

Tudor Rickards

Gower

© Tudor Rickards 1988

All rights reserved. No part of this publication may be reproduced, stored in a retrieval system, or transmitted in any form or by any means, electronic, mechanical, photocopying, recording, or otherwise without the prior permission of Gower Publishing Company Limited.

Published by
Gower Publishing Company Limited,
Gower House,
Croft Road,
Aldershot
Hants GU11 3HR,
England

Gower Publishing Company,
Old Post Road,
Brookfield,
Vermont 05036
U.S.A.

British Library Cataloguing in Publication Data

Rickards, Tudor
   Creativity at work.
   1. Management   2. Problem solving
   I. Title
   658.4'03   HD38

ISBN 0 566 02756 9

Contents

Preface vii
Acknowledgements xi
Introduction 1

PART I THE NATURE OF CREATIVE ANALYSIS

1 What we know about creativity 9
2 Opening up your options creatively 24
3 Dealing with too many options 43
4 How to remain creative 58

PART II PROCESS AND PROCEDURE

5 Blockbusting 73
6 Brainstorming and its relations 91
7 Frameworks for thinking 115
8 Implementation 127

PART III CREATIVITY IN ACTION

9	A tale of two projects	147
10	In search of diversification	159
11	The Magnolite story	166
12	Introducing new technology	179
13	Changing corporate culture	192
14	Some long-term applications	202

Appendix: Computer-aided creativity　219

Glossary　223

Recommended reading　231

Index　235

Preface

The term 'creative analysis' was coined some years ago by an American Professor of English. He wanted to encourage students to dig more deeply and imaginatively into the meanings of a given piece of English literature. For whatever reason, the term fell into misuse. So much so that I re-invented the phrase, in ignorance of its provenance, for the direct ancestor of this book, *Problem Solving through Creative Analysis*. History repeated itself, as the phrase again demonstrated its instant forgetability. Fellow academics did not so much attack it as ignore it, and that during a period when creativity and techniques such as brainstorming and lateral thinking were gaining popular attention.

Nevertheless I thought, and still think, that the phrase 'creative analysis' captures an important relationship between two aspects of human behaviour often assumed to be alternatives, or opposite modes of thinking. Both, however, are needed if we are to deepen understanding of our creative experiences in order to maintain and develop even greater creative abilities.

The point is this: creative behaviour (leaving definitions aside for the moment) is always a once-and-for-all event. The act of creation has its own built-in seeds of destruction, because it is required to reveal some freshness and originality in the stated product. It follows that exact procedures cannot be 'routinized'. After all, the scientist who makes a breakthrough will not be able to spend the rest of his/her life going through the same experiments and reaching the same conclusions. Nor can a poet rewrite the same sonnet.

To retain freshness, we have to analyse our creative impulses. Hence 'creative analysis'. I can find no better way of describing how it is possible to use a technique for stimulating creativity, and yet retain flexibility as we become increasingly familiar with the steps of the technique.

Creativity can be accidental, capricious, unexpected. But after the event we can review, analyse and prepare ourselves the better for more deliberate attempts to stimulate the creative process. In *Problem Solving through Creative Analysis* I explained the process as one in which a creativity technique with various 'subroutines' could be used in one context, and then analysed. As a consequence, the 'creative analyst' can consciously think about possible changes in the subroutines.

Recent research into human information processing has suggested that we act as if we acquire a small number of mental strategies or formulae which we call up and press into service to deal with everyday situations. Although the strategies are more or less fixed, they can be influenced through experience. This is an analogous concept to creative analysis, which involves examination of our own creative 'strategies', thus discovering ways of improving them through deliberate introduction of procedures and structures. If we believe that we are all creative and can develop our potential further through personal efforts, it follows that human beings of all kinds could benefit from a course in creative analysis. As a pragmatist, I decided to write a book that would reach rather smaller segments of the planet's inhabitants: organizational consultants (especially process consultants and change agents), researchers, trainers, and professionals with responsibilities for assisting and directing change throughout organizations of all kinds. Students of business and other social studies will also find relevant material on how individuals and systems resist change, and how the resistances can be overcome. It would be valuable for top managers, too, if they would only read it. I have rather despaired of the reading habits of top managers, who are usually too busy being top to have time to study material that has not been predigested. So in many cases it will be up to the rest of the readership to pass on the messages to the required Olympian heights.

WHY AN UPDATE?

Several aspects of human problem-solving have become clearer in the fifteen years since *PSTCA* was written. Very importantly, more has become known about the nature of consciousness. Although controversial, the 'left brain/right brain' distinction has been assimilated into popular understanding. Writing in 1973 I followed the 'scientific' traditions of emphasizing the more logical components of problem-solving. The essential 'right-brain' component of the creative act was played down to the extent that it was virtually non-existent. The update has more of a 'whole-brain' flavour. Secondly, there is no longer any need to catalogue all the so-called creativity techniques, with blow-by-blow details of operating mechanisms. Instead I have concentrated on fewer techniques, and given more explanation of their practical uses, and technical rationale (i.e. the what, how, and why), although I followed the advice of readers of *PSTCA* and avoided the academic inclination to equip every idea with footnotes and biographical references. This makes the whole book thoroughly unreliable and unrespectable academically, a health warning I trust all readers will note.

The case examples described in *Problem Solving through Creative Analysis* still read quite well, but more recent examples have largely replaced them. Finally, the human side of problem-solving has been made more explicit. People cause problems; people solve problems. Techniques are as useful as their users are prepared to make them.

During the rewriting of the original book the line between a new edition and a new work was crossed. The core idea of creative analysis remains, but in emphasis, style, and content the differences are so great that they suggested the need for a new title more in keeping with the changed product. In 1973 I was a closet believer in creativity and creativity techniques. Although suspicions of the concept, and even of the word creativity, are still strong among the forces of orthodoxy, it is time for me to come out of the closet and make that belief explicit. This book is about the workings of creativity, and about deliberate attempts to stimulate the process in work contexts. It is about creativity at work. That is how it got its name.

Acknowledgements

In previous books I went to great pains to acknowledge all those people I did not want to offend: especially the great and the good. This is known as the Matthew effect (to them that hath shall it be given . . .). Here I would like to take as read the debt we all owe to the founding fathers of creative problem-solving. Finally my thanks to friends and colleagues at Tudor Rickards and Associates Ltd for technical and moral support, and to Dr Scott Isaksen and the department of Studies in Creativity, State University of New York, Buffalo for making my visits in 1977–8 so enjoyable and educational.

Furthermore, I supplied earlier drafts to students taking a creative problem-solving option at Manchester Business School. Their fearless criticisms of the weaknesses of the work were as valuable as their more constructive and positive suggestions. Shuichi and Jean-Pascal helped in the removal of the most idiomatic expressions. Warren and Rob cut my paragraphs down to size, and made several important suggestions that improved the structuring of the material. And Clare helped both by providing creative suggestions and by pointing out the examples that were going out of date at about the time some readers of the finished work were being born.

Tudor Rickards

Introduction

A trainer I know used to teach creative problem-solving techniques to industrial managers. He would often be halfway through an introduction to some set of procedures for carrying out a technique when one of his trainees would interrupt with a question which required more experience of later aspects of the course before it could be answered in a helpful way. The trainer liked to make an analogy with someone about to play a game of golf for the first time standing nervously on the first tee. He or she begins to quiz the instructor about problems that might crop up during the round. The golf tyro would be better off delaying most of the questions at least until they have taken a walk around the golf course. The creative problem-solving trainer went on to suggest that his training course was a bit like learning how to play golf. 'Let's walk around this course', he would say, 'before we get ourselves stuck on the first tee worrying about all sorts of traps and bunkers'.

That was good advice, although rather hard to take when you are beset with doubts about what is shortly going to happen to you. The advice is valid for golfers taking on their first full round, and it is valid for readers of a book offering a new challenge to master. The introduction gives you a chance to take a quick walk around the creative analysis golf course, familiarizing yourself in broad outline with its fourteen 'holes', or chapters.

The book is divided into three parts.

Part I (chapters 1 to 4) deals with basic concepts needed to improve understanding of creativity and how the process might be influenced. In golfing terms we are offered awareness of what it takes to become a good golf player, and why.

Part II (chapters 5 to 8) describes the various families of creative problem-solving techniques. To continue our golfing analogy, these holes are where we learn the use of the different clubs, where to use them and what to do in different situations.

Part III (chapters 9 to 14) focuses on creativity at work – examples of creative problem-solving in organizational settings. These chapters might be likened to learning golf vicariously by watching how other golfers, some more professional than others, have dealt with typical challenges they have encountered in their playing careers.

The specific 'holes' that you play in Part One are as follows: Chapter 1 looks at creativity as a universal human capacity for escaping mental habits or mind sets. We all find ourselves in mental bunkers from time to time, hacking away helplessly. Fortunately we usually escape, by rediscovering an old approach, or more rarely as a result of improving our technique by discovering a new way out of the sand traps.

Chapters 2 and 3 deal with two complementary aspects of creative behaviour – the processes of opening up and closing down your options in problem-solving. A range of simple but effective ways of opening up thinking are illustrated in Chapter 2, based on reducing evaluation during the search stage, or through deliberately structuring the problem-solving process to make the opening up and closing down stages more obvious. Chapter 3 presents assorted methods of 'closing down', particularly as this applies to innovative search and decision-making.

Chapter 4 goes into the notion of creative analysis in more detail. It is of greatest importance to readers who wish to understand the process of creative problem-solving better and would like to design approaches for enhancing their own performance and those of teams with which they are involved. It offers a way of reviewing creative performance by studying the operational steps and their theoretical justifications. The creative analysis chapter ends Part I of the book.

Part II begins with Chapter 5, which covers the various 'blockbusting techniques' for triggering individual creativity, including the best known, attributed to Edward de Bono through his elegant writings on lateral thinking.

Chapter 6 briefly covers the enormous body of knowledge on brainstorming and related approaches. This much maligned technique has spawned many others, and we trace the family tree, from Osborn's simple idea for reducing the effect of status on group meetings through deferring judgement, to later variants.

Chapter 7 outlines some methods of structuring complicated systems as a first stage towards understanding and insights. The approaches can be seen as conceptual models for triggering new ideas. They are frequently mentioned as a family of creativity aids, and it has been necessary to be selective, concentrating on those techniques for which there is evidence of widespread and satisfactory applications for creativity at work.

In Chapter 8, the last concentrating on methods, we come to implementation, which is another subject of great practical and theoretical interest. Very recent work is presented here which suggests that implementation is difficult because most people persist in approaches that are over-influenced by a dominant implementation strategy or mind set. Even when the mind set is broken, we may fail to consider sufficiently widely the available strategies, and resort to a favoured fallback strategy.

The implementation chapter concludes the section on procedures and processes for stimulating creativity at work, and the final section of the book, Chapters 9–14, contains practical illustrations of creative problem-solving reported from a range of organizational experiences. For every attempt to stimulate innovation which produces a significant innovation there will be thousands of attempts that give lesser results. For reasons outlined in the text we are more concerned with descriptions which reflect good industrial practice than with the very few available examples of creativity at work out of which significant innovations are claimed to have arisen. Readers are urged to study the mechanics of sessions which ended less conclusively, as these can often provide instruction for what to copy, and what to avoid.

Chapter 9 is a bridge between the case examples in my earlier *Problem-solving though Creative Analysis* and more recent work. It concentrates on the mechanics of operating creative problem-solving techniques within an industrial new products group, comparing an engineering problem with a consumer-oriented one.

Chapter 10 describes another structuring technique in practice, mind-mapping. Through its use a management team was able to devise a diversification strategy for its company.

Chapter 11 covers work with a small engineering company about to start a new products search. It illustrates typical applications of creative problem-solving – initial planning, climate setting, techniques for opening up and closing down . . . . At the end of the case some promising ideas had been discovered in a cost-effective manner.

Chapter 12 outlines the introduction of new technology backed by regular creative problem-solving sessions. The case shows how, in the management of technology, the biggest problems may prove to be human rather than technical.

Chapter 13 deals with a chemicals company which had set up an unsuccessful new ventures team. A programme of creativity training and developmental problem-solving was established. Considerable organizational and technological gains have been attributed to this programme. As so often happens, the 'real' issues emerged well into the programme, when the managers began to think of their problems in new ways. An implementation model was explicitly used to guide the company to more effective and realizable strategies for change.

Chapter 14 looks at more ambitious programmes designed to help organizational innovation and change. Updates are given of three important European initiatives. Each of these has a well documented track record of success amounting to hundreds of new products worth tens of millions of pounds, as well as successes in implementation.

GETTING THE BEST OUT OF THE BOOK

Learning, whether we retain our golf analogy or whether we are concerned with creativity at work, goes beyond acquiring facts and information. The most important and personalized learning can be blocked by our own beliefs and assumptions. These blocks are partly unconscious, and therefore have to be tackled in ways that are not always straightforward.

The broad themes of getting started, what techniques to use, and illustrations through case studies, are presented as the factual information which can be studied in a conventional way – that is, starting with Chapter 1 and progressing through the chapters at your own pace. Anyone prepared to follow this path would acquire a lot of knowledge in what is described in the book as a left brain way (a logical, step-by-step approach).

Sometimes a point on the journey offers you the opportunity to explore a byway for a while before returning to the main path. These excursions have been separated from the main text, so that they can be studied, or not, according to the interests of the reader. Some of them go into more detail than is strictly needed on a first pass. Others offer various diversions – puzzles to practise your problem-solving skills on, even stories which, like the best folk-tales, can offer considerable food for thought.

As a general principle, the main text contains messages which I believe to be important, and which I have tried to communicate in

The golf course

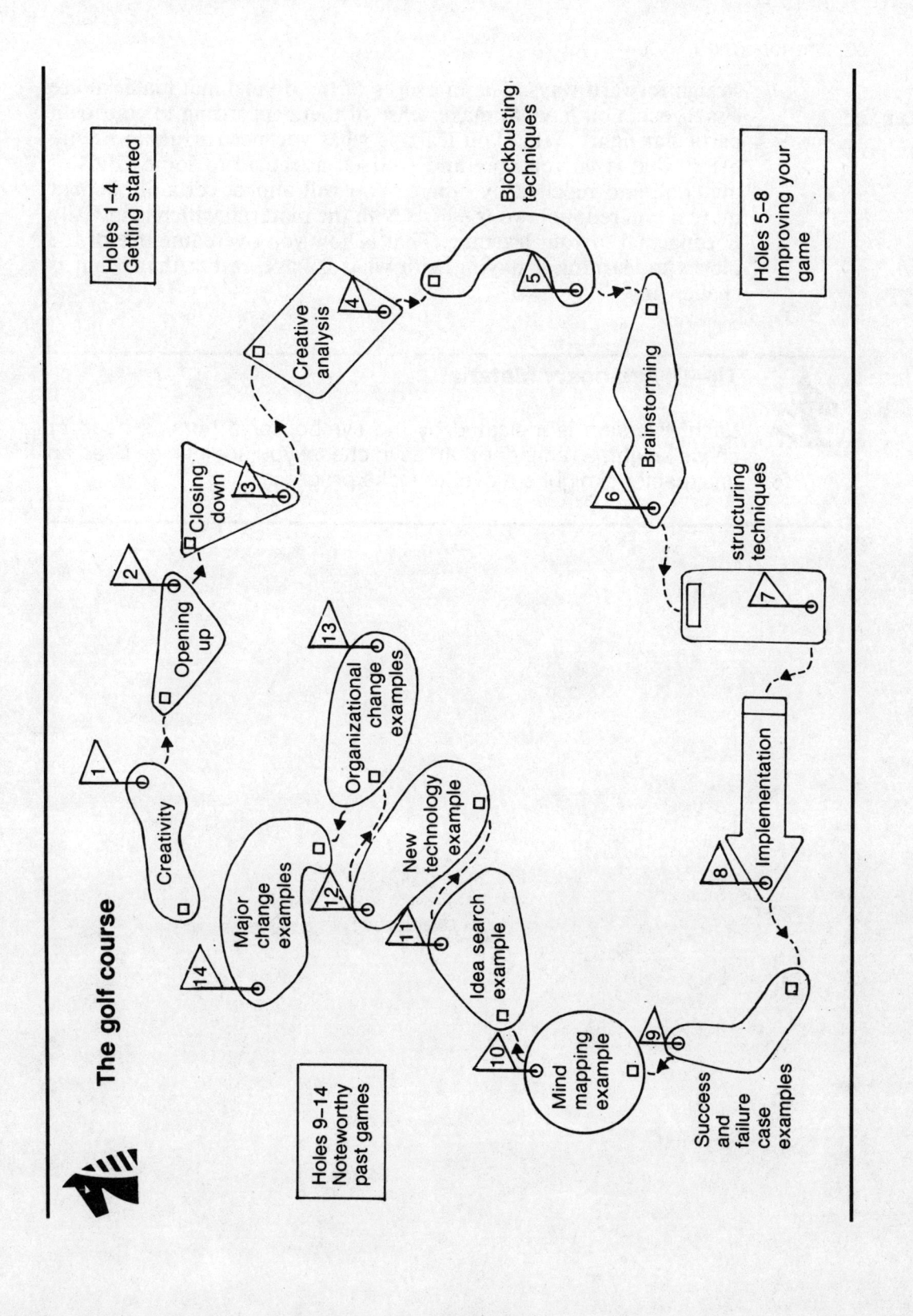

Holes 1–4 Getting started

1. Creativity
2. Opening up
3. Closing down
4. Creative analysis

Holes 5–8 Improving your game

5. Blockbusting techniques
6. Brainstorming
7. structuring techniques
8. Implementation

Holes 9–14 Noteworthy past games

9. Success and failure case examples
10. Mind mapping example
11. Idea search example
12. New technology example
13. Organizational change examples
14. Major change examples

straightforward ways. The messages of the diversional material are less direct. You have to make sense of them according to your own particular lights. What you learn is what you need. Human nature being what it is, you may find yourself attracted to some kinds of material, and repelled by others. You will almost certainly benefit more if you redouble your efforts with the material which is initially uncongenial to your learning. That is how you overcome one of the blocks to learning – staying with what is easy, rather than what is challenging.

The Diversionary Material

Each diversion is indicated by the symbol for a horse's head or chess knight, a reminder that, as in chess, you sometimes need an unexpected 'knight's move' to make progress.

Part I
THE NATURE OF CREATIVE ANALYSIS

"RIGHT! ANYONE GOT A NEW IDEA WE CAN BOUNCE AROUND?"

1 What we know about creativity

What do we mean when we say someone is being creative? Here is a little exercise I have tried out on hundreds of people attending courses on creative problem-solving, which will give us a starting point to answering the question.

> Try to build up a mental picture of someone actually creating something... What did you see? My guess is that you thought of an inventor dreaming up a new product, or a painter being inspired to produce a work of art, or maybe a scriptwriter coming up with ideas for a television show. If you did you would be in good company, for these are the commonest responses. It turns out that most people who carry out this experiment reveal a view of creativity as a special mental process carried out by rather special people to produce important new products in the arts and sciences. For whatever reason we equate creativity with the highest form of achievement in such fields.

It is significant that very few people imagine themselves as the people doing the creating. This is a pity, because creativity is a gift which we all possess, and which can be developed by appropriate training and application. If this seems contrary to our everyday observations, it is because we have fallen into a definition trap. Once we define creativity as 'something which special people do', it follows that whatever the something is, we shall not find examples in everyday life.

Many studies have been made of the creative behaviour of musicians, great scientists, architects, poets and painters. It turns out that the creative process is the same regardless of the field of excellence, which is surprising in itself. Even more surprising results emerge when 'ordinary' people are studied, because the process is essentially the same, whether the creativity is concerned with day-to-day problem-solving, or highly specialized scientific discovery.

For many years the process has been described as four stages:

> preparation
> incubation
> insight
> validation.

In the preparation stage a conscious attempt is made to understand and deal with some personal need. This is rarely sufficient to resolve the need, and a fallow period follows. This is the time when we may sleep on a problem, or leave it for some other task – the second or incubation stage. Then, in a moment of enlightenment or insight, we break through to a new understanding. Finally, the discovery seems to give us the energy to realize our creative idea – the validation or implementation stage.

CREATIVITY IN EVERYDAY LIFE

Although the four stages have been recognized in the titanic struggles of great creative geniuses to produce their works of art or creative breakthroughs, the process is not confined to the gifted few. We all have our little triumphs of imagination after a period when some problem seemed impossible to solve.

For example, it may be all-important to find a way into your house after you have mislaid your door key. Discovering how to break in using a garden cane and a discarded coathanger may produce all the exhilaration of a 'eureka moment'. The process can be classed a creative problem-solving one. In a thousand everyday situations such as this we have responded creatively.

When considering this very practical form of creativity we see that it entails escaping from assumptions and beliefs which block us from seeing a solution that with hindsight might appear obvious. That is to say, we move from old habits of thought to new ones. As with physical habits, mental habits may be hard to shift.

We all have our little triumphs of imagination after a period when some problem seemed impossible to solve.

The more we become immersed in a subject, the more likely we are to form mental filters about what is true, and what is possible. So, during the preparation stage of problem solving, we may simply be unable to see the possible solution. What seems to happen in the incubation stage is a relaxation of these mental filters which permits the new understanding or insight.

CREATIVITY AND PROBLEM-SOLVING

Creativity is often linked with problem-solving. Problems come in all shapes and sizes including crossword puzzles, scientific paradoxes, industrial relations conflicts, ethical issues, difficult managerial decisions, and global questions such as Third World famine. In this book we take the view that problems are what people have when they want something and don't know how to get it. A distinction can be made between 'close-ended' and 'open-ended' problems. Close-ended problems have answers that are the logical consequences of the nature of the problem 'givens'. Open-ended problems do not have correct answers, because for example, they are not precisely enough defined, or because there is disagreement about the nature of the problem, with different people seeing it in different ways.

There is more scope for creativity in open-ended problems, although, as a scientist or a chess player will confirm, their problem-solving, a kind of intellectual detective process, involves the processes associated with creativity, including periods where they feel stuck, the transcending of habitual thought, and the emotional pleasure at the moment of insight. Indeed, although problems come in various forms, all offer scope for new insights, and therefore for creativity.

1 One right answer problems

The classic problems of our school days: many people continue to assume that all problems have a right answer. Such a belief will block off many opportunities for creativity, and is all too often quite wrong. Problems with one correct answer are rarer than most people imagine, as they have to be quite unambiguously defined and stable over time.

However, we must not forget that when we discover the answer to a crossword puzzle or a chess problem we are being creative – even if hundreds of people have had their own moments of discovery before us.

2 Insight problems, or 'aha' problems

These problems turn out to have unexpected answers which are sometimes discovered through the classic ('eureka') moment of insight. The result may be a new perspective on the nature of the problem and the assumptions we have been making.

This phenomenon occurs regularly in business – e.g. in finding a competitive response, or a marketing strategy, or when a problem is suddenly seen as an opportunity. Insight puzzles may not have a demonstrably correct answer. Instead, they may have various possible solutions, of which one has something special which appeals to people (sometimes called an elegant solution). Insight problems are solved once the elegant solution has been discovered, and usually do not require great efforts to persuade other people to accept the new idea. They have a creative logic about them. These problems are often found on creative thinking courses, as they reflect the stages of creative struggle and discovery.

3 Wicked problems

These problems are ones for which the potential solution cannot be proved until the problem has been tackled. The test of the solution is in its execution ('I think this rope bridge will bear our weight, Colonel; are you ready to go?'). Complex social engineering problems which cannot be tested in pilot schemes are of this kind. Most organizational restructuring schemes and business acquisitions fall into this category. Engaging in action requires courage, creativity as intuition, and follow up creativity to solve the unexpected happenings as the solution is implemented. Those people who need logical proof before acting may avoid wicked problem-solving, but will never achieve significant innovation (which always has an element of potentially wicked problem-solving about it).

4 Vicious problems

These are a bit like wicked problems. Here the problems involve people, and they may appear to have obvious answers. However, when conventional remedies are applied they turn out to produce solutions which in turn create even bigger problems than the ones that were there originally. Numerous and varied business problems turn vicious, especially in industrial relations and other situations where there is scope for 'lose–lose' behaviours. The opportunity for creativity is great, particularly in avoiding premature actions before looking beyond the obvious for solutions with potentially less vicious consequences.

5 Fuzzy problems

This term has become popular with the growing importance of and interest in computer-aided problem-solving. Fuzzy problems have very unclear boundaries which makes them difficult to resolve using logical analytical approaches, but well suited to attack by creative problem-solving. Wicked and vicious problems are also examples of fuzzy problems, as are most other non-trivial difficulties we encounter in our work and personal lives.

All these kinds of problem, and more besides, require creative thinking. Sometimes the problem itself is a block, sometimes the block arises from the attitude of the solver . . . .

'WHOLE-BRAIN' THINKING

Over the last few years creativity has sometimes been likened to 'right-brain' thinking. This is an example of a confused interpretation of results about the brain. The very complicated story of how the brain works is far from fully understood. We know that the last part of the brain to evolve was the neo-cortex, the convoluted mass of cells where the most recent thinking and reasoning processes take place. The neo-cortex is divided in two, the left hemisphere and right hemisphere, connected by a bundle of nerve fibres.

For many people the left side of the neo-cortex processes speech. As a shorthand, we say that left-brain thinking is verbal, logical, and step-by-step. By contrast, the right side of the neo-cortex processes information without us being aware of verbal reasoning processes. 'Right-brain thinking' has been described as more visual, more pattern manipulating, and more intuitive, and therefore superficially like creative thinking.

However, creativity is better explained as a process which takes us away from left-brain logic, which operates within a set of unchallenged assumptions. At the moment of insight creativity may well be the result of both sides of the brain working together, so that a new pattern of beliefs emerges.

In view of uncertainties about the mechanisms of mind we should regard concepts such as left brain and right brain as working hypotheses, and convenient to explain the dual importance of logic and intuition in creative problem-solving.

MIND SET: PERSONAL DIFFERENCES IN PERCEPTION

Human beings make sense of the world by an information-processing trick of pattern recognition. We carry around with us memories of past experiences against which we match present events. The more

Mind set

Mind set is the condition of being over-sensitized to some part of the information available, at the expense of other parts. It is an inevitable human condition.

When mind set helps us

Mind sets help us become sensitized to important repeated patterns of events, including potential problems. For survival the mind sets are helpful, as we can recognize dangers very rapidly, and with incomplete information. A flashing red light sets off our alarm systems, and we become alert and ready to react. Learning from experience provides more useful mind sets. We are sensitized to patterns that remind us of successful problems solved. So we do not have to re-invent the wheel. We automatically act under the influence of our unconscious 'set'. This could involve dealing with work problems, or operating a machine, or doing a crossword puzzle.

When mind set blocks us

Mind sets can lead to a sorry state of 'stuckness' when things have changed but everything looks the same as before. We are too ready to accept the similarities with the past, so that, if we have made an incorrect assumption, we may carry on for far too long before discovering our error.

Early work on aircraft pilot error, for example, showed how pilots expected the dials to be showing their normal readings, and failed to notice when they showed abnormal readings. It is typical that high stress reinforces mind sets and adds to stuckness. For example, blocks to creativity can become harder to challenge. They include:

- One correct answer thinking – Remedy: 'There must be other ways: there might be better ways'
- Negative or 'yes but' thinking – Remedy: 'yes and' thinking
- Over-regard for logical thinking – Remedy: Accept the need for intuition as well as logic
- Over-reliance on experience ('we've always done it this way') – Remedy: 'Then let's find a better way'

A particularly valuable 'set to break set' is a habit of reminding yourself during difficulties of the general remedy 'when stuck, challenge assumptions'.

emotionally powerful the past experience, the easier the match. This makes us over-sensitive to similarities between past and present (we recognize our children as rapidly disappearing specks on the holiday landscape), and inevitably under-sensitive to new patterns, which we seek to relate to our repertoire of past experiences. The term mind set has been coined to describe the condition of experience-biased perception (the mental filters described earlier).

When our mind sets let us down we are in a state which I like to call 'stuckness'. We may persist in a false belief that we understand what is going on, failing to realize that our beliefs are over-influencing our understanding. Our actions will then be based on dubious assumptions, and although there may be increasing evidence of error, an element of vicious problem-solving arises. The harder we try to solve the problem, the more we reinforce the mind set, and the harder it becomes to recognize the error of our assumptions. Hence stuckness: the greater the effort the greater the stuckness in a mental morass of our own making.

In problem-solving, our starting position indicates a dominant mind set, and a potential for stuckness. This brings us to the possibly surprising conclusion that a problem will to some degree be as open-ended or close-ended as the problem-solver perceives it. Furthermore, creativity, or escape from old ways of thinking, typically requires individuals to discover more about their assumptions or mind sets.

The more dogmatically someone insists on the 'right' way of looking at the problem, the greater the likelihood of a mind set obstructing creative solutions from emerging. As mind sets operate at a below-conscious level, the mechanisms for releasing them require special 'tricks of the trade' which include the techniques of creative problem-solving.

TRICKING YOUR WAY OUT OF THINKING BLOCKS

The concepts of mind set and whole-brain thinking help explain blocks to problem-solving and suggest ways of overcoming these blocks. Suppose you have a problem – you are stuck and can't find any satisfactory ideas for solving it. Obvious strategies based on past experience do not work. Perhaps the feelings of stuckness have been reinforced by redoubling efforts in some way that is proving wrong.

> Anyone who has tried to make progress on an unfriendly piece of computer software will recognize this description. Recently I came across a vivid example of someone who was 'stuck' for a month with a new word-processing package in attempting to centralize a

title in a practical document, being quite unable to proceed to the
next line of the text during all that time, and going round and round
the same cycles of errors.

In these cases there may be 'obvious' and 'logical' solutions, but what is obvious to the outsider remains concealed from the person in the state of stuckness. Robert Ornstein in his book *The Psychology of Consciousness'* shows us that for enlightenment we have to find mechanisms to take us to a different level of consciousness. The methods often involve distracting the dominant 'left brain' with its intense focus inside a set of assumptions so that a more 'right-brain' contribution can be made. Notice that we cannot easily use 'left-brain methods' (e.g. reasoning) to escape from left-brain dominance. It is not sufficient to say to oneself – or anyone else – 'I must find which of my assumptions is wrong'. A better way to discover a false assumption is to distract the mind from the immediate problem.

The left brain can be distracted by various diversionary tactics, and it does not matter which specific mechanism is used. To take an obvious example, physical exercise reduces mental stress and assists in loosening the unhelpful mind sets which have produced stuckness. Some find a game of golf works wonders in resolving a tricky work problem. For others it may be tennis, or jogging. The exact type of exercise is not so important as the principle of distracting the over-active left brain which is reinforcing the assumptions and mind sets involved in the state of mental stuckness.

The creative problem-solving techniques for helping 'switch off' the left brain temporarily should be approached in the light of this understanding. Someone who asks 'What is the best technique for getting more creative ideas?' is looking for a left-brain answer where it would be better to look for an 'escape from left brain' answer. It is important to realize that there will be a variety of techniques, with superficial differences, all of which can trick the brain into revealing its assumptions. The eventual choice will be to a degree a matter of personal preference.

Other techniques that have been used for temporarily switching off an over-active left brain include drugs, meditation, yoga, fasting, dreaming, exercise and assorted 'non-intellectual' group activities from sport to encounter groups. Some of my Scandinavian colleagues swear by repeated cycles of sauna/cold swim/sauna – which reminds one of the old story of Archimedes in his bath relaxing and then getting the famous 'Eureka' insight.

Later in the book we shall come across various problem-solving techniques which, according to their advocates, also stimulate creativity. They all have the potential to change our levels of consciousness temporarily away from left-brain dominance. Sadly, many of the 'how to do it' texts miss this point completely and focus on the mechanics of the techniques, which can result in left-brain descriptions, and continued left-brain attempts to execute the techniques.

> The American author Roger von Oech likened the process to gaining enlightenment. When a novice is studying the way of Zen he has to learn the uselesssness of direct questions to his problems. His mentor will find very unexpected ways of demonstrating this point which help to bring enlightenment.
>
> 'What is knowledge?' the novice might ask. The answer might be a quite unexpected whack on the side of the novice's head. I had a mathematics teacher who used the whack-on-the-head technique, but as this was as predictable as hangovers after a night's drinking the effect was not mind-expanding. What the Buddhist novice receives is sudden and unexpected upsetting of mind sets. Logical left-brain information processing is thrown into confusion by an idea which cannot be fitted into the former pattern.

Perhaps the most comprehensive series of experiments on tricking mental censors comes from the work of the Synectics corporation at Cambridge Massachusetts which shows how, in a search for new ideas, a block or problem can be overcome by disguising it. The disguised problem or metaphor is tackled so that 'the strange becomes familiar and then the familiar becomes strange'. The process weakens the tyranny of excessive left-brain thinking, perhaps because metaphoric images are likely to have right-brain contributions. We shall come across this and many other ways of achieving a whack on the inside of our head in the rest of the book.

In summary, the creativity trickster achieves results by indirect means. The balance changes from 'left-brain' to 'whole-brain' thinking and the psychological climate changes to greater receptiveness to novelty. Indeed, the purpose of the techniques is partly to break through some assumption that is producing stuckness. But even more important, groups which regularly practise creative problem-solving develop a greater level of receptivity to creative ideas. In other words, a more creative climate emerges.

SETTING A CLIMATE FOR CREATIVITY

An organization's climate results from assorted general factors which produce a general mood for better or worse. They might include the congeniality of the work practices, the pressures of work, the management style, and reward systems. A poor climate for creativity would be one which leads people to avoid risks, be over-critical of new ideas, and resist attempts to introduce change. A creative climate would be one in which people trust each other so that they can take the psychological risks of being open and revealing their deeper needs and fears.

It is difficult to change the attitudes and climate of an organization (although there are documented examples of change programmes that have set out to do just that, and have succeeded). One strategy is to change 'micro-climates' until there is an increasing number of locations receptive to creative ideas. This strategy requires 'cues' that encourage a willingness to work on new ideas, and to escape from the old enemy of premature judgement.

Some clues to positive climate-setting can be found in the excellent book *The One Minute Manager* (Blanchard and Johnson). There we are told how a good manager can reinforce behaviours by recognizing and rewarding them. In practical terms this means we have to separate out our approval of the process that has produced a new idea from our reactions to potential weaknesses in that idea. This is a threatening concept for many managers.

'If we reward bad ideas don't we reinforce sloppy thinking?' is a common question. The answer is that you do not reward bad ideas, but the habit of sharing new ideas, regardless of their apparent weakness. The skill lies in responding so as to send out two messages simultaneously:

1 It is always a good thing to come up with new ideas; and
2 This particular idea needs working on, but don't give up.

The process can be helped by genuine efforts to look for the merits in new ideas. Here is a recipe which will pay dividends in the long run in producing a creative climate. I have seen it work with hundreds of managers and students, and I have never seen it lead to creativity running amok and causing more trouble than it was worth (a common concern of managers with a high need for control).

> Approach any new idea with a positive assumption – that in the vast majority of cases someone is only prepared to share an idea which they believe to have considerable merit. If you can't see that merit you probably have a blocking mind set about it (or the person concerned). Do not evaluate the idea until you have some feel for the motivation behind the suggestion (this may take a while, but you become more sensitive with practice). Then, and only then, can you begin the process of appraising the idea. Appraise it not in 'good' or 'bad' terms, but in terms of its acceptable strengths, and

then in terms of its weaknesses. The key to climate setting is to convey your own desire to convert the weaknesses into improvements that will be acceptable to the proposer, to you and to those you have responsibility over.

There are quite simple ways which with practice help you acquire the habit of positive thinking. One of my colleagues has a printed sign on his desk reading WGAI. It reminds him to ask 'What's good about it?' in his work. Another powerful device described in the next chapter is to resist 'yes/no' thinking, and practice 'yes and' thinking, in which weaknesses of ideas are built upon, thereby strengthening both the idea and the climate for future ideas.

Climate setting is a process which takes time and considerable effort. But it lies at the heart of the deliberate practice of creative behaviour – and is worth all the trouble, because without a creative climate new ideas have little chance of support or survival. It is a personal discipline, and it is also a component in the leadership style which is needed to stimulate creativity in work situations.

CREATIVE LEADERSHIP

Creativity can be managed and stimulated. The skills required, as in other areas, may not be evenly shared out around the population. They can develop through experience, application and learning (creative analysis). Or they can shrivel, become warped and misapplied. The obvious way to be a creative manager is through example – sparking off ideas which can be developed and implemented. Unfortunately, this strategy rarely succeeds. If the 'creative' leader is truly outstanding as a creative individual, he or she is rarely equally able to manage the creative ideas, and might therefore be better off as a team member producing an outstanding flow of stimuli. If, on the other hand, the leader is no better at producing ideas than the others, then the unconscious favouring given to the leader's ideas demotivates the others. It can send out cues that are negative for the creative climate – 'there's no need for you lot to be creative, just leave that to me.'

There is a quite different way of operating as a creative leader. It is to concentrate on 'ideas about ideas'. The concern should be how to get the best out of other people's talents, so that the emphasis is on the management of people. The style has been called a facilitating, or process-oriented, one. To develop this kind of leadership style you must learn to pay attention to the signals which people give out regarding their needs and beliefs. You must learn that sometimes the best way to help people solve problems is not to supply your own solutions – even if it is quite obvious to you what needs to be done. Creative leaders make things happen, but their approach is subtle – more like a midwife than a surgeon.

This is how one successful businessman summed up creative leadership:

> It's a kind of willingness to accept it when an employee says 'your way is not working'. It should make you really want to put things right . . . . Creative leaders develop procedures and practices which enable people to participate. When run properly, Quality Circles do that, for instance. The most successful leaders also are able to offer a precise shared understanding from time to time of their vision of the company leaving scope for those involved to own their part of the proceedings.

This style of leadership emerges in its most clear-cut form in group creativity sessions like brainstorming, where the leader concentrates on stimulating ideas and does not put in any of his or her own. And one of the spin-off benefits of practising such creative problem-solving sessions is that is helps develop the liberating leadership attitude, not just within the brainstorming session but in the wider work context.

SUMMARY

In this chapter some assumptions about creativity have been challenged. The common view is that creativity is a special mental gift which enables a few gifted people to make great discoveries. This élitist view can be replaced with a generalist one, viz, that we are all creative.

According to this view, creativity is escape from old beliefs and assumptions, particularly as a means of solving problems. Different problem types require different treatments, although creative problem-solving involves a repeated pattern of preparation, incubation, insight and validation. These stages involve a mix of left-brain (verbal) and right-brain (visual) components.

Mind sets are personal perspectives based on past experience. Over-rigid mind sets produce stuckness, so that creativity can be seen as escape from some dominant mind set. Escape from mind set often requires unexpected ways of tricking the brain (having a 'whack on the head').

A constructive work climate can help loosen mind sets, and conversely a negative climate can strengthen them. One of the roles of creative leaders is to establish a constructive climate, thereby liberating the creative talents of their people.

Puxxles

A puxxle is a puzzle with added ingredients to whet the creative appetite. Don't be fooled into putting puxxles into a box labelled 'trivial, silly, no-use-for-work problems'. Fooling around with puxxles can be a risk-free way of building up positive mind sets that help us escape from 'stuckness' when dealing with more important problems. Here are some puxxles set me over the years by puxxle-lovers. All you need to succeed is confidence that if at first you don't succeed – challenge assumptions and you'll eventually get there.

Puxxle 1

A city in Europe has ten trees planted in five rows. Now the surprising point to the story is that each of the five rows has four trees in it. In tackling this puxxle you may find it interesting to keep a record of your attempts, and then reconstruct the process from initial stuckness (ten trees and five rows must mean two trees per row?), to increasing awareness of the possibilities for tree planters and puxxle solvers.

Puxxle 2

Innovations require a starting trigger point. Look around you and notice more acutely some personal dissatisfaction. There is a good chance that others share your dissatisfaction. Think of ten ways of removing that dissatisfaction, remembering to postpone judgement. Take the wildest idea and improve it until it is both realistic and imaginative.

Puxxle 3

I went to the cinema yesterday with a friend. On the way out he said to me 'Why do people make such a noise with their crisp wrappers?' I was going to say something like 'What do you expect? There's no consideration for others.' Before I could, my friend said, 'Why does paper have to make a noise?'

I'd never thought of that. Once the need has been spotted the problem becomes a puxxle. There are many ways of solving the problem. Some of them are things to do to paper to make it less noisy. We came up with several dozen ideas, some of them new and promising. Can you dream up some new inventions for silent wrappers? Set a target of twenty starting ideas.

Puxxle 4

Can you think of a birthday present that people all over the world would agree was absolutely useless? You can?

Now try to think of at least three reasons why the idea is not absolutely useless.

(This puxxle is itself useful as well as a mind-teaser. From time to time we hear an idea which we consider absolutely useless. Can that really be the case, or are there some merits in the idea – if only we could change our perspective?).

Puxxle 5

Imagine you are a research chemist who found a way of making incredibly cheap superglue from harmless ingredients. You told your bosses, who immediately promoted you and raised money to turn the idea into an innovation. Unfortunately, while they were away talking to their bankers, you carried out more experiments and found that you could not reproduce your result. You feel stuck – nothing to do with the glue, which refuses to stick at all. There seems nothing to do. Or is there? Can you find a dozen different ways of looking at the problem, some of which might be better than remaining stuck with the non-sticking glue problem?

Puxxle 6

When you are tackling puxxles you know there is a problem, and that someone knows the answer or some of the possible solutions. In real life most problems creep up on us. Can you think of an early warning system for alerting people who are blissfully unaware of their stuckness? Think of three or more approaches.

Puxxle 7

Business is sometimes like fitting together a jigsaw puzzle without the picture on the box. If you are given a jigsaw without any further guidance and find you can't fit all the pieces together, you may have to challenge your assumptions. What assumptions might be challenged? Does this suggest ways of solving more important problems?

2 Opening up your options creatively

Creativity involves escaping from stuckness and opening up new possibilities. This chapter is concerned with various ways of wriggling free from the constraints of mind sets which are interfering with effective problem-solving. We shall thus be dealing with stuckness which arises from a deficiency of options. (Another kind of stuckness, arising from a surplus of options, is covered in Chapter 3.)

The key to obtaining sufficient options to break out of stuckness is the principle of deferment of judgement. We shall see the principle at work for problem-stuckness in the approach known as goal orientation: a powerful way of reappraising problems in terms of dominant mind sets or goals which once discovered can be challenged.

If you are working in a climate that requires some opening up, then you will find the 'yes and' approach valuable, while a third opening up device is the deliberate practice of seeking right-brain and visual metaphors to break out of left-brain logic traps.

Finally some more general observations are made about opening up and closing down opportunities in work situations, and the importance of escaping from mental habits.

OPENING UP AND CLOSING DOWN OPTIONS

There are two important types of stuckness that are more related than they seem at first sight:

Creativity involves escaping from stuckness and opening up new possibilities.

1   stuckness because of a shortage of options; and
2   stuckness because we have too many options.

Stuckness often arises when we are so short of ideas that we can see no satisfactory way out of our problems. This is option-deficiency stuckness, and we shall be concentrating on its nature and mechanisms for generating acceptable options in this chapter.

Sometimes we find we are overwhelmed with possibilities, a state which can induce feelings of stuckness arising from the difficulties in selecting the most promising one to act upon. This is option-surfeit stuckness, to be dealt with in Chapter 3.

The two forms of stuckness are linked, because from a starting position of option-deficient stuckness there is a natural tendency to avoid generating too many options lest we find ourselves in the equally unpleasant state of not knowing how to select the best. As a result, search for new options can be inhibited, often stopping as soon as the first promising idea is thought of. Unfortunately this is likely to leave some of the most firmly held assumptions unchallenged, and the idea will be close to previous ones.

This leads to one of the most powerful principles of creative problem-solving – search widely for new ideas, for quantity and variety of options are needed to increase the chances of escape from option-deficient stuckness. Put another way, we must not start judging the quality of the options until we have a sufficiency of them – which can sometimes mean dozens or even hundreds of ideas in competitive situations. To widen out search processes you must defer judgement – 'stay loose till rigour counts' as one trainer put it.

Later we shall see how creativity techniques have series of mechanisms for generating options and selecting the most appropriate ones. A linked pair of option opening/option closing procedures can be thought of as a diverge/converge couple.

Deferment of judgement

Repeated studies of idea generation have shown us one fundamental human behaviour which reduces our creative outputs. That is the impulse to evaluate prematurely when we come across a new idea. The roots of the behaviour are unconscious rather than conscious, and may be a defence against the uncertainties of change. The behaviour is very likely associated with personal mind sets, the signals of which are apparently rational statements, rational because that is how we are 'supposed' to behave. But listen more carefully and we detect the irrational fear of the new idea in the response, which

Opening up and closing down: the diverge – converge couple

Creative problem-solving techniques can be seen as a series of opening up and closing down sequences. Typically, opening up involves postponing judgement, using techniques to challenge mind-sets, and accumulating a range of possibilities. Closing down involves selection, focusing, and development. This diagram shows the three diverge/converge stages in the Problems–Ideas–Solution (PIS) approach to structuring problem-solving. Note how the last stage can lead to 'recycling' to stage 1.

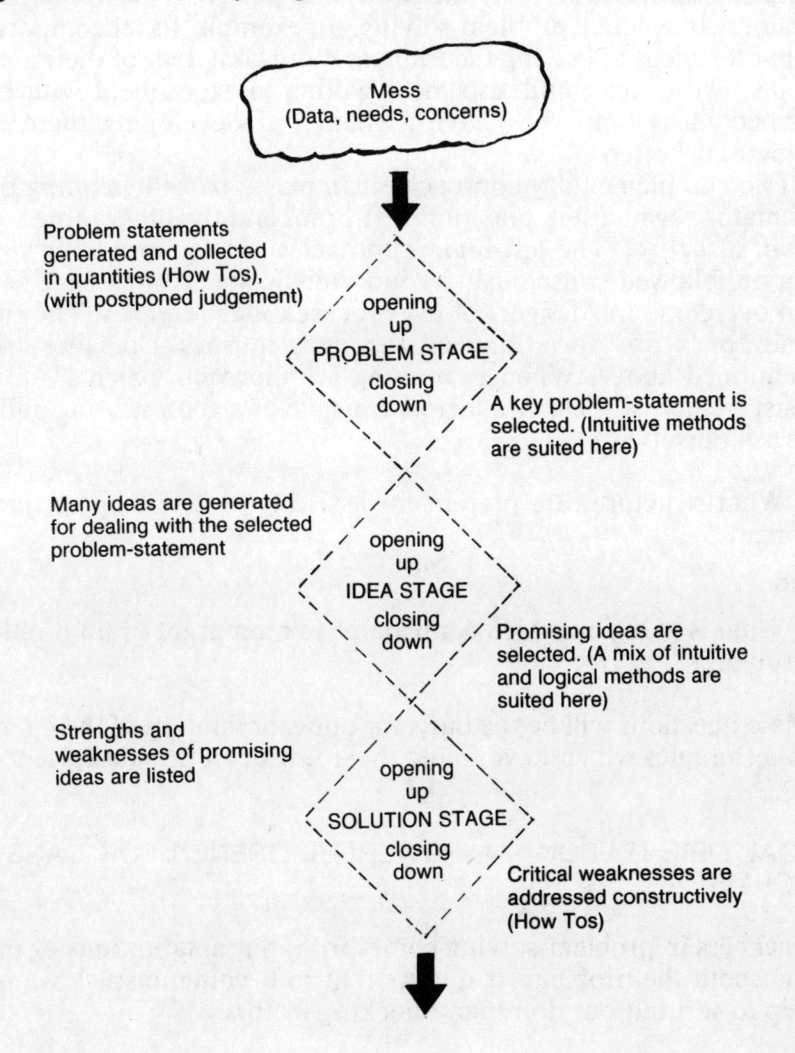

Mess
(Data, needs, concerns)

Problem statements generated and collected in quantities (How Tos), (with postponed judgement)

opening up
PROBLEM STAGE
closing down

A key problem-statement is selected. (Intuitive methods are suited here)

Many ideas are generated for dealing with the selected problem-statement

opening up
IDEA STAGE
closing down

Promising ideas are selected. (A mix of intuitive and logical methods are suited here)

Strengths and weaknesses of promising ideas are listed

opening up
SOLUTION STAGE
closing down

Critical weaknesses are addressed constructively (How Tos)

can be a 'killer phrase' such as:

> 'It will never work.'
> 'It will cost too much.'
> 'We can't do that.'

or the most widespread of all:

> 'Yes but'.

Research on creative problem-solving groups suggests that rejecting behaviours are learned rather than innate. It follows that people can unlearn the behaviours that lead to impulsive rejection of ideas. Training in creative problem-solving, for example, has the important spin-off benefit of leaving the trainees more confident of their ability to deal with ideas, and also more willing to experiment with half-formed ideas until they have a chance of developing them into something better.

Two complementary approaches can play a part in escaping from premature evaluation, one more left-brain and the other more right-brain in nature. The left-brain approaches set up structures which can be followed consciously by individuals and groups, and which can overcome the dangers of over-focused idea searches. The right-brain ones are variations of the consciousness-changing tricks mentioned above. When examining an approach which claims to assist creativity, these two factors can give us a good starting point if we ask ourselves:

> 'What structures are present for assisting in deferment of judgement?'

and

> 'What is going on which contributes to more right-brain problem-solving?'

These questions will be the basis for our examination of the opening up techniques which have found most favour in the workplace.

GOAL ORIENTATION – A POWERFUL OPENER FOR CANS OF WORMS

Stuckness in problem-solving comes from our assumptions or mind sets about the problem. It follows that to become unstuck we need help to sort out our dominant blocking factors.

Goal orientation

Goal orientation is both an attitude of mind, and a technique to encourage the attitude. Open-ended problems can be seen as situations where the boundaries are unclear, but in which there may be fairly well-defined needs and obstacles to overcome. There may also be areas which, after examination, are accepted as close-ended (i.e. the solver does not wish to challenge the boundaries around these areas). The close-ended parts are often described as constraints.

The Goal-oriented solver is constantly seeking goals ('what I want'), and obstacles ('what's stopping me from getting what I want'). The technique is simply to adopt the habit, conscious at first, of asking 'What are the goals or objectives of the situation; what are the acceptable constraints; what are the obstacles?'

A very good technique for clarifying goals is to use the 'how to' approach. In time it becomes possible to find a whole range of 'how to' statements which indicate differing ways of looking at a problem. It may be important to escape from our initial 'how to', if it is blocking us off from finding ideas. (It is probably a mind set.) Remember there are a range of 'how to' ways of looking at problems, including metaphorical ones, which are useful for stimulating more imaginative thinking.

Example:

I want to persuade my client to accept my proposal.

Goal statements:

How to persuade my client to accept my proposal.
How to win his confidence.
How to show him what is better about the new approach.
How to arouse his enthusiasm.
How to turn him on.
How to find the right bait to hook his interest.
How to reduce his fears of change.
How to break down his resistance.
How to . . . (Find other examples for yourself)

Goal orientation (GO for short) can be practised daily and will rapidly prove its value as as means of escaping from stuckness which is due to failure to study the problem carefully enough. It can be used as a structured technique for groups or individuals. Or it can be developed into an attitude of mind which is increasingly able to challenge and go beyond initial assumptions.

GO operates on the premiss that important problems at work are 'owned' by people who want to do something, but may be blocked or stuck by unchallenged assumptions. In order to generate new ideas about the problem it is important for those involved to find out as much as they can about their assumptions (opening up options), after which they have the possibility of accepting their set of assumptions, or of moving to a new perspective (closing down options).

The simple mechanism which characterizes GO is known as a 'how to' statement.

> Whenever a complex fuzzy problem has revealed a dominant mind set, the problem can be expressed in terms of that mind set by a single and clearly focused 'how to' statement.

Actually, if you encourage someone to describe a work problem, including details of what is needed, and what has been tried, the information can often be split into scores of 'how to' statements, some overlapping, some discrete. So why the insistence that within this mess there is a single 'how to' summing up the problem? Answer: because we are looking for a summing up of the right brain's view of the problem. The 'how to' is in the verbal mode of the left brain, but in seeking a key or dominant 'how to' we are trying to link up with the right brain's feelings for the nature of the problem. So what we feel about the problem and what we would like are as important as what we know.

When trying to help someone solve a problem in my role as an educator or a consultant I listen very carefully to his or her description of the case before us. Usually very early on in the conversation there are clues to the dominant mind set. After a while I can check my suspicion by some such comment as: 'So is one important thing about the problem how to get this new technology working before your budget is cut'? Or I may confess 'I can't quite see ... are you mainly wondering how to speed up production or is it how to match marketing demand better?' These questions are intended to trigger off awareness of the dominant mind set of the problem-owner, and are not suggestions of the right way to think about the problem. After all, my own mind sets are in as good a working order as anyone else's and I do not want to impose them any more than I can help.

Over a period of years the discipline of using GO on a near daily basis means that I follow its steps almost automatically working alone or in groups. I'm at least aware when I return time and again to an unhelpful starting position that I'm stuck and this awareness is a clue to what the mind sets are.

My writing was interrupted a few moments ago by a possible consultancy client with the news that he expected the costs to his organization to be roughly half what I had quoted. Is my problem 'How to agree a price within his budget'? Or is it 'How to get a decent contribution to my business after paying off the expenses'? Or 'How to use this as a "loss leader"'? Or 'How to help him bring his fee structure more into line with our other clients'? Or 'How to pass the business on to someone else to mutual benefit'? I'm still stuck, but before I speak to him again this practical application of goal orientation will make it much easier for me to deal with the problem. (Twenty-four hours, and several discussions, later a totally new perspective emerged, namely 'How to lower the daily rate to mutual benefit'. It emerged that the client perceived the original daily rate as high because of our accountancy procedure of incorporating development charges. The problem-solving logic was to spread these over additional days' work, which could be offered to the client, but which had not even been considered in our earlier discussion.)

Later we shall see how goal orientation is also an excellent mechanism for groups to deploy as the first (problem-exploring) stage in brainstorming. Such exercises reveal how different are the perspectives of the team members, and how easy it is for someone with a problem to be stuck and narrowly constrained by his/her starting mind sets. The brainstorming approach can open up possibilities and offer an invitation to escape from the confines of blocking mind sets.

DEALING WITH IDEA KILLERS: THE 'YES AND' APPROACH

In Chapter 2 it was suggested that positivity can be fostered, thereby leading to a climate in which new ideas flourish. This philosophy can be put into practice through opening up ideas using the 'yes and' formula: 'two little words', according to one consultant, 'which can change your life for the better'. Why should he share with so many other creativity trainers such a deep conviction of the importance of 'yes anding'. It happens to demonstrate the structure and workings of effective simple opening up techniques. Let's see how it works, and why.

It is primarily a technique which works first on your own mind sets and only then on other people's. It has a simple operational form and easy-to-recognize conditions where it can be put to use. Finally, it can be practised frequently and permits rapid reinforcement and feedback. The sign of stuckness is your reaction to an idea as being wrong or worthless. You make every effort to find the core of your objection. If you like, the objection can be treated as a problem definition or 'how to' statement. You then look for ways of dealing with the objection, expressing the idea or ideas as a 'yes and' statement.

'Yes and'

'Yes and' is a method of beating premature evaluation and negativity. It works in the following way.

As a shorthand we talk about a 'yes but' climate, and a 'yes and' climate. A 'yes but' climate is one in which people are prone to respond to any new idea with a 'yes but'. This is one of the well-known killer phrases which are themselves signals of a negative mind set.

The negative mind set is based on unconsciously held beliefs, and we can weaken these by becoming conscious, to the extent of becoming self-conscious, of 'yes butting'.

We begin to reduce the damage caused by excessive 'yes butting', by substituting 'yes and'.

'Yes but' implies 'There is something wrong with this idea. I want nothing further to do with this bad idea'. 'Yes and' implies 'There is something that can be improved about this idea. I am willing to work at it to improve it as best I can.'

To take a simple example: 'I have just had the idea of a flypaper to go in cars to stop insects distracting you when you are driving.'

'Yes but . . . wherever you put it someone would get stuck sooner or later.'

'Yes and . . . if you could design it so that passengers never get stuck it would be even better. How about an insecticide block, or the paper inside a mesh with fly attractant? Or how about combining it with the air freshener?'

Note: in follow-up studies of participants on our courses, more find they have applied 'yes and' with benefit than any other technique.

Here is a quite complicated version of 'yes and' from a real life case study.

Suppose you have come across an idea for reducing road fatalities which involves weakening lamp standards so that they break away

Developing an idea using a 'yes and' approach

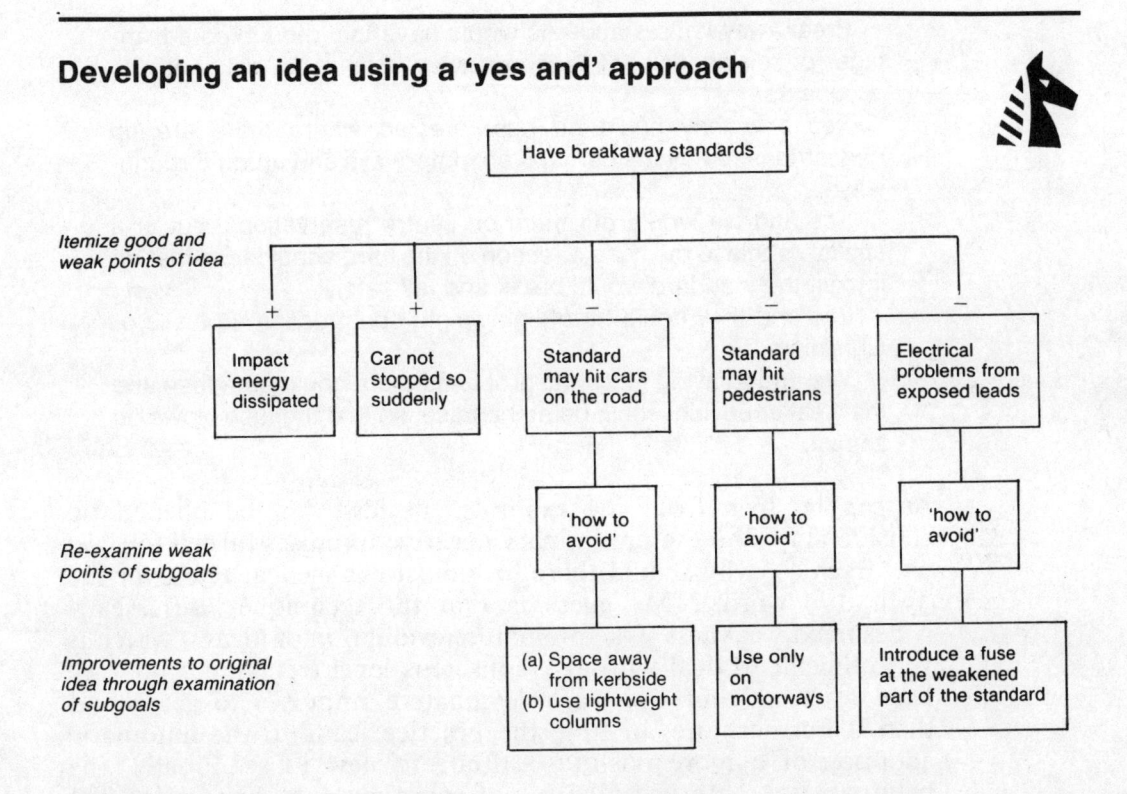

```
                        Have breakaway standards
                                 │
        ┌────────┬────────┬──────┴──────┬────────────┐
        +        +        −             −            −
Itemize good and
weak points of idea
        │        │        │             │            │
    ┌───────┐ ┌───────┐ ┌───────┐   ┌───────┐   ┌───────────┐
    │Impact │ │Car not│ │Standard│  │Standard│  │Electrical │
    │energy │ │stopped│ │may hit │  │may hit │  │problems   │
    │dissi- │ │so sud-│ │cars on │  │pedes-  │  │from exposed│
    │pated  │ │denly  │ │the road│  │trians  │  │leads      │
    └───────┘ └───────┘ └───────┘   └───────┘   └───────────┘
                            │           │             │
Re-examine weak         ┌───────┐   ┌───────┐   ┌───────┐
points of subgoals      │'how to│   │'how to│   │'how to│
                        │avoid' │   │avoid' │   │avoid' │
                        └───────┘   └───────┘   └───────┘
                            │           │             │
Improvements to original ┌─────────┐ ┌─────────┐ ┌──────────┐
idea through examination │(a) Space│ │Use only │ │Introduce │
of subgoals              │away from│ │on       │ │a fuse at │
                         │kerbside │ │motorways│ │the weak- │
                         │(b) use  │ │         │ │ened part │
                         │lightwt. │ │         │ │of the    │
                         │columns  │ │         │ │standard  │
                         └─────────┘ └─────────┘ └──────────┘
```

An idea for improving road safety: have breakaway lamp standards. The diagram shows how this potentially valuable idea can be made more practical through the 'yes and' approach.

---

on impact. A habitual reaction would be to discard the idea because of its obvious shortcomings:

'Yes, but if you did that you would be hitting other cars on the road, and pedestrians as well. There would also be electrical problems with exposed leads after the lamp standard had broken away.'

A 'yes and' approach would look for the advantages of the idea as they might have been in the mind of the inventor. Thus reassured of some merits in the idea we can then look for modifications to our own concerns (which may, of course, arise from a different interpretation of the idea to the one intended by the inventor):

'Breakaway lamp-standards would have the undoubted advantage of dissipation of energy away from the car and its occupants . . .'

'Yes and they could be best erected where there are no pedestrians to be hit – perhaps on motorways and urban throughways.

'Yes and we would put them on centre reservations, but at a shallow angle to the car's direction on the hard shoulder so that on impact the standard would break and fall safely.'

'Yes and they could be of lightweight construction – plastic or aluminium.'

'Yes and to avoid electrical problems there could be a fuse and the weakened joint could be at the base, so that the fuse blows on impact.'

As can be seen from the example, an idea can be opened up considerably, and the preliminary negative impulses turned to good use. Even so, why should there be almost evangelical zeal over the 'two little words'? My guess is that the technique addresses a widespread weakness – the premature evaluation of ideas – which is very difficult to deal with at a conscious level (remember how we have to 'trick' our over-eager evaluative impulses to get round them?) Furthermore, in time the practice leads to the automatic adoption of a more positive attitude to new ideas. Finally, the habitual user observes others, self-consciously at first, using the expression in his or her presence, which is a sign of success, and evidence of a climate that is becoming more open to change.

The actual form of words does not matter all that much. When students ask me whether some other expression would be better I reply 'Yes and it's up to you to find one that you feel comfortable with.' It is important to set up a trigger or cue that reminds you, and other people, that you are trying to be positive and helpful.

I will go so far as to say that the concept of 'yes and' thinking is a vital one for you to work through as a stage in developing understanding of the principles of developing creative problem-solving skills. If the technique has raised doubts in your mind, stop at this point. Practise the 'yes and' approach to explore those concerns until you are satisfied you are ready for the next section, which is otherwise likely to reinforce the feelings that all this creativity stuff is not for you after all.

METAPHORIC THINKING – THE ROYAL ROAD TO THE UNCONSCIOUS

Freud said that dreams were the royal road to understanding the unconscious mind. From Freud we have the idea of a personal problem arising because we repress some unpleasant idea. Then, in the healthy individual, the repressed idea re-emerges in disguised form – perhaps in a dream. If you like, the dream is the metaphor for the repressed problem. Freud believed that the repression arose because of the painfulness of sexual self-awareness, so that the metaphors were of a sexual kind. It was a short step to attribute explanations to dreamed symbols such as snakes (penises), railway trains (penises), guns (penises). But it is easy to make fun of the excessive attention Freud paid to sex. What still seems convincing is that:

1 We can repress a solution to a problem.
2 We can first glimpse the solution in a disguised or metaphorical way.

> A very famous and important example of this is the case of the scientist Kekule, who was searching for a structure that explained the formula for the benzene molecule. Kekule, along with his comtemporaries, knew that fitting the six carbons and the six hydrogens together would not work. The conditions are typical. Kekule, in accepting the body of scientific knowledge, might be seen as rejecting ('suppressing') the new possibility – that maybe the atoms form, not a linear chain, but a closed ring.
>
> Eventually this possibility came to him – in a dream – which he documented. His metaphor was of snakes (again the Freudian motif). The snakes were dancing and catching each other by the tail, forming the circle of atoms. The recognition of the dream as a disguised solution to his problem brought him back to full consciousness. That which had been suppressed was now confronted – carbon atoms can form rings as well as chains.

The significant points of the tale include:

- A strong urge to solve the problem
- Failure to solve it conventionally
- Refusal to consider a 'counter-intuitive' solution
- Suppression of the 'counter-intuitive' solution
- Revelation of the 'disguised' solution as a powerful visual image
- Making the connection between the disguised and the actual problems.

This general pattern of discovery has been described many times by different people. Perhaps the unconscious mind helps to reconstruct the problem that has been passed to it. The 'incubation' takes time. Then often when the critical facilities have been relaxed (e.g. when daydreaming) the idea 'comes to consciousness', perhaps in its disguised form.

Sometimes the process can be triggered by an external stimulus which provides its own metaphor.

> Barnes Wallis, inventor of the bouncing bomb of World War Two, thought of his sighting device when attending the theatre. The twin spotlights trained on a performer triggered off the idea of lights on the front and rear of the plane to provide precise focusing.

Psychologists have suggested that the trigger mechanism for insights obtained through metaphor is at its most sensitive in a state midway between concentration and dreamless deep sleep. Thus, daydreaming, 'relaxed attention', and the twilight zone before sleep and just on waking up are particularly productive.

To sum up, there is a body of evidence suggesting that:

- Metaphors play a part in some acts of creative problem-solving.
- The metaphors may reveal insights that are then 'known' to be right.
- Environmental conditions can make it easier or harder for the metaphors to emerge.

If metaphors arising spontaneously are associated with creativity, can creativity be deliberately stimulated through the conscious seeking of powerful metaphors and relating the material back to the problem?

The answer for many thousands of people is an unequivocal yes. The evidence comes from practical demonstrations in creative problem-solving sessions where it has become common practice to seek out metaphors as a means of arriving at more right-brain material. Research studies have backed up the experimental results. Today there are institutes concentrating on techniques for 'visioning', and for developing the practical skills for deliberately stimulating images and metaphors.

Putting together these various ideas, we can see conditions which may assist in the generation of powerful blockbusting metaphors.

- Visualization (use of right-brain thinking).
- Deliberate seeking of analogies and metaphors.
- Relaxation of conscious attention ('excursions').

For any given problem there is a range of ways of 'loosening up' your thinking. When the new idea emerges it has some logic of its own which has much to do with the problem, and perhaps little to do with the choice of metaphor. That is why with conscious searching it is possible to envisage several different metaphors, and that is also why it is generally a waste of energy worrying about which will 'work' best. The first step towards developing a powerful metaphor is to express the problem as a short, active statement indicating the primary need or objective of the person with the problem. Our old friend a 'how to' statement serves very well. The action word – the verb – is important, and the less clichéd and more evocative it is the better the metaphors you will obtain. Then you transplant the essence of the 'how to' (indicated by the verb) into a different context. For example, 'how to find a hijack victim' might be turned into the metaphor 'how to find a needle in a haystack'.

Here is an example of creativity in work which involved the generation and exploration of a metaphor.

> A chief executive of a department in a public authority had been appointed after a change of political power controlling the authority. The new political group had little experience of office and invited their senior officers to draw up strategy proposals within very lightly sketched-in policy statements. The new chief executive found the absence of guidelines a mixed blessing. He invited his senior team to help him design a new strategy, but their reactions puzzled him. They wanted more guidelines before they could make any proposals.
>
> He became increasingly convinced that the problem was how to organize a drifting department and help it find a sense of direction. He articulated this as a direct analogy – first, at a senior executive workshop. He then raised the matter at a team-building and problem-solving workshop with his own most senior staff. The team joined in enthusiastically, and in an hour-long session explored the analogy of a drifting supertanker. For the first half of the session the team listed page after page of ideas about the troubled ship, using the left-hand side of pages – about a dozen in all. Then on the right-hand side of the pages they proposed their ideas and plans for dealing with the problem. The group went on to set priorities and establish a timetable for achieving the most important tasks.

One of the benefits of metaphoric language is that it permits an indirect approach to subjects that might otherwise be too painful to broach. In our example the team members were very articulate about the need for the captain of the supertanker to take decisions. They were then able to discuss the direct issue of how much responsibility could be delegated in the department.

This illustration of the practical use of an extended metaphor is typical of a procedure that can be applied by creative problem-solving groups when opening up opportunities, particularly when there is a perceived need for some substantial shift in thinking, and for challenge to existing mind sets. For engineering problems analogies from biological systems are particularly powerful because they challenge the conventional mind sets of engineering technology. It might be expected that managerial and organizational problems could be solved using engineering and other technical metaphors. 'How to speed up a trainee's learning' might be turned into 'how to speed up a car engine', or 'how to speed up the children's bedtime rituals'.

The selection of the metaphor will in each case produce many interesting ideas. If you were to follow through the process you would discover that in the first example the ideas are rather mechanistic, and in the second case more paternalistic. It is easy to find a metaphor giving new ideas. Care must be taken that the unconscious desires which lead us to select a metaphor are not continuing to direct us in a particular mind set way.

Metaphoric thinking lies at the heart of creative problem-solving. Its systematic practice is to be highly recommended for all those who wish to develop creative skills, for themselves, and as guides and trainers for others. The evidence of practical products emerging from deliberate use of metaphors is growing as experiments are carried out in an increasing number of organizations. For individuals involved in this kind of work there is great satisfaction at the practical skills that can be gained. Unfortunately, at present, there is also one great problem – challenge, if you like – to be faced. Unlike the simple 'yes and' technique, acceptance of metaphoric thinking procedures in typical work situations is not easy. A certain amount of climate-setting is needed, which is far easier in the context of a creative problem-solving session.

However, there are important, albeit specific, circumstances where skills in metaphoric thinking will enhance effectiveness in managerial roles. For instance, sometimes a manager has to communicate a message in a memorable way. The most memorable messages have a metaphoric content. Great orators, like Winston Churchill and Martin Luther King, instinctively drew on metaphors to capture the imagination of their audiences. They invite us to follow their vision or dream, and from that shared vision comes understanding and commitment.

It has been found that most people respond to what has been called an 'imaging' style of presentation. For those of us with a natural imaging style, studying metaphoric thinking can enhance an existing skill. For those who prefer a more reasoned logical style, metaphoric thinking offers an opportunity to acquire a different style of thinking which will be particularly useful where our habitual left-brain approach is not working.

HOW OPPORTUNITIES OPEN UP AND CLOSE DOWN

It is sometimes said of an idea that it was 'ripe for its time'. There do seem to be times when an idea is attended to, and times when it is ignored, regardless of the logic of its presentation. The phenomenon of ripeness can be crucial in launching a new product, or promotional campaign, and it can be important for an individual trying to point out to a group that there is a better way of proceeding, if only they could escape from their assumptions and mind sets.

> In one of the currently popular outdoor training exercises a team is required to cross a stream using whatever equipment is available. The team may keep trying to build a bridge, although this is a near impossible task, ignoring the repeated suggestions from one member that they might be able to float across one by one. The frenzy of activity, together with the belief that progress is being made, conceals an increasing state of stuckness. In such a state, the group redoubles its efforts in frantic struggling which often prompts the group member with an alternative approach to drop out of the work altogether. At some point, in some groups, there is a period of calm, and a growing suspicion arises that the group is on the wrong track. If the alternative idea is then suggested, particularly by someone in the group who had originally supported the previous idea, the group starts again, rather slowly, but building up momentum again behind the new idea.

Here we have an important point about ripeness of ideas. It is necessary to become sensitive to the dynamics which will influence acceptance of an idea. Notice in our example, as in real life, that in the absence of structure such as a period of brainstorming, the group needs the certainty of direction offered by a single idea, and would not welcome too much opening up.

'There is a tide in the affairs of men, which, taken at the flood, leads on to fortune.' By recognizing the ebb and flow – the relative opening and closing of sensitivity towards ideas – in social groupings, we can improve our skills in getting ideas accepted.

We can all learn from the senior manager who would never intervene in meetings until the discussion became bogged down. Then he would summarize the failed efforts and only then make his own view clear. He enjoyed a career as a respected and unusually imaginative administrator.

Opening up and closing down : the loose–tight organization

In their management best seller *In Search of Excellence,* authors Peters and Waterman describe one of the characteristics of excellent firms as a 'simultaneous loose–tight' structure. These firms had at the same time some very clear tight objectives, with individual freedom to operate in creative ways to achieve those objectives.

Most organizations worry about control and direction lest they lose the tightness needed to achieve corporate goals. Corporate tightness might represent a common belief system or mind set and most of the time creativity is directed to getting new ideas and possibilities within the implied corporate goals. But the corporate mission itself may have to change, and the successful organizations are those which cope with new challenges by changing their strategic positions. The old 'tightness' is first loosened, then displaced by a new idea which is rapidly accepted as the new orthodoxy.

Many top managers still have to learn that tight control structures must be accompanied by individual freedoms and responsibilities ('yes and', not 'either/or'). They have to play a part in ensuring that the organization has mechanisms for opening up new possibilities, and for conscious and regular reappraisal of the corporate vision or mission. Creativity in a changing environment is a corporate necessity, not an add-on luxury.

OTHER WAYS OF OPENING-UP PROBLEMS: DEVELOPING A FALL BACK STRATEGY

Our habitual way of dealing with problems is sometimes called our dominant problem-solving style. Because it is automatic, we repeatedly miss opportunities of responding in ways that are different from our dominant style. If we can become aware of our dominant behaviours we can practise those less-favoured approaches until we eventually have a wider set of available skills.

It is likely that we shall still favour our original style, but now we have a fall back strategy. For example, a technically trained person may have a rather left-brain approach to all problems. He or she will respond to problems initially by looking for logical explanations based on past experience. Such a person may want to develop a more right-brain fall back strategy so that, if logic fails, more imagination may be brought to bear on the problem.

For the more analytical thinker, initial problem-formulations are likely to be precise and unambiguous. Even listing other possibilities as 'how to's will probably result in additional logical statements closely linked to the original concept. A desirable fall back strategy would be one which increased contributions from right-brain impulses which are being repressed by the problem-solver's need for rationality. Consciousness-changing 'tricks' rather than structures are called for.

Conversely, a very intuitive person may recognize that his right-brain dominant problem-solving style tends to be impulsive and sometimes leads to trouble. He may look for ways of developing a more considered and logical approach, so that if trouble is brewing he can switch to being a little more left-brain as a fall back strategy. Stuckness may result because the intuitions are not grounded in reality. This bias can be helped by introducing more structure into his fall back strategy. ('When all else fails read the manual'.)

For example, it may be a good discipline for such a person to set up a written routine for analysing problems. Justifying the commercial logic of a decision sharpens the analytic powers – even if you choose to confront only yourself.

What actually happens is that we favour our dominant strategies in our attempts to improve our problem-solving. The volunteers on idea-generation courses tend to be fluent in idea generation before the course starts. Similarly, those people with a well-developed and structured style of problem-solving are the most enthusiastic for even more structures, such as time management systems. For the left-brain and right-brain biased person alike the most beneficial fall back style is one that is uncongenial to existing personal patterns of behaviour. They are therefore difficult to embrace, and may never be fully internalized. The more stressful the situation the more likely we are to retreat to our favoured habits of mind. Nevertheless, it is possible to become sensitized to signs of stuckness, and therefore better able to make conscious attempts to escape from our mind sets and dominant problem-solving styles. The reward is far greater flexibility and creativity.

Finally, a different tactic. If you remain unconvinced of your own capacity to adopt a conflicting problem-solving style, you can achieve equivalent results if you are prepared to consult someone with a quite different style to yours. Too often we seek out people of a similar disposition, so you will have to be careful in choosing your confidant. Learn to accept the key principle for escaping a dominant mind set and problem-solving style: 'My way is my way, not the way.'

SUMMARY

This chapter has been mainly concerned with ways of opening up our options, without introducing complex techniques. This leads to escape from stuckness due to a deficiency of options.

The state of mind for effective opening up of problems or ideas is that of deferred judgement.

Goal orientation is an approach to identifying the dominant mindset in problem-solving by listing goals as 'how to' statements.

'Yes and' is a method of overcoming negativity towards ideas, by treating weaknesses as opportunities for more creative problem-solving (perhaps using the goal orientation technique).

Metaphoric thinking is a particularly powerful way of tricking the left brain so as to reveal suppressed ideas. Working on disguised problems can reduce the internal censorship, assist deferment of judgement, and lead to new and valuable ideas.

Dominant problem-solving strategies are habitual ways of tackling problems which reflect personal mindsets. A more flexible style can follow deliberate attempts to practise strategies that are less congenial (fallback strategies). For example, if you prefer a left-brain strategy you could practise the right-brain approaches such as metaphor as a fallback in problem-solving.

Another way of broadening one's range of problem-solving strategies is to become more receptive to people with opposing problem-solving styles. ('My way is my way, not the way'.)

3 Dealing with too many options

Life is a complicated business. Every moment of every day we are bombarded with information about the world, which we take in through our eyes, ears, and sense receptors. In principle this means that there are also many ways of interpreting and responding to the information. Something as simple as putting on our overcoat and buttoning it up would be quite a problem if we had to consider all the thousands of different combinations of ways that are possible. We would never get to work if we had to decide on the best possible route from among the millions of theoretical options. And opening the morning's mail and replying to it would be quite out of the question, with the billions of sentences we actually could consider.

One way of coping with the enormous number of possibilities open to us is to deny the existence of many of the options. That is what the mechanism of mind set does, by taking information and coding the elements into categories that can be recognized and related to past experience, and conveniently ignoring information that does not fit into these patterns. Indeed, people can feel very uncomfortable if they are faced with large numbers of possibilities without any indication of which are the most important. It has been suggested that suspicion and dislike of creative problem-solving techniques may arise from uncertainties of dealing with scores of new ideas.

This is a quite unnecessary concern, for there are well-established ways of reducing the variety generated, as we shall now see. Some of the methods are more disposed towards a left-brain treatment, and others try to bring in the right brain's capacity for creative insight and vision.

The ones found most frequently in reports of creative problem-solving are:

> intuitive judgement ('gut feel')
> voting
> hurdles
> grouping (clustering or mapping)
> weighting methods

There have been few attempts to examine why one particular technique is used in preference to another. Techniques seem to be used in specific circumstances according to personal taste, and previously established custom and practice. Let's take a look at their operating mechanisms, and try to establish some ground rules for selecting one rather than another of the closing down, or convergent, techniques according to personal information-processing style, and specific circumstances.

INTUITIVE JUDGEMENT (GUT FEEL)

Gut feel is shorthand for relying on the right brain's intuitive kinds of information processing to reach a judgement. In the past, intuition has been regarded as a feminine characteristic, a kind of sixth sense which sometimes turns out well, but which may also be contrary to the logic of a given situation. We now know that a proportion of people, male as well as female, prefer to process information in a way which deals more in relationships and possibilities, rather than with facts and figures. We also know that such an intuitive style is particularly valuable in dealing with 'fuzzy problems' for which there may be no reliable factual data available.

Intuition is an essential component of creative problem-solving. In routine situations logical step-by-step methods may be adequate to reason a way to a routine answer. However, in the examples we gave in Chapter 1 of different kinds of open-ended problems, the creative leap is in the first instance an intuitive one. Once the leap has been made it may be possible to work out a logical justification for it.

In some situations the evidence suggests that the intuitive problem-solver has actually taken a short cut and somehow arrived at a decision that could have been reached through conscious deliberations. Chess masters, for example, reach a rapid and intuitive decision about the move they intend to play, and then spend as much time as they are allowed checking the logic and consequences of the move. More often than not they confirm their intuition and play the move they first thought of. Some financial trading jobs put even greater demands on the professionals involved, whose intuitive decisions can involve millions of pounds each time they give a buy or sell order. Gamblers who can hardly explain why can offer or take complex combinations of bets in less time than it takes to punch the data into a computer terminal. And at work, managerial decisions often have to be based on what the manager might call experience or judgement, which are more socially accepted terms for gut feel.

We have already seen how opening up a problem can lead to large numbers of differing perspectives, from a starting position of stuckness. This occurs when a fuzzy problem is turned into a series of possible new perspectives or 'how to' statements, for example, as part of a creative problem-solving exercise. Under such circumstances the person looking for new insights is invited to select a small number of promising starting points. If the problem-owner is willing to trust intuition, he or she will have no difficulty making a rapid scan of the material – even if there are scores of problem statements – and picking out a few candidates.

In a similar fashion, a brainstorming session may result in fifty or a hundred ideas, usually uncomplicated ones, to be sure. But during the process an idea is sometimes suggested which produces a spontaneous reaction of pleasure and approval from the group. An 'instant winner' has been found which has triggered off the right brain and intuitive approval. Under these circumstances it is normal after the brainstorming session for the originally acclaimed 'instant winner' idea to emerge triumphant, even when more analytical evaluation methods are applied.

It must be said that when gut feel is wrong it can be horribly wrong. There is a history of misguided inspirations which have led inventors to pursue an intuitively held belief well beyond any justifiable limits. Nevertheless, among more rational (left-brain) types there is a prejudice against intuitive methods of reaching decisions which deserves to be challenged. We can actually train ourselves to become more aware of the signals from our below conscious thoughts, and in this way become more sensitive to their messages.

If you would not of choice rely on gut feel to select a few instant winners from a list of 'how to' statements you probably have a more left-brain decision-taking style. And here is some good news. You are among the people most likely to benefit from introducing a little gut feel into your decision-making, when the situation is appropriate (as it is when you are looking for new ideas, for example). Why? Because it provides you with a fallback style of decision-making that is so different from your habitual style that it will help break you out of dominant mind sets and assumptions in your decision-making which even left-brain styles are prone to. What's more you will be well placed to check out the ideas in a more logical left-brain fashion when the information becomes available to you.

Finally, a consoling word to those who have a naturally intuitive decision-style. You have no difficulties trusting your intuition in problem-solving. If it sometimes leads you astray force yourself to read on, as you may decide to build in some more structured methods of closing down to avoid the excessive pursuit of false inspirations.

VOTING

It is a deep-rooted mind set to resort to voting when a group of people are gathered together trying to reach a decision. As with other mind sets, it can blinker us to the assumptions we make. Voting is generally assumed to be: (a) fair and (b) a logical means of reaching a decision. But, as many hardened organizational in-fighters know, voting can be a manipulative device in the hands of an unscrupulous chairperson. Nor is it as logical as it seems. After all, suppose a board of directors vote nine to seven to close down a factory. Does that make it the correct decision? Of course it doesn't. Correctness is an attribute of left-brain procedures. The more examples we think of, the more we can see voting as an expression of right-brain thinking dressed up in the left-brain guise of numbers.

Essentially, voting is a symbolic act – a powerful ritual associated with participation, commitment and democracy. In a creative problem-solving meeting that has generated a large number of ideas (let's say from a brainstorming) someone in the group often suggests taking a vote to help decide which ideas they should concentrate on. If I am involved I am quite happy to go along with the voting – as long as it is understood that the result relates to the acceptability of the ideas, not their quality.

There are two important reasons why voting can improve the quality of decision making. First, it can reduce the effects of status. Most of us have experienced the powerful effect of status in workgroups – either from senior managers present, or from professional 'experts' called in to give advice. Voting has been shown to lead to decisions that are less heavily influenced by one or two powerful individuals.

A second and more powerful way in which voting can lead to improved decision making is when the procedure permits reappraisal in the light of additional information. Voting is used as the closing down technique of first choice in several group decision-making techniques which will be covered more fully in the chapter on the brainstorming family of techniques, when it is important to establish viewpoints on issues of common interest.

To summarize, voting is often an unthinking strategy during decision making which may be more, or less, effective according to directors vote nine to seven to close down a factory. Does that make it the correct decision? Of course it doesn't. Correctness is an attribute of left-brain procedures. The more examples we think of, because of time pressures, it is tolerable. If it is a device to cut short views that are uncomfortable to the majority of the group, the process is uncreative and will lead to rigid group behaviours, the outcome of which is failure to react to opportunities and threats.

In the specific context of creative problem-solving techniques a good rule is to use voting to indicate individual commitment, rather than as a means of identifying 'best' options. For example, an agenda could be derived by inviting each member of a meeting to nominate his or her preferred 'how to' item, from a previously collected list. The voting then entails accepting ownership of the problems associated with the agenda item, and can assist in showing who will be expected to act subsequent to ideas being suggested.

CLUSTERING

Clustering is a quite different closing down mechanism which relies on the creative process of pattern discovery – very much a right-brain activity. If a large number of ideas needs to be examined – for example, after a brainstorming – clustering attempts to create a smaller number of groups of ideas. It is much easier then to make evaluative judgements about the groupings, and about the relationships between groupings. We can use our understanding of blocks to creativity to design procedures for effective clustering. The process should avoid premature evaluation, over-dominant and unhelpful mind sets, one-right-answer thinking, and so on. Also, we know that warm-up, incubation and a positive constructive climate enhance right-brain performance. These principles can be put to work to discover unexpected and valuable groupings of ideas.

Working alone with a set of fifty to a hundred ideas, I find it valuable to write each item down as a brief phrase on a card. Then I spread out the cards and look for obvious and less obvious groups. I promise myself that, if I start feeling increasingly 'stuck', I shall give the problem time to incubate – in which case I prefer to collect up the cards, destroying the half-formed clusters which may be contributing to the stuckness. This personal contract may have a liberating effect in itself as it reduces any compulsive need for closure.

Unlike voting, which cuts down on options by a process of elimination, clustering does not eliminate. It incorporates. In systems terms, it refocuses our attention on higher levels of classification – with the individual ideas as subsets of the clusters. It becomes easier to understand – not just the importance of each of the clusters, but the possible interrelationships.

Clustering can be considered as any process of creating a smaller number of groupings from a larger set of undifferentiated elements. It crops up in various techniques. One advocate called it 'morphological creativity'. An example is given in Chapter 10 of clustering procedures in a diversification exercise. In a survey of methods of idea generation in Japan a version of clustering (the KJ technique) was found to be, with brainstorming, the most frequently mentioned technique.

HURDLES

In some idea-collection activities such as suggestion schemes, ideas arrive at irregular intervals, and it may not be possible to arrange team meetings to deal rapidly enough with the flow of ideas. In these cases, a preferred method of closing down is to confront the ideas with a series of challenges or hurdles of increasing severity. (Cheap tests first; more costly tests on smaller numbers of surviving ideas. The same applies in most personnel screening and selection work.)

In the Grand National horse race, the hurdles do sort out the relatively weak from the better horses (although favourites still fall at the first fence). But unlike horses, ideas can be modified even as the race is taking place.

Furthermore, they arrive with differing degrees of refinement, so that some may have confirming evidence (for or against) and others will not. And the hurdles themselves may not be straightforward. Each hurdle attempts to reduce the issue for each idea to 'does it go on, or doesn't it?', the either/or question that only applies when right-brain possibilities and 'maybe's are suppressed.

One simple but effective two-stage screen has been tested extensively for new product groups when ideas of different types are being regularly screened. Stage one is to set a three-in-one screen with the questions:

Is it new?
Is it relevant?
Can we see a clear and simple first action step?

This screen standardizes the ideas that get through and removes wishful ideas. (Of course, a wishful idea with a committed champion might be reworked and reintroduced.) A second screen is then set to test whether the ideas are as easy to put into practice as they are believed to be. A deadline is set for each idea to be converted into a tangible prototype or demonstration – 'a product in a bottle'. Once the time has elapsed without the tangible product being produced, the idea is put on the backburner, and attention is turned to the next idea.

A new products team can screen hundreds of ideas rapidly in this way. It has been found that the discipline of deadlines reduces the dangers of 'pet ideas'. However, such advice should be used for guidance, and not as absolute laws. The exceptional idea will crop up from time to time, when intuitive feelings need to be balanced against the left-brain logic of the screening results.

WEIGHTING SYSTEMS

Quantitative approaches to decision taking are the most common methods found in books of management decision theory. If gut feel is the essence of right-brain closing down, weighting methods are their mirror-image – the essence of left-brain information processing. Furthermore, the methods are very acceptable to professionally trained people, as they seem to offer certainties, and pointers to discriminate between the best idea and the others.

The well-known Kepner–Tregoe method of problem-solving advocates that, to reach a ranking among a set of options, a set of necessary criteria (i.e. hurdles) or 'musts' should be established. Then a set of desirable criteria should also be established ('needs'). Each 'must' receives a maximum weighting (say 10 out of 10); each 'need' is allocated a smaller weight, according to perceived importance, some being close to 10, others closer to 1.

Ideas are then graded. First the hurdles technique eliminates ideas that fail one of the necessary criteria. Remaining ideas are all systematically examined and coded according to their merits on each need. By adding together the weighted mean scores, a total score for each idea is obtained. The whole thing appears so logical . . .

In practice, the system works particularly well when the items being compared have been standardized and when the criteria for evaluation, taken together, make up an accurate statement of most of the factors that contribute to the perceived value of an item. The intuitive (i.e. 'gut feel') decision of experts can be converted into such a set of criteria in an expert system which thereafter, in a computer, can outperform less experienced decision takers – and sometimes outperform the expert whose decision rules it incorporates.

Individuals use such systems to complete those competitions on the back of cereal packets of the 'put these statements in order of

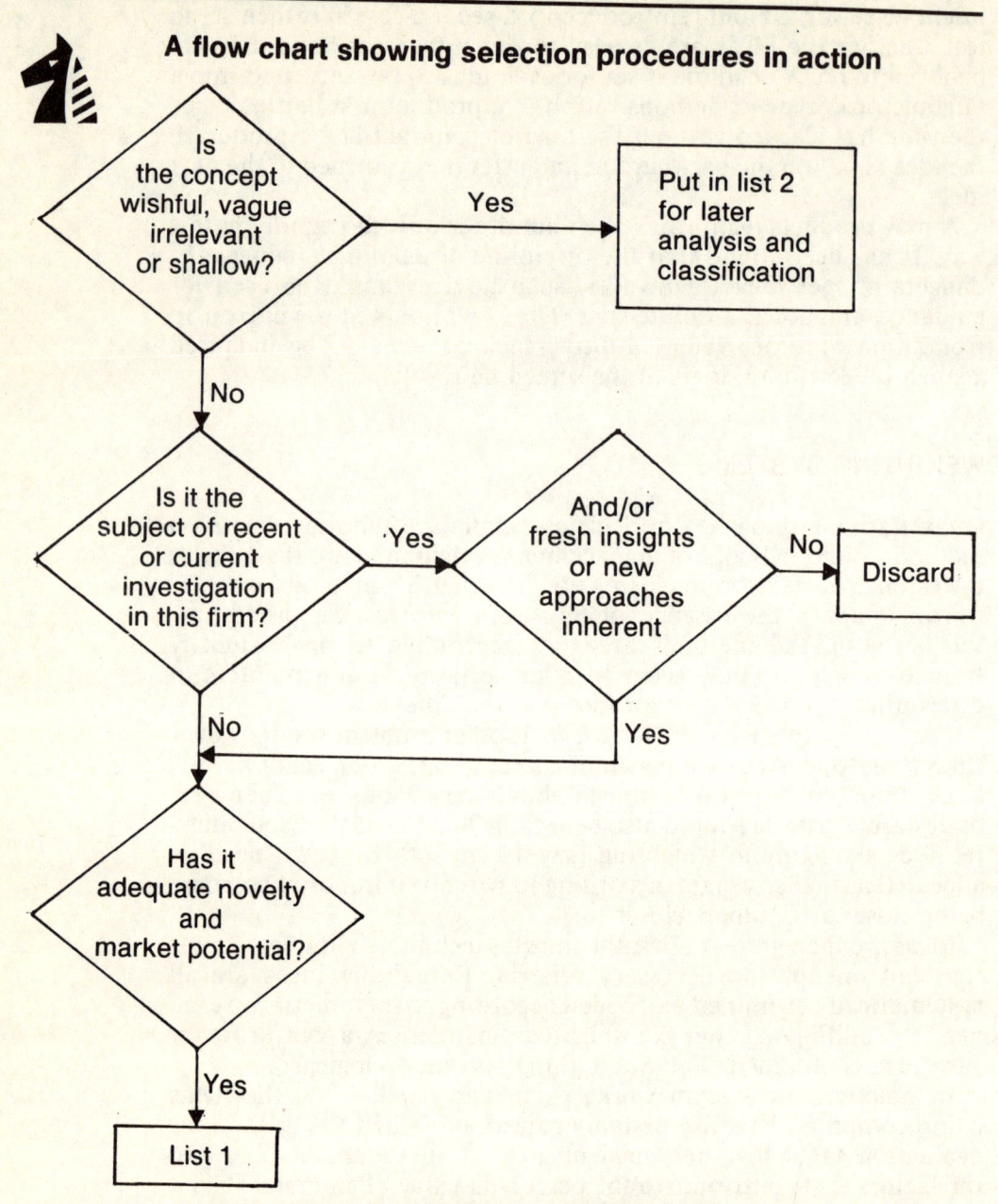

A flow chart showing selection procedures in action

- **Is the concept wishful, vague, irrelevant or shallow?**
  - Yes → Put in list 2 for later analysis and classification
  - No ↓
- **Is it the subject of recent or current investigation in this firm?**
  - Yes → **And/or fresh insights or new approaches inherent**
    - No → Discard
    - Yes ↓
  - No ↓
- **Has it adequate novelty and market potential?**
  - Yes → List 1

The first screen introduces a hurdle which separates wishful ideas. The second screen tests for novelty and market potential.
List 1 has relatively homogeneous ideas in it, and these can be treated to more quantitative methods.

importance' kind. Other applications reported include deciding which car, which holiday, even which house to buy. I even knew someone who claimed he had followed the system when he was in the process of selecting a wife. It is somewhere between choosing a rank order of ideas on a cornflakes packet and choosing a life partner that the technique stops being helpful for most of us, as the criteria become less clear and the items less standardized. At the extreme, a really novel idea creates its own criteria of excellence, rewriting the weighting system.

THE CENTRAL ISSUE: WHICH TECHNIQUE WHERE?

It would be useful to know which is the best technique for closing down options. Readers will by now realize that such a question does not command a simple answer. Personal preference comes into consideration – are you comfortable with more logical approaches, or more intuitive ones? The technique of choice will be influenced by personal preference. However, there are circumstances (and some have been indicated in the text) which favour one technique over others, from which we may be able to draw up some selection rules.

Gut feel is a way of breaking out of stuckness that comes from needing a decision in the absence of hard facts. It is at the same time a powerful creative decision-making mechanism, and the hardest to explain and justify to other people. It follows that, if there are more reasoned ways of reaching a decision, gut feel may be a liability from the point of view of acceptance seeking. But many complex business problems do require intuition. It has been suggested that routine planning problems may be best tackled in more left-brain ways, but general management decision-making will always require a contribution from right-brain thinking, as there is always an element of personal judgement that cannot be quantified.

Voting in creative problem-solving techniques can be found in the Delphi technique and nominal group methods of brainstorming in which individuals generate ideas in isolation from each other. In these techniques voting tests for consensus when there is no obvious agreement about a logical 'best' decision. Often the voters have a share of responsibility for the problem under discussion, or are likely to be influenced by what is decided at the vote. In contrast, when a single person has responsibility for solving the problem, the decision-making mode is more usually through intuition and gut feel. The difference lies in the existence of an acknowledged client or problem-owner whose acceptance of problem-ownership is related to the right to decide on the ideas that appeal to him or her. The rest of the group has no right to interfere with the selection process, which is concerned with helping the client break out of private mind sets which can hardly be challenged by outsiders, particularly through voting.

In competitive sports and in evaluating ideas, hurdles provide an unbiased method of sorting out the front runners from the rest. We have seen how they are efficient when the ideas are arriving over periods of time, and some mechanistic process is needed. The benefits are greater if the ideas are very diverse, as the hurdles can quickly remove the difficult-to-assess ones. The disadvantage of this arises if you need to be sure that you do not lose any extremely good idea. In many evaluation schemes there is a compromise between avoiding the loss of a small number of 'good' products, and letting too many 'bad' items slip through the net. So if the nature of the problem suggests that there is a very small number of ultimately acceptable ideas, accidental loss of a potential winner is bad. Hurdles are therefore best if there is a very large number of promising ideas to choose among.

Clustering seems to be particularly valuable if there is a need to transform the data in a qualitative way – for greater ease of understanding or decision-making. In particular, the technique helps if the purpose of the exercise is to understand the broad picture – the system and the interrelationships between the parts, rather than wanting to select out a small number of ideas from among the larger available set. Clustering helps to make some initial sense of a mass of details.

Weighting methods are most useful when the factors of importance for evaluation are all known and can be quantified. The conditions for effectiveness of such a left-brain approach are almost exactly the opposite to those favouring gut feel. Difficulties arise if some of the items are non-standard, as subsequent interpretation of the significance of the weightings relies on an assumption that all the items can be treated equivalently.

The difficulties in sorting out 'which technique when' arise because several factors come into the decision. From the above we can summarize the following important ones:

- Situation bias towards left-brain or right-brain methods.
- Whether the material being evaluated is all available at the start or arrives over periods of time.
- Whether the problem-solving need is to gain a broad picture or to find a smaller number of key items.
- Whether the decision is primarily one of individual insight or one of shared consensus.

It is possible to draw up a decision tree which shows how taking these factors into account leads to the selection of one technique over the others.

Unfortunately, such a tree over-simplifies the decision process. It makes assumptions about which are the most important factors, and is at best a description of how many selection decisions appear to be made at present, rather than suggesting whether there are other equally valid decisions. In other words we are still some way away from having a simple rule which removes the need for creative thinking.

SUMMARY

In creative problem-solving some people have been put off by the difficulties in 'closing down' and are deterred from search processes which throw up more than a few options.

It is important to know that there are excellent methods of closing down, so that we need not restrict our creative idea-generation for that reason.

The gut feel technique appeals to those who favour a more right-brain mode of decision making. It is particularly appropriate if the information is unclear and difficult to obtain.

Voting is a good way of establishing consensus, although care must be taken to avoid its manipulative uses, which restrict outcomes to a few politically acceptable ones.

Clustering reveals important patterns within sets of information and is of particular use when understanding of these patterns is more important than finding winners from a set of ideas.

Hurdles are a means of sorting out ideas which arrive over a period of time. Hurdles can act as a course filter for ideas of different kinds, e.g. with different amounts of information available about them.

Weighting is a technique which appeals to those who favour a more left-brain mode of decision making. It is particularly appropriate if the items being weighted are similar, and comparable.

These simple rules will provide guidelines regarding 'which technique where', but there will often be a need to experiment with more than one technique, to develop a greater understanding of their scope and limitations.

Factors influencing choice of a closing down technique

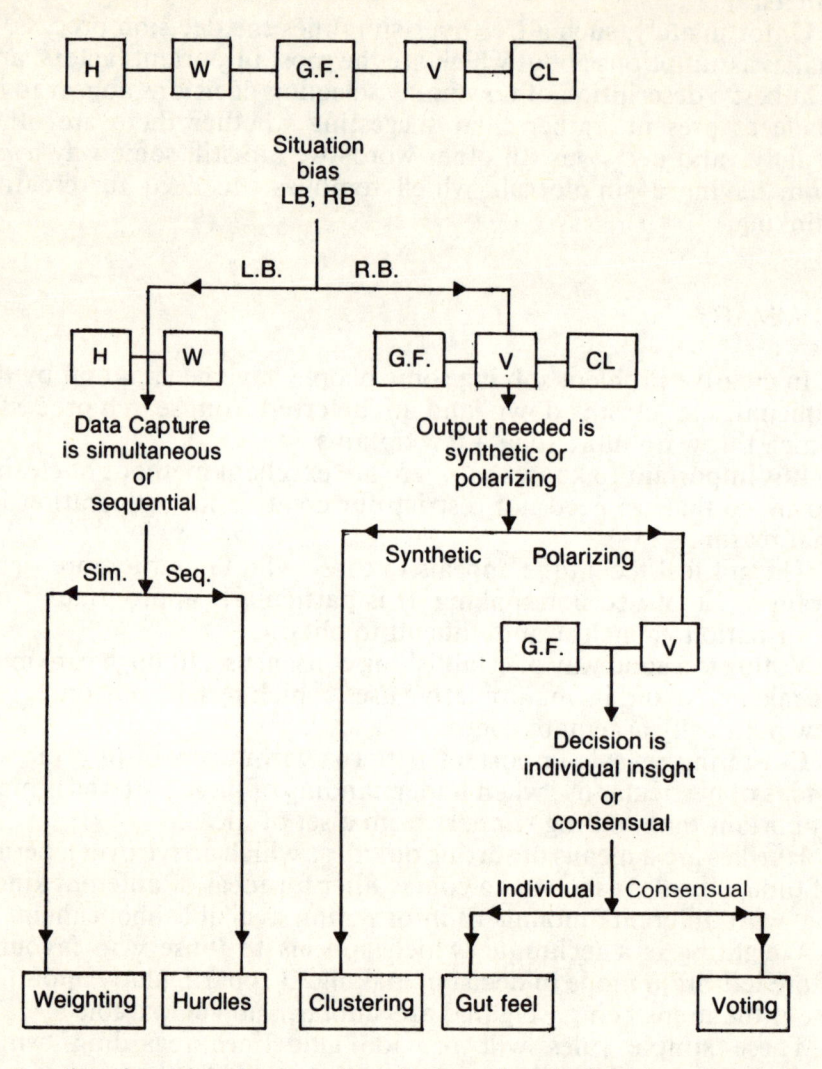

In practice there is a logic to the choice of a closing down technique which can be displayed as a decision-tree. The 'branches' arise according to the type of situation. Does it favour left-brain or right-brain approaches? Is data capture simultaneous or sequential? Is the output to be synthetic – including all the data at some level of generalization, or polarizing? i.e. eliminating unwanted data. Finally, the importance of individual versus group contributions may influence the final selection decision.

DEALING WITH TOO MANY OPTIONS   55

Factors influencing the decision to use a closing down technique: A 'fuzzier' view

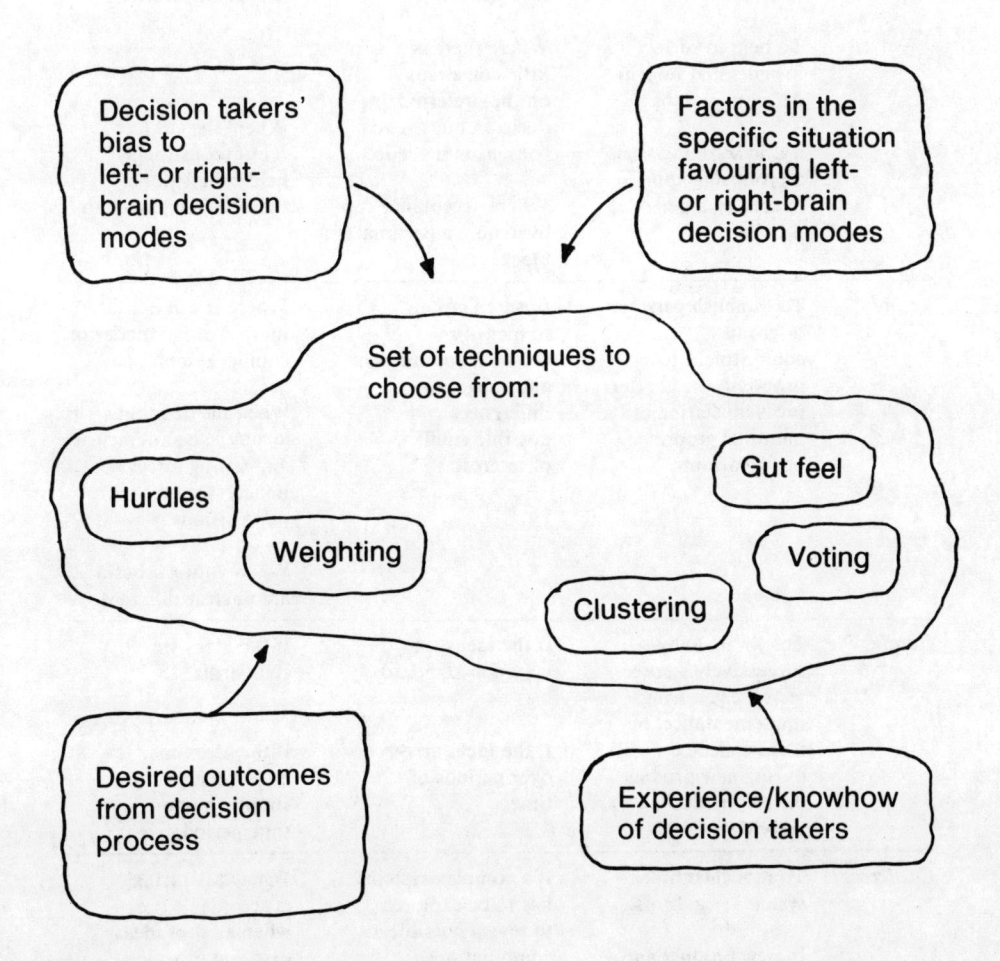

- Decision takers' bias to left- or right-brain decision modes
- Factors in the specific situation favouring left- or right-brain decision modes

Set of techniques to choose from:
- Hurdles
- Weighting
- Clustering
- Gut feel
- Voting

- Desired outcomes from decision process
- Experience/knowhow of decision takers

It is not possible in practice to give the 'right answer' to the question 'which (closing down) technique when?' The diagram shows factors which will influence different individuals in different ways.

COMPARISON OF CLOSING DOWN TECHNIQUES IN CREATIVE PROBLEM-SOLVING

Technique	Preferred usage	Suitable situations for its use	Unsuitable situations for its use
Gut feel	To make decisions in the absence of 'hard data'. To help to surface insights that inform decision making. e.g. in selecting a promising approach to solving a personal problem	Where personal insight and belief are important. Where there is little consensus on the preferred decision but where consensus is needed. Where acceptance can overcome a personal block.	Where there is a demonstrable logical 'imperative'. Where the gut feel reinforces strongly held beliefs rather than challenging them.
Voting	To establish personal or group commitment to proposals – e.g. after problem stating in 'nominal group' brainstorming	In small groups, to identify personal commitment and subgroup differences and possible conflicts of interest.	Where it will inhibit more creative modes of conflict resolution. When the decision set is incomplete and unclear and voting forces unnecessary 'either or' decisions When voting criteria are unclear/different.
Hurdles	To eliminate by successively sterner tests – e.g. during implementation of ideas collected during new product development activities	If the ideas are very non-standard. If the ideas arrive over periods of time.	If the ideas are standardized. If the ideas can be screened more simply in one time period.
Clustering	To model complex systems (e.g. firms). In new product and design projects. Can be relatively 'loose' or 'tight' sets; personal or group activity.	If a complex system has to be explored to reveal possible combinations. If the complexity of a system has to be controlled without losing any elements.	When 'satisficing' is acceptable (i.e. when a set of ideas exist out of which any idea reaching minimal criteria 'solves' the problem. When modelling the system is an over-sophistication.

Weighting	To rank a set of ideas	If the ideas are standardized, and representing a sample from a well-characterized population: e.g. technical properties or raw materials; financial criteria for investment decisions.	If the ideas are not standardized.
	To establish priorities across a portfolio of ideas		If the criteria are unclear.
			If the ideas are unclear.

4 How to remain creative

This chapter shows why we need a mixture of creative behaviours, and subsequent analysis of those behaviours, if we want to go on developing imaginative responses to problems.

WHAT IS CREATIVE ANALYSIS

Creative analysis is a conscious attempt to understand and analyse creative behaviours, particularly those associated with some conscious strategy for being creative, with the goal of providing new and modified approaches for future attempts to stimulate creativity.

In particular, the strategies 'consciously identified' for stimulating creativity involve the various creative problem-solving techniques such as brainstorming and lateral thinking which we shall be looking at in more detail in the next part of the book. One of the complications of analysing the techniques is the nature of the creative process, which is not itself entirely under conscious control. We cannot actually monitor what is going on as it is taking place. To understand and analyse such techniques it is important to have a view on the following aspects of creative problem-solving, some of which have been covered already, some of which we introduce now:

How do we get ideas?
What causes 'idea stuckness'?

How are techniques used to escape from idea stuckness?
What causes 'technique stuckness'?
What can be done to escape from 'technique stuckness'?

HOW DO WE GET IDEAS?

What distinguishes an idea from a fact, or a feeling, or a belief? When we say 'that's an idea', we do not usually pause to consider just what we mean. In common parlance an idea goes beyond any old thought that comes into consciousness. Observations of the world 'out there' are usually described as facts. Emotions triggered off by those facts are called feelings, which themselves can be linked to earlier facts and associated feeling through memory. Ideas go beyond our recollections and observations of the world out there. In the first instance an idea is the result of somebody interpreting or making sense of observed facts or feelings. An idea adds meaning to facts. (In communications theory a similar distinction is made between data, or observations 'out there', and information, or interpreted data.)

So – to answer the question posed at the start of the section – we get ideas by discovering meaning where previously there was no meaning, or perhaps a different meaning. The act of getting an idea is a creative act.

WHAT CAUSES IDEA STUCKNESS?

We have described the process of getting stuck as increasingly rigid thinking under the influence of distorting mind sets. Sometimes these arise because our previous efforts at getting ideas have actually been successful. An idea that was recognized as important ('a really good idea') can actually be a powerful blocker for future ideas. It may predispose us to repeat as closely as possible the conditions that surrounded the discovery of the previous idea.

The freshness and spontaneity of the early discovery is lost, as the repeated attempts become automatic. It becomes a matter of habit to follow the familiar path, and habit, with its implicit unchallenged assumptions, is the enemy of renewed creativity.

The author who writes a successful first book faces all these pressures from publishers and public – 'give us more of the same', they cry. The increasingly affluent scribbler may be quite happy to oblige, and to do so sticks closely to a formula, until loyal readers can predict more or less what will happen from the first few pages of the latest work. There are many trigger-points in everyday life, and as the author needs only a marginal modification for each new book, he or

Most of us live in a world that is changing fast enough to pose fresh problems regularly.

she can afford to wait for the 'idea' to turn up. Even so, 'writer's block' is the nightmare of even the most prolific author.

Journalists who have to meet deadlines six days a week regularly suffer 'stuckness'. Advertising agencies tolerate the tantrums of their so-called 'creative' staff in recognition of the agonies of a related stuckness as they seek their sixth campaign theme of the year. Most politicians searching for a lively phrase to enrich their campaign message are usually so stuck that they settle for the clichés that have become their travelling companions.

The factors associated with stuckness can be summed up as follows. People are particularly prone to stuckness if there is a repeated demand on them to produce new ideas, particularly if they rely on 'accidental' stimuli to provide the marginal modifications to the formula, and if they have no conscious understanding of the nature of the primitive idea-seeking strategy of 'just waiting for inspiration'.

This is not to suggest that the stuckness is permanent. Writers escape from their blocks, sometimes discovering factors which assist the process, sometimes in ignorance of contributive factors. Nevertheless, leaving the discovery of ideas to chance, if there is a regular need for new ideas, is far from satisfactory. Furthermore, most of us live in a world that is changing fast enough to pose fresh problems regularly. This may in principle offer fresh stimuli for change – or it may lead to failure of our habitual responses to produce workable results. We become stuck, and need new ways of dealing with the world.

HOW ARE TECHNIQUES USED TO ESCAPE FROM IDEA STUCKNESS?

To understand how techniques work (or how they are intended to work), we have to begin with how techniques are created. First there is someone trying to solve problems in a normal, that is to say habitual, way. Either deliberately or by accident he or she escapes from stuckness. Then comes the important step of reflecting on the whole process in order to understand what happened. If this creative analysis reveals a series of steps that can be re-applied to future problems we have the basis for a strategy, or generalizable approach. In some cases the steps can be described so that other people can experiment with them as well.

A creative problem-solving technique is made up of a series of steps, each of which can be described and put into practice. The describable steps are operational mechanisms. We have come across two kinds of operational mechanism – those for opening up options (divergent procedures), and those for closing down options (convergent procedures). It is also important that the description gives an indication of the context for use of the technique, which will guide its future users. Techniques pass into common use when someone describes those operational mechanisms in sufficient detail to allow others to experiment with them.

So a creativity spurring technique is a describable set of procedures which enabled the original user to escape from stuckness, and which have been followed in related circumstances, or contexts.

> Some unidentified early wise man observed that when he was worried about a problem he often found the answer after a good night's sleep. Or maybe it was discovered by a woman, who shared her observation with her sisters. In any event, the excellent advice 'let's sleep on this problem' emerged as an operational mechanism, and the context as 'when someone seems too close to the problem to think clearly'. This particular technique has resulted in enough successes for its gradual acceptance into popular folk-wisdom.

More complex techniques evolved, all with identified operational procedures and contexts. Brainstorming came about because Alex Osborn observed that the conventional behaviours in business meetings killed ideas, especially those of low status. This is the context in which brainstorming still operates. He proposed some simple operational mechanisms to break the inhibiting factors, such as 'no criticism of ideas . . . go for large numbers of ideas . . . build on each other's ideas . . . don't be afraid to freewheel.'

When these rules were followed it was found that dozens of ideas could be produced in a short space of time, sometimes including novel and valuable ones. The results were obviously an improvement on the outputs of meetings that had gone before, and the technique gained popularity very quickly.

WHAT CAUSES TECHNIQUE STUCKNESS

Our story does not end with the discovery of techniques which help us produce new and useful ideas. We have already come across the problems that follow the successful production of a good idea. The very success of the act of creation biases future behaviours. The good idea becomes the enemy of different kinds of idea. Similarly, the successful use of a technique can carry its own built-in seeds of destruction.

The brainstorming technique can continue to serve as an illustration. The first time it is used, the comparison with previous meetings is particularly striking. There is an incentive to try again, following the same procedures. The process becomes more and more automatic or habit forming. If the results are not satisfactory, the group of habitual brainstormers have only two options: trying again, or giving up. In other words they are in the same position with their technique as someone struggling against a blocking mind set: stuck, and becoming increasingly stuck through redoubled efforts.

Technique stuckness is common, and can be expected because of the decreasing impact of any experience with repetition. Furthermore, previous success will increase willingness to try the technique in different settings, so that, unnoticed, the contexts will change. Brainstorming worked for our team looking for new marketing ideas for cosmetics? Let's try it with a team of designers building a chemicals plant. Or let's see if we can brainstorm to find a new chairman of the company...

The parallel with idea stuckness is clear. Although brainstormings can be successful, the group has no mechanisms for learning from bad experiences, so as to discover ways of escaping from technique stuckness.

WHAT CAN BE DONE TO ESCAPE FROM TECHNIQUE STUCKNESS?

An argument has been constructed for using techniques to escape from idea stuckness, and for the need to find some other way of escape from technique stuckness. It should come as no surprise that the proposed approach is through creative analysis, which we described early in the chapter as a conscious attempt to understand and analyse creative behaviours, with the goal of providing new and modified approaches for future attempts to stimulate creativity. More specifically we suggested it was applicable to creativity techniques ('conscious strategies for being creative'), thus becoming a process for inventing new and modified creativity techniques.

In principle creative analysis is easy. Following the deliberate use of a technique, we can analyse the operational mechanisms, precepts, context, and outcomes. This suggests modified approaches for different contexts.

There is a natural tendency to avoid reflecting on past experience in a systematic way. We head for the next experience, taking with us an increasingly faint recollection of the details of the earlier creative activity. The discipline of recording and evaluating the event is one that has to be cultivated, so that it becomes a matter of habit.

Representation of Creative Analysis as escape from a general and automatic problem-solving strategy

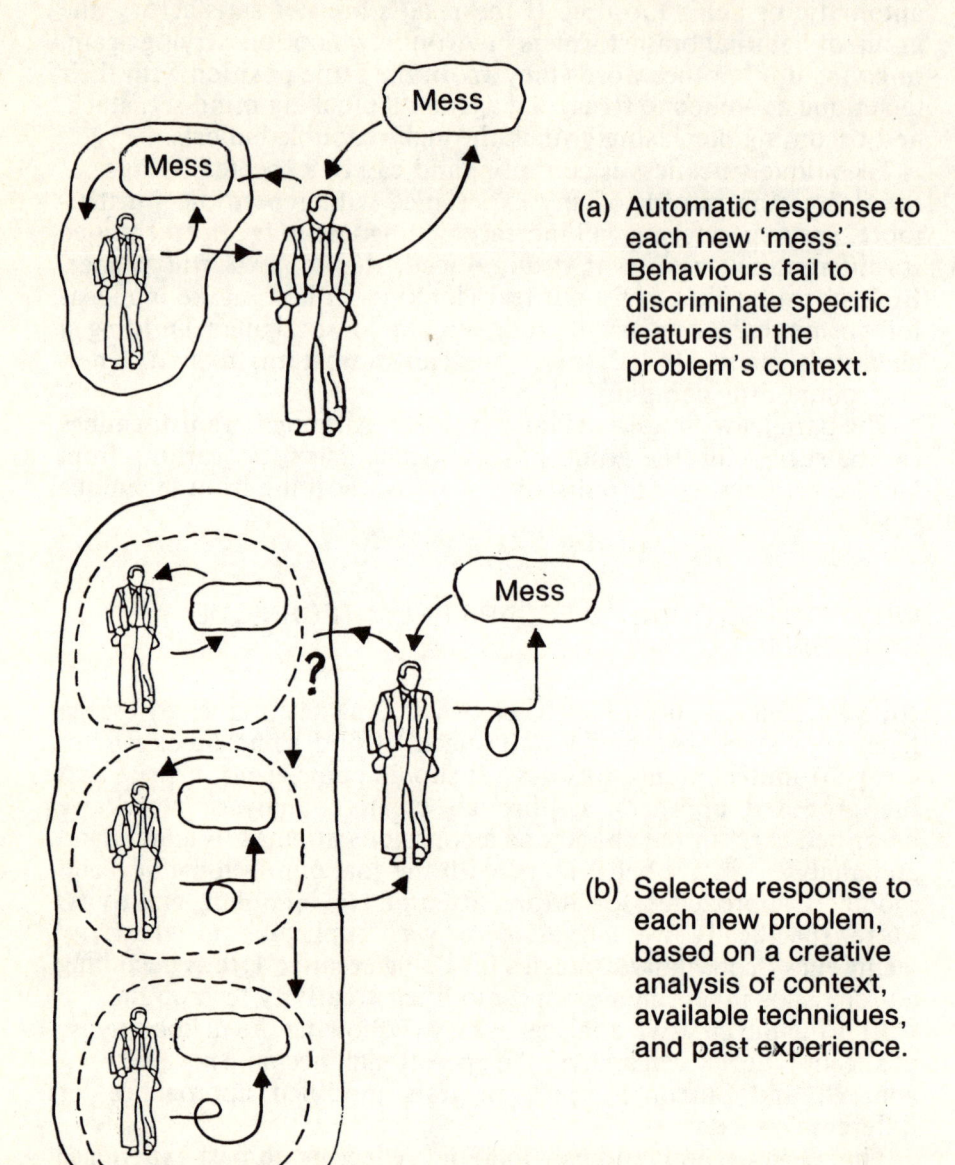

(a) Automatic response to each new 'mess'. Behaviours fail to discriminate specific features in the problem's context.

(b) Selected response to each new problem, based on a creative analysis of context, available techniques, and past experience.

Here are two examples showing how new techniques can emerge from a creative analysis of practical experiences of creative problem-solving exercises.

1 From brainstorming to minibrainstorming. Over a period of years, teaching and consultancy work have given me many opportunities to be involved in brainstorming sessions. From time to time some experience suggested a possible change or improvement for future trials. One simple deliberate technique modification occurred when I acquired an office that was too small to incorporate the habitual apparatus of flipchart stand, easy chairs, and six to eight brainstormers. I frequently convened meetings in that office with subjects suited to brainstorming, but with only two or three associates or students.

Of necessity, the context of the meetings differed from most 'full-blooded' ideas sessions. An analysis of typical situations suggests that we often had only ten or fifteen minutes to deal with a topic such as 'how to find new clients for student projects' or 'how to advertise our new training product'. Partly logically and partly by trial and error we began experimenting with smaller groups, simple alternatives to a flipchart, shorter brainstormings.

At the moment anyone in a group during a discussion may shift into a minibrainstorming mode simply by taping a sheet of paper to the back of the office door, and listing the ideas that are being discussed. This rather trivial example shows how we eventually broke a mind set shared with many other brainstormers, that the technique requires the team to generate fifty or a hundred ideas (we may stop at ten or even five). We also challenged the assumptions that brainstorming requires six people and a flipchart. (Another example of minibrainstorming is found in Chapter 12).

2 From excursions to split-page problem-solving. In the 1970s many practitioners of creative problem-solving techniques were influenced by work on deliberate metaphor-seeking. Examples can be found in Chapter 9, where the characteristic of the approach is revealed as taking a team of people away from the 'real' problem in a series of stages. Other researchers independently found ways of shortening the excursion without losing its impact. Our own creative analysis again did not happen as the result of a single analytical investigation, but was a mix of analysis of sessions that failed, and trials of modifications.

It was clear that the format of successful excursion involved left-brain and right-brain activities. Typically, a visual image (right-brain) is shared by a group in discussion (left-brain). As was shown in Chapter 2, the metaphor or excursion has to distract the attention away from the real problem long enough to loosen the hold of habitual ideas. Unsuccessful sessions result when team members forget the metaphor and let their concern for the problem return too rapidly to their conscious attention.

One of the trainers had been experimenting during this period with a split-page technique for evaluating ideas. He would encourage a problem-solving team to evaluate an idea by splitting a page vertically, and writing the positive points on the left side of the line, and the negatives on the right. We also tried splitting ideas further by writing the negatives on the left side of a fresh page, and trying to overcome as many of them as possible on the right side of the page. It emerged that previously difficult groups could quickly deal with many of the negatives using this split-page format.

At some stage we realized (as a group of trainers/creativity consultants) that the split-page technique was worth testing as a means of 'force-fitting' elements of a disguised problem back to the real problem. When we experimented we found that the technique had an unexpected power. When groups are presented with a dozen or so briefly stated ideas dealing with the disguised problem on the left side of the page, they are strongly motivated to relate each idea quickly to the real problem. It seems relatively easy for groups to move from disguised problem idea to real problem idea, repeatedly. Furthermore, our expectations as group leaders have changed. We are now confident that each new group will be able to find links with the problem triggered by every one of the elements of the disguised problem. This kind of confidence in a technique is, of itself, a self-fulfilling prophecy, and our expectations are being confirmed.

DEVELOPING EXPERIENCE IN CREATIVE ANALYSIS

The examples show how a little analysis can suggest modifications to creative problem-solving techniques. For research into creativity and its techniques the analysis has to be more rigorous, and include careful study of the various elements of a technique, and the possible intended and unintended consequences of the elements. Fortunately, for most practical purposes, a less formal approach will still be of value. The following practical tips may assist in developing creative analysis skills, and thereby deriving more benefits from using creativity techniques.

1 *Plan*. Make it a habit to plan any attempt to generate ideas. This is when you have a conscious choice of the type of technique to use, taking into the context the objectives, who should be

involved, timescales, location, and so on. The choice of technique system then will be more considered, and less reliant on your first impulse or dominant mind set. For more complex group exercises I find it useful to carry out a mental 'dummy run' of what might actually happen.

2 *Keep creative exercises and analysis apart.* Analysis before and after the session is vital. During a session, attention to the 'why' keeps the left brain too active and engaged on the process. Even the group leader, who attends to the mechanics of group process, should attend during the meeting to how the group is progressing, not why things are turning out well or badly.

3 *Review.* Immediately after the session it is excellent practice to check the feelings and observations of participants. Instructive suggestions for future approaches often emerge.

4 *Keep records.* Most practitioners of creative problem-solving techniques do not like the discipline of careful recording of sessions. There are few reported comprehensive case examples out of the thousands of activities that take place every year in dozens of different countries. These sessions should be treated at least as seriously as any other project, and descriptions should be written for future reference and analysis.

Beware of electronic recording. Attempts to hold information through audio and video tapes have not been successful – there's too much real time packed into the accumulated set of discs/tapes, and evaluating takes at least twice as long as each original recording.

5 *Understand what you are doing and why.* The 'what' comes from studying the practical activities and outcomes, that is, the operational mechanisms; the 'why' from the less tangible reasons or theoretical justifications we called precepts. In addition the context has always to be remembered.

6 *Learn from the experiences of others.* The remainder of the book offers opportunities to do this. As far as possible the techniques have been explained with indications of all three components required for a creative analysis – the operational mechanisms, the precepts and the context.

7 *Experiment.* Creative problem-solving is still an emerging subject, needing more experiments, as well as closer links between theories and practice. The need may be not for new techniques, but for more enlightened application of existing families of techniques followed by analysis and modifications. The outlined approach to a creative analysis is just one of many investigative

A form for monitoring group problem-solving processes

1. Meeting date _____ 2. Code _____ 3. Client _____
4. Problem title _____
5. Problem category _____ 6. Organizer _____
7. Composition of the group: names, background, familiarity with problem (F_P) and with the techniques (F_t)

Name	Background	F_P	F_t	Name	Background	F_P	F_t

8. Pre-meeting observations _____
9. The meeting
9.1 Cooperation
9.2 Positivity
9.3 Acceptance of procedure
9.4 Level of speculation
9.5 Orientation time
9.6 Idea-generation time
9.7 Total ideas produced
9.8 Types of subroutines (SR) _____
SR(0) Pre-meeting orientation _____
SR(1) _____
SR(2) _____
SR(3) _____
SR(4) _____
SR(5) _____
10. Main objective(s) of the exercise _____

11. Post-meeting comments by participants _____

12. Meeting recorded by _____
13. Key individuals – idea development   names F_P F_t

14. Key individuals – evaluation   names F_P F_t

15. Evaluation procedures _____
16. Details of short-listed ideas _____
    _____
    _____
17. Approximate times for development and evaluation stages _____
18. Impact of exercise on client's actions
    (a) Within a month _____
    (b) After six months _____
19. Impact of meeting on client's perception of the problem
    (a) Immediately _____
    (b) After one month _____
    (c) After six months _____
20. Summary of the exercise and how it might have been improved

Signed _____ Date _____

---

paths that might be taken. 'There must be other ways, there might be better ways.'

SUMMARY

Creative analysis is a conscious attempt to understand and analyse creative behaviours, particularly those associated with some conscious strategy for being creative, with the goal of providing new and modified approaches for future attempts to stimulate creativity.

We get ideas by discovering meaning in matters of personal significance. We are blocked from getting ideas by unhelpful mind sets and thought habits.

Creativity techniques provide a 'set to break set', thus liberating fresh ideas. However, with repeated use techniques themselves become ritualized habits, and lose their ability to help participants break out of their unhelpful mind sets.

Creative analysis is an approach for maintaining the power of creativity techniques through modifying them after experiments and analysis.

Creative analysis can be assisted by: good planning, keeping creative and analytical stages apart; reviewing and recording creativity exercises; and by experimenting with modifications which suggest themselves over time.

Part II
PROCESS AND PROCEDURE

5 Blockbusting

Creativity is escape from stuckness or self-imposed mental blocks. We saw in Part I a few ways of 'tricking' the mind into different perspectives. We also came across a few climate-modifying techniques such as 'yes and' which prevent premature rejection of ideas. It is now time to look at a wider range of methods for stimulating creative thinking at an individual level. The techniques work by conceptual blockbusting – helping us break out of our self-imposed blocks to arrive at important and novel personal insights. In this chapter we examine the following techniques which represent a sample of the most widely applicable ones:

- Lateral thinking:
    Intermediate impossible, or finding stepping stones from one perception of reality to a new one.
    Random juxtaposition, which forces you to extend the horizons of your thinking by the deliberate introduction of evocative and random extra ideas.
    Concept challenge, which focuses attention on the assumptions behind assertions of fact and belief.
- Reversing perspective as a means of turning 'threats into opportunities, weaknesses into strengths'.
- Bunches of bananas, a provocative introduction of irrelevant material when idea searches are only producing unimaginative ideas.

- Wishful thinking, or expressing suppressed but deeply held goals as a starting point to achieving them.
- Knight's move thinking, which finds imaginative ways of escaping from either/or thinking.
- Force-fitting ideas, so that two ideas become merged into a powerful new concept combining the virtues of each of the original ideas.

These techniques will be covered in sufficient detail to enable readers to try them out whenever the need for blockbusting has been recognized.

LATERAL THINKING

Lateral thinking is firmly linked to the name of Edward de Bono. His ideas came to wide public attention in the late 1960s and early 1970s. According to his early books lateral thinking is a process and a set of techniques which demystify the creative process by providing thinking tools and a conceptual framework. In a well-known metaphor, he describes a typical problem-solving process as 'digging a hole deeper'. This is vertical thinking and it is only through the use of lateral thinking that we can escape from the hole and 'find somewhere else to dig'.

For de Bono, the need for lateral thinking arises because the mind does not record successive data in an objective way, but produces understanding through creating patterns. New data are fitted into older patterns, and also influence and reorganize the older patterns. We therefore have a bias towards interpreting current experiences in the light of past experiences. He suggests various mechanisms for restructuring the thinking process. These are the techniques of lateral thinking. We shall look at three of the most widespread applications.

The intermediate impossible

This is an idea which would be rejected by the logical conventions of either/or thinking. However, when we are learning to use lateral thinking it is useful to have a label such as 'intermediate impossible' to remind us that we are not operating in our normal yes/no thinking mode, and that an impossible idea is impossible only according to the assumptions of our mind sets. In this way we can treat such an idea as a stepping stone from one view of reality to a new one.

The operational procedure is to set about finding a totally outrageous idea. Then, preferably without an undue rush back to reality, you play around wth the idea, understanding it more deeply, looking for modifications to return you to a new and useful reality.

The context which suggests trying out an intermediate impossible is whenever you have recognized you are stuck, perhaps an inner voice telling you that you have to break out of the confines of your thinking on some issue.

Suppose your original problem was people wasting your time with trivial enquiries. You have tried the obvious ways of dealing with the problem without success. You remain stuck until you recognize that you are stuck and that you need some new ideas. This allows you consciously to think of an intermediate impossible:

> I'd like to find out if these people are serious. When someone calls me up I'd like to hook them up to a lie detector to find out.'

Not bad, but not totally impossible, and the weirder we make our stepping stone, the further away from the confines of our past thinking we can take ourselves. How about:

> 'When somebody calls I transmit a signal which paralyses the centres of the brain where they convert truth into lies'?

That's impossible enough. Now how might we take this as a stepping stone back to a new reality? Our thought processes might take the following direction.

> 'Perhaps the truth-triggering signal is one which makes the person want to tell me the truth. So I have to do more to win their trust. Maybe I've got to be more truthful as well .... Yes, and most people won't answer a direct question with a direct lie, so the way to obtain honest answers is to ask direct questions about what the problem really is, and what is the real purpose of their visit or phone call.'

Practising the intermediate impossible technique leads to greater ability to unearth assumptions which previously had led us to assume something to be impossible. And it is through such discoveries that we break out of our conceptual blocks.

Random juxtaposition

This approach breaks out of mind sets by bringing together current thinking and an unexpected and random additional focus or concept. It becomes possible to find connections that are remote from our habitual thought combinations. Instead of waiting for rare new experiences to happen we create them deliberately and attempt to link them to past experience.

When we do this we are creating a new idea which makes sense to us, rather than uncovering something that already existed. This is what happens millions of times every day as regular readers of such things turn to their horoscopes. From a few bland assertions we create our own reality, by taking a random statement and juxtaposing it with our hopes and fears.

There are several ways of deliberately stimulating ideas through juxtaposition of unexpected material. Seeking out new environments rich in different stimuli is a simple approach. A walk around a museum or a supermarket is guaranteed to trigger off fresh thoughts for the prepared mind. A more contrived method is to open a book at random, and pick a word. The very simple pronouns (I, you, me etc) and link words (and, because, but) may be excluded, but otherwise set yourself the rule that you will work with any word that you find. (Otherwise you will be trapped into looking for words that are close enough for you to trigger off close associations with existing ideas, bounded by your assumptions of reality that block you from new ideas.)

You can use any words that are far enough away from the core concepts of your working life, provided you are prepared to manipulate them. From a random page in my dictionary I found the following trigger words which will all bring fresh thinking to my current problem of improving a distribution system.

Random word	Ideas on distribution triggered by the random words
hardy	Toughen up rules, packaging, dealerships
hare	Speed up communications; use hare as our slogan
harem	New way to select and keep our dealers?
haricot	Sustains the soil it grows in. How do this for customers?
harlequin	Find two different geographic niches for our product.
harlot	People come to her. Attract people to cash and carry?
harm	Collect data of harm caused by bad practices, and correct.

In selecting the words I rejected 'hareld', 'harigal', 'Harijan' as being too little known, and I would have ignored 'he', and 'hah', as being too simple. Most words 'work' in triggering ideas, although simple nouns, and verbs suggesting activities, seem to have particular power.

Concept challenge

This technique operates by challenging what is usually taken for granted. If progress is deliberately blocked off temporarily in one direction it becomes easier to find an alternative direction or a lateral leap. Once again, the important first step to convert the principle into a deliberate thinking aid is recognition of the need for challenging concepts. Useful practice can be obtained by taking a closer look at 'logical' arguments in business reports. Recommendations, in particular, are fruitful places for surfacing assumptions.

From a letter to a national newspaper:

> 'Inflation can be contained in two ways: indirectly by wage restraint; or directly by controlling prices.'

By systematically challenging all the assumptions behind just one such statement it is possible even for a layman to see much more than otherwise meets the eye. The example can be taken as if it had appeared in a company report as a recommendation.

> We leave inflation as the focus of the concept, and challenge as much as we can of the rest of the sentence. Can be contained, or might be contained? Contained – for ever, for a day? Contained at today's levels, regardless of external forces of innovation, technology, or financial market disorders? Would 'influenced' be a better word than 'contained'? In two ways – only two? Might there be other ways based on changing attitudes and expectations? Indirectly by wage restraint – this assumes that the only indirect way is by wage restraint. Are there other indirect ways (there are, some might even be acceptable ways, such as the ones just mentioned)? Directly by controlling prices – a similar assumption, that the only direct way to 'contain' inflation is to control prices. Indirect or direct. A popular assumption – the either/or trap. How about considering a mix of indirect and direct methods?

Concept challenge is at the same time analytical and creative. It is hard work, but the rewards are escape from sloppy thinking and hidden assumptions.

There are other techniques which show a family resemblance to the three lateral thinking ones described here. The following five have been widely tested in individual and group creativity sessions.

THE REVERSALS TECHNIQUE

Most of us have had the pleasure from time to time of discovering something by turning conventional logic upside down. In this section we shall look at examples of how this occurs and then consider mechanisms for making it happen on a more regular basis.

> *Reversals example 1.* One of my favourite examples comes from a company that was plagued by pilferage. The managers were

concerned that the toy cars they were manufacturing were being stolen while awaiting distribution. Conventional methods of reducing the pilferage had a partial effect, but still quantities were being stolen. At some point, the cost of stopping the problem would have risen beyond the benefits of stopping the cars from being stolen. In the end a bright idea struck one of the managers, and careful figures were collected of the nature of the pilferage. The result was as hoped for. The most popular targets of pilferage were those cars in greatest demand in the marketplace. It turned out that the residual pilferage served as a very convenient market research indicator.

Reversals example 2. Another famous story relates how Alexander Fleming made the initial discovery of the penicillin mould. He came across a contamination in some of his experimental dishes. He also noticed an inhibition of the mould that was growing there. While many more tidy personalities would have demanded better and cleaner laboratory conditions, Fleming was able to reverse this perspective. Far from seeing dirty conditions uncongenial to scientific research, he was able to see an opportunity which has made a great contribution to the wellbeing of mankind.

At a humble level, many industrial breakthroughs emerge through the turning of conventional wisdom on its head. Waste products sometimes turn out to be best sellers. 'Blu-tak', the all-purpose adhesive, began life as the dregs of a polymerization process.

Reversals example 3. From my own experience comes the story of a researcher who was very concerned about his failure to produce a certain chemical reaction. His failure resulted in the deposit of a thin film of material resistant to acids and solvents, which would cohere to his reaction vessel. It emerged that he had arrived at a means of producing a kind of non-stick material with great commercial possibilities. Unfortunately for his company he failed to switch his thinking into reverse, and never turned the perceived problem (of unwanted solvent-resisting material), into the opportunity of a new kind of resistant and adhesive surface coating.

Reversals example 4. A new technology instance comes from the records of a company manufacturing lasers. At first they were concerned that their particular laser could not match those of their competitors in certain characteristics. At some point, however, they recognized the enormous benefits in that, while they could not imitate their competitors, it was equally impossible for the competitors to achieve some of the results they could arrive at. This gave them greater protectability than any patent by itself. They have successfully established a profitable niche in the market.

All these examples (and many more could be added) suggest that reversing perspective can lead to valuable new ideas. But how can we 'reverse to order'?

Reversals often involve a motivated search to overcome a problem or perceived need. Fleming had an obsession about cataloguing and studying moulds. These are conditions of increasingly restrictive mind set. Reversals seem to be the mechanism to escape from some dominant mind sets. Very often the escape follows a period of stuckness and struggle.

I have come across three different strategies which can be applied in many industrial contexts to break out of stuckness using reversals.

1 Problem challenge
2 Problem swotting
3 Amplifying SOS signals

Problem challenge

Quite a few managers – and some entire companies – refuse to recognize problems. 'Never talk about a problem, think about an opportunity.' This can be a signal of problem evasion, a company as ostrich. Under these circumstances senior managers are never told what is going wrong because their staff are afraid to mention that a problem is arising. The company spirals into a set of uncreative behaviours designed to protect individuals from retribution as 'problem-mongers'. However, approached sensibly, a problem can be attacked as a disguised opportunity. If there is a climate in which problems are repeatedly examined for possibilities and opportunities, then the company becomes increasingly sensitive to imaginative ways of dealing with its problems.

Swotting problems

This term is a reference to SWOT analysis, a technique in corporate strategy where company strengths, weaknesses, opportunities and threats are examined. If this is done systematically, it is quickly apparent that a strength or a weakness is very much a matter of perspective. Often discussion springs up as to whether a stated factor is indeed a strength or a weakness. Even the knowledge that a weakness is more a matter of perspective than of absolute classification helps people to make the reversal or switch in perspective. One of my own favourite trigger questions is: 'How can we turn that threat into an opportunity?'

Amplifying SOS signals

SOS signals are signs of stuckness. We can become more sensitive to mind sets that are resulting in stuckness. It is far easier, of course, to recognize SOS signals coming from other people than to recognize that we ourselves are struggling. This is a clue which is ironically enough in the form of a reversal. If we have trouble recognizing our stuckness, we should encourage other people to point out when we seem to be getting stuck. Be grateful for the advice, and you will find you will need it less and less.

Here is another powerful mechanism for reversing your way out of a thinking cul-de-sac: next time you are discussing a problem, or even thinking one over by yourself, ask the question 'What is the worst possible solution we can think of?' Give yourself time to be creative about this negative perspective. You have to work at it because the dominant mind set may continue to block you from being negatively creative. When you have a particularly horrific worst case, see if you can find the germ of a good idea, especially one arising from a reversed perspective.

BUNCHES OF BANANAS

We have already seen how the lateral thinking technique of random juxtaposition creates new combinations of ideas. This is but one version of a broader series of intervention strategies intended to trigger off a change in perception. The triggering mechanisms often have the effect of reducing excessive left-brain attention to a problem, which might have been reinforcing a mind set. Many people instinctively liven up meetings by deliberate interventions to provoke discussion and comment. One senior manager confessed to a penchant for 'rolling in a hand grenade' if a meeting was not making any progress. Another expression is to throw in a bunch of bananas.

This term was coined by a successful leader of a new products team who found it important to challenge the group to more unconventional thinking. At first it became a joke that whenever ideas were running out he would say, 'A bunch of bananas would solve that problem.' Initially the results were quite gratifying – perhaps because his team members had seen a creative idea connected with a bunch of bananas. This type of blind faith gradually disappeared but the leader was able to keep ahead of the game by throwing in unexpected comments or suggestions. This encouraged the group members to treat any suggestion as having potential, and so acted as a creativity-spurring aid.

Some practical tips for successful banana-throwing to help individuals or groups find new ideas:

1. Spend time assessing the mood and climate, and whether there are any signs of stuckness.
2. Give some thought to the kind of thing you can say and do to help bring the group out of that state of stuckness. You will be creating your own bunches of bananas to suit your personality and style.
3. Remember that you are engaging in a 'whole-brain' activity. Just as with a comedian, it is as much the delivery as the idea which produces the effect.
4. For groups with little experience of creativity techniques, the approach may have to be appropriately signalled: 'I know this is going to sound a little crazy, but bear with me a minute or so. Sometimes you can get out of a rut in the most unexpected ways...'

Banana throwing cropped up during a meeting for marketing new products to Australia from the UK.

> The small group had exhausted the obvious possibilities and seemed to be in a state of stuckness. 'We don't seem to be getting very far marketing to Australian consumers,' someone said. 'What I'd like to do would be to find a product that every Australian sheep would be clamouring to buy.' In any conventional meeting this would have been met with derision or polite silence, after which the person suggesting such an obviously stupid idea would have been ignored for the rest of the meeting. He had, however, timed his bunch of bananas quite cleverly, and someone picked up the idea. 'Sheep? Oh, you mean for us to find large numbers of customers who can be influenced easily. Perhaps we have been concentrating too hard on too few clients...'
>
> Eventually a new product strategy for marketing to Australia emerged along lines triggered off by the bunch of bananas (or bunch of sheep) intervention.
>
> A second example concerns a dreary academic meeting that had been adjourned for lunch. The mood of the meeting was bad and getting worse. Over lunch, people were becoming increasingly depressed about current job uncertainties and future prospects. I had withdrawn for about an hour, frustrated and unable to make any contribution of value. It struck me how much easier it was to help as an outsider (I was a member of this particular working group.) I could recognize the state of stuckness we were in and began consciously to look for an opening to throw in a bunch of bananas. Just when we had finished our meal, it seemed worth a

> try. I commented that we were all in a heavy mood of gloom and despondency, quite unlike the times together when we used to tell jokes and have a general good time as a team. I told a very bad joke very badly. We all laughed and someone else told another equally bad joke and we laughed again. A few minutes later we were discussing very positively steps towards solving our problem.

These cases show that bunches of bananas can come in very different forms. In many ways, the actual content of the intervention is not important. In the example, almost any joke or anecdote would have worked in the same way, provided the timing were right. The process is a whole-brain one. It is concerned more with mood than with correctness of content. And it does involve some risk and uncertainty, as you can never predict the effect the intervention will have.

WISHFUL THINKING

Practical jobs and a technical or professional training reinforce beliefs in the importance of being practical. As a consequence we may have to force ourselves to escape from the trap of the obvious and logical. The relation of wishful thinking to lateral thinking, and the intermediate impossible technique is clear, although wishful thinking need not be impossible, but rather a discovery process which reveals that previously suppressed wishes can be profitable starting points for new ideas. To cultivate wishful thinking as a worthwhile habit we have to find some practical situations, and a few procedures to help the process when it is needed. The situations which are particularly suitable are those in which a person is trying to work through personal or career goals.

In its most acute form the stuckness may arise from a career change, or personal crisis. Wishful thinking can be introduced in two stages. Stage one is to recognize and clarify a goal, as a 'how to' statement. Stage two is to seek more wishful goals by repeated investigation of 'What I really want out of this'. Here is a reconstruction of a job counselling discussion:

> 'All I want to do is get my job back,' the redundant steel worker kept repeating. As steel jobs were severely declining this was a sad but typical example of being stuck with a problem definition that offered few possibilities for creative ideas. He needed help to arrive at stage two. At first he insisted that all he really wanted was his old job. Later he began to loosen up.
>
> 'I suppose what I really want is my dignity. You are rubbish if you're on the dole.'

'How to get your dignity back?'
'That's it. A job. Not any kind of job, though.'
'If you could have any job you wanted except in steel, what would you go for?'
'With my skills all I could do is labour.'
'If there were ways you could pick up any new skills you liked, what would you really want to do?'
'I might try for an HGV licence.'

The principle can be extended to personal goal setting. A simple aid to such personal planning is to draw up a wants list for the year ahead, to include some wishful goals and some bankers (i.e. more easily attainable ones). Make sure you consult your list from time to time. The clearer the want, the stronger becomes the mind set towards opportunities around you for advancing towards your goal. (We have perhaps said too little about mind sets as positive features in problem-solving. Here is a good example of deliberately emphasizing a helpful mind set.)

A word of caution. Wishful thinking may be a substitute for direct action. There are people who escape into fantasy easily, but never return to earth. If you enjoy juggling with ideas, and find it easy to identify your goals as imaginative wishes, you may be more advised to concentrate on finding actionable steps to make your dreams come true. The real benefits of practising the technique will accrue to those who are more literally minded, and who therefore would have a more flexible range of strategies if they would practise a little wishful thinking as a fallback strategy.

KNIGHT'S MOVE THINKING

In 1985, Peter Elliott, a former medical doctor studying creativity at Manchester Business School, made an interesting observation. He had been working with schizophrenics. The schizophrenic patient makes unpredictable statements without obvious reason behind them. For some time the process was considered totally illogical; later it was realized that the thinking was logical but that several steps had been omitted in the logic. Doctors had called this 'knight's move' thinking, an allusion to the way the knight jumps over pieces in a non-linear fashion in chess.

Elliott reasoned that knight's move thinking, far from being a handicap, could be an asset in business situations. It could produce unexpected results which would not be easily anticipated by business competitors. He set about finding methods of achieving knight's move thinking, and the contexts in which it would be most useful.

Knight's move thinking

If neither alternative is pleasant:

1 Look for 'third' option

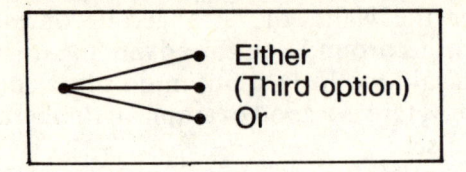

```
Either
(Third option)
Or
```

perhaps combining best features of both

2 Look for knight's move,
   asking 'what do we really' want?

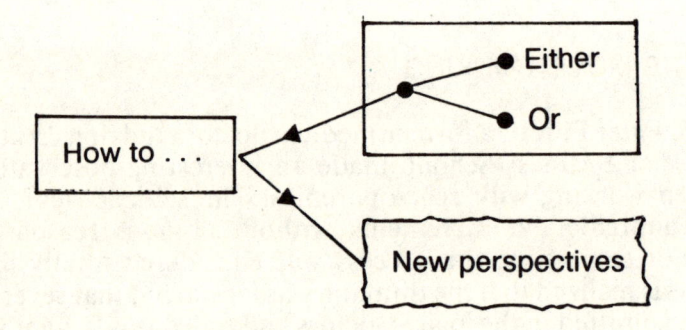

```
How to . . .  →  Either / Or
              →  New perspectives
```

Remember: There will always be alternatives.
There might be better options.

Knight's move thinking combines logical or vertical thinking with unexpected divergent ideas, sometimes called lateral thinking. Like the knight's move in chess it enables you to jump around and over obstacles, and also to escape from false either/or logic traps.

Example

A sales executive gets a telephone call from a customer who complains bitterly that the company's product is very expensive for what he wants it to do. An 'instant' response would be to point out that it is the best there is, and cheaper products do not work so well. This is unsatisfactory and can lose a customer. So the flexible executive looks for a new approach, via a knight's move.

He is very aware of an unpleasant 'either/or'. Either we drop our price, or we risk losing the customer and others to a competitive product. He looks for a 'how to'.

Habitual thinking leading to 'either/or' dilemma

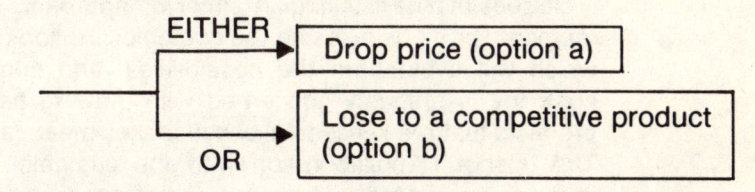

EITHER → Drop price (option a)

OR → Lose to a competitive product (option b)

Knight's move breaks out of either/or thinking

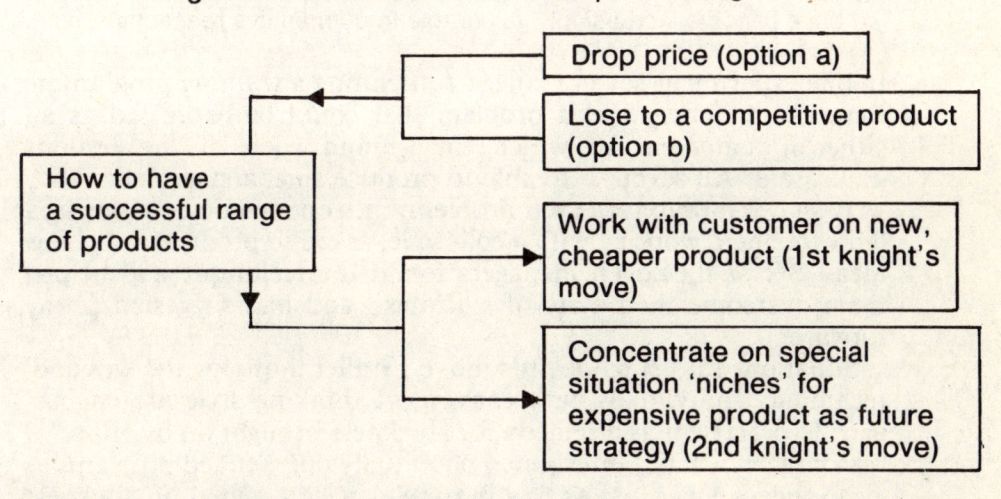

How to have a successful range of products:
- Drop price (option a)
- Lose to a competitive product (option b)
- Work with customer on new, cheaper product (1st knight's move)
- Concentrate on special situation 'niches' for expensive product as future strategy (2nd knight's move)

One context is particularly worth noting. In many situations we can reach a state of stuckness because we have reduced something into a false either/or. As we have seen, either/or thinking is close-ended and usually inhibits the production of creative ideas. Any mechanism which helps move from either/or thinking to open-ended thinking will produce a knight's move. An excellent mechanism is already known to us in the form of our old friend goal orientation or 'how to' thinking. We have discovered that any either/or statement can be converted into an open-ended statement by the use of 'how to', as in the following example:

> A sales executive for a company selling dyestuffs has a telephone call from a major buyer of a speciality material. The customer complains bitterly that the price is unreasonably high for what she wants the product to do. The executive's impulsive response is to point out that cheaper products are not so reliable, and that if you want quality you have to pay for it. He also realizes that he is in danger of losing the customer – either immediately, or as soon as she can find another supplier.
>
> He sees that he is taking an 'either/or' approach. Either he drops the price, or he risks losing the customer. He looks for a 'how to' which will avoid both the possibilities, and suggests that his company is primarily concerned with 'how to have a range of products that are successful because they meet customer needs'. The upshot is collaboration with the customer to produce a cheaper version for her less-demanding needs, while finding more specialized niches for the original product, which would otherwise have become increasingly vulnerable to competitive reactions.

In one experiment seven managers attending a training programme were asked if they had a problem that could be expressed as an either/or statement in which they found each of the options unpleasant. All seven were able to produce such a statement. They were shown how to turn their problems into open-ended ones using a 'how to', then, working with a colleague, asked to produce some new ideas. Six of the seven managers found the technique had helped them overcome their state of stuckness, and had suggested a way forward.

Situations for using knight's move parallel those for the 'yes and' technique. Individuals with convergent thinking style are encouraged to practise it as a remedy for stuckness brought on by either/or reasoning which has interpreted potentially open-ended problems as close-ended ones. Just as 'yes butting' can be a signal of stuckness calling for a 'yes and', so can an unpleasant either/or be a signal calling for a 'how to' and a knight's move.

FORCE FITTING: 'MOVEMENT TOWARDS, NOT ARRIVAL AT'

Force fitting is a deliberate attempt to arrive at a powerful new idea from two previously unconnected, or partially connected, ideas. When this happens spontaneously we have the 'eureka moment', the coming together of two thoughts in a meaningful way. The practice of creativity techniques requires that we give the spontaneous process a nudge by introducing procedures as a matter of strategy.

Force fitting is implicit in the 'yes and' technique, as a weakness is worked on until the idea becomes stronger. It is also essential if a metaphor – a disguised problem – is to be linked with the specific needs of the problem-solver. We can see the need for a similar process in the lateral thinking techniques: the intermediate impossible is impossible until links are created which bridge the gap between reality and fantasy. Random juxtaposition and bunches of bananas both rely on connections being made between two previously unconnected elements.

The conscious 'nudge' to help the creative process is to look for step-by-step marginal changes in one or both components of the ideas being dealt with. You are interested in 'movement towards', in the absence of a eureka moment and immediate 'arrival at' a satisfactory idea. As with the other techniques, a new habit will be helped by a repeatable signal to reinforce it. For force fitting, it helps to use a formula such as 'I wonder if this idea moves us towards . . .'

Specific circumstances for force fitting crop up when two viewpoints are being explored in the hope of finding a 'win – win' formula in discussions. This is the key to industrial relations successes. Another example is the matching of technical means with customer needs when new product concepts are being developed.

RELEASING YOUR INSIGHT-SEEKING POTENTIAL

In this chapter we have talked a lot about SOS – the state of stuckness. We must not imagine that a state of stuckness is a character defect and a sign of an uncreative personality. Rather, it is a temporary condition that everyone encounters from time to time, and which can be overcome – sometimes through the use of acquirable techniques.

When we become aware of our condition of stuckness we can make a conscious effort to do something about it, and we can help others in similar positions. Notice that the techniques can come consciously into play only after we become aware of stuckness. However, practice and success with the insight-seeking techniques reduce the worse

Force fit technique

In force fitting two ideas are integrated to create a new opportunity. In new product work one of the ideas is often an identified need, the other a piece of technology or similar corporate means.

In seeking ideas it is important to realize that any idea can be modified in many ways while retaining its essential characteristics. The need can be modified to match the means; the means can be modified to match the need; or even both can be modified.

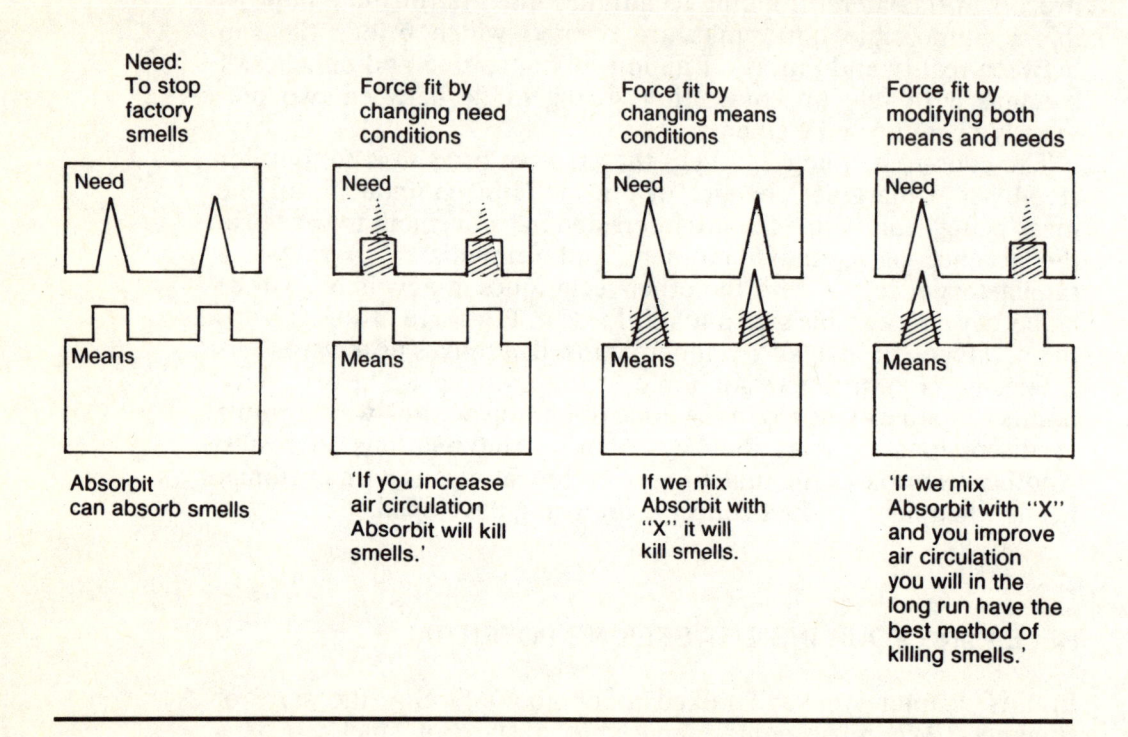

Need: To stop factory smells	Force fit by changing need conditions	Force fit by changing means conditions	Force fit by modifying both means and needs
Need / Means	Need / Means	Need / Means	Need / Means
Absorbit can absorb smells	'If you increase air circulation Absorbit will kill smells.'	If we mix Absorbit with "X" it will kill smells.	'If we mix Absorbit with "X" and you improve air circulation you will in the long run have the best method of killing smells.'

excesses of stuckness, and make us increasingly aware of inappropriate and ineffectual behaviours.

To develop more automatic behaviours we have to learn to recognize those patterns of circumstances in which one or more of the techniques has worked for us. A start can be made by experimenting as suggested in this chapter – each technique has been described with illustrations of where and how it has been used. It is also a good plan to build up new habits – 'catchphrases', if you like – to be brought out as the operating procedure for the insight-seeking technique. You will have your own way of saying and thinking these trigger phrases. Some of mine are as follows:

Intermediate impossible	'Let's imagine there are no logic rules for a while.'
Random juxtaposition	'We could do with a complete break from our thinking... here's a random thought to toy with...'
Concept challenge	'I've written down what you claim to be conclusions. Now I want us to challenge everything we can.'
Reversals	'If you turn it upside down and take the opposite view you might get...'
Bunches of bananas	(Sometimes the bananas are thrown in without explanation for 'whack on the head' effect.) 'I think we should stop looking for new products and hire a science fiction writer.'
Wishful thinking	'What I'd really like to do is...'
Knight's move	'We don't like the "either", we don't like the "or", what we need is a "how to".'
Force fit	'Can we get any movement towards something if...?'

SUMMARY

Creativity is escape from personal stuckness, and the various blockbusting techniques represent invented means of helping this process.

The best known are the lateral thinking techniques, and the three considered in this chapter were

- Intermediate impossible, or finding stepping stones from one perception of reality to a new one.
- Random juxtaposition, which forces you to extend the horizons of your thinking by the deliberate introduction of evocative and random extra ideas.
- Concept challenge, which focuses attention on the assumptions behind assertions of fact and belief.

Reversals is a technique for producing a switch away from a blocking viewpoint to a different one, so that a perceived threat reveals an unnoticed opportunity. Bunches of bananas is a technique related to random juxtaposition. It is often an intervention to provide 'a whack on the head' and break people loose from a dominant mind set.

Wishful thinking induces more right-brain efforts, and challenges reality assumptions. It is related to the intermediate impossibles technique.

Knight's Move thinking jumps over obstacles and especially helps escape from unpleasant either/or dilemmas, thus turning close-ended views of problems into more open-ended ones (Chapter 1).

Force-fitting implies deliberate attempts to merge two ideas to get an unexpected and valuable result. The process is a vital part of effective use of the other blockbusting techniques, such as intermediate impossibles, random juxtaposition, bunches of bananas, and the climate setting 'yes and' approach (Chapter 2).

Practising the techniques using a trigger phrase can assist the process of acquiring a wider set of creative responses to stuckness.

6 Brainstorming and its relations

Brainstorming is a widely used term. Most readers will have heard of the technique, and the chances are that you will have taken part in a meeting in which the intention was for the participants to come up with ideas following a brainstorming approach. A smaller number of readers will have been involved in the planning and running of brainstorming meetings on a regular basis.

Many thousands of brainstormings take place every year, as part of activities such as cost-savings, customer relations, organizational development, innovation seeking, fund raising, and advertising campaigns. Such projects have recorded millions of pounds in new business sales or cost savings. However, the technique is all too often misunderstood, clumsily applied, and quickly written off by individuals and organizations disappointed with the results obtained from their bungled efforts.

This chapter contains background information to complement the practice of brainstorming. For best results the reader should have the motive and opportunity to become involved in brainstorming sessions – initially as a group member, and subsequently as someone able to plan and run such meetings. We shall take a look at how brainstorming in its modern form started, and at a few of the many related species that have evolved subsequently. Some practical advice is then offered on setting up and running brainstormings, including suggestions about when, and when not, to use such techniques.

"BINGO, ANYONE?"

MADAME ZORA SEANCES HOROSCOPES

Not every search for ideas should be treated according to the freewheeling rules of brainstorming.

HOW BRAINSTORMING STARTED

A form of brainstorming was practised in Asia over three thousand years ago, but in modern times the technique is attributed to an advertising executive, Alex Osborn, who popularized it in the 1940s and 1950s. He described his approach in his book *Applied Imagination*, in which he quoted this dictionary definition of the verb 'brainstorm': 'to practise a conference technique by which a group attempts to find a solution for a specific problem by amassing all the ideas spontaneously by its members'.

He emphasized that a meeting cannot be called a brainstorming unless specific rules are included which require that the idea-generation stages are deliberately separated from the evaluation stages. It is incorrect to assume that during a brainstorming session there is no control at all over what is said, and that such a technique is illogical and the practitioners lacking in judgement.

> A famous but ill-informed criticism made in *Fortune* magazine some years ago described it as 'cerebral popcorn', with the result that sponsorship from industry for creative problem-solving courses plummeted for a period of years. As we shall see, it is true that during the idea-generation stage of a brainstorming no evaluation is permitted. But judgement is postponed, not abandoned, and in the subsequent analytical stages of the technique evaluation of ideas is at least as rigorous as in a conventional meeting.

Brainstorming became popular through the 1960s, pioneered by Osborn at the Creative Problem-Solving Institute at Buffalo, and for many years afterwards by his successor there, Professor Sidney Parnes. At its simplest, the technique involved a group of people (originally ten to twelve in number), with two people writing down ideas on large sheets of paper.

Osborn had developed his approach to beat the stultifying effects of status in business meetings, and the technique must have liberated enormous amounts of previously repressed energy and creativity. The 'rules' were:

- Quantity breeds quality (go for many ideas)
- Hitchhike each other's suggestions (i.e. build in a positive way)
- Freewheel (be prepared to make lateral changes in direction).
- The fundamental principle was summed up in the slogan 'postpone judgement'.

Brainstorming: the bottom line

Most regular users of brainstorming are convinced of the value of the technique, which in its assorted versions is used in thousands of different situations globally every year. Practitioners find its benefits obvious. Unfortunately there are few documented studies of the impact of the technique, and because the approach is often part of a longer-term project, it is hard to 'prove' direct links between brainstorming and corporate gains. However, here are some 'bottom line results' authenticated in some recent follow-up work instigated by the Creative Problem-Solving Institute, Buffalo, New York.

$10 million (Canadian) cost-savings in 6 months by a Canadian manufacturing company (1983).

M.S. Barados & Associates followed up training programmes for senior executives in 1983 with further training in eleven operating plants. Hourly paid workers as well as managers were included in the schemes, which covered cost-savings and distribution ideas. In six months targets of 750,000,000-dollar savings over five years were revised upwards, as the first year's target had already been surpassed.

$10 million (US) savings by an engineering firm in 5 years (1978–83).

Johnson Controls reported an approach to value engineering involving brainstorming in each of its stages. The approach included training of team members in quality circles, work improvement, and product improvement projects. As well as the economic impact, the company believes longer-term gains will come from developing people and achieving a creative climate and higher motivation across the company.

$50 million (Canadian) cost reduction programme in an energy corporation.

BC Coal (British Columbia) claimed $50 million cost savings in 1984 with considerable proportions of ideas from brainstorming sessions. Typical 'hard' results included:

$400,000 savings for a coal haulage idea
$136,000 savings on costs of high turnover items in stores

Other ideas led to improvements in :

safety records
quality of metallurgical coal

communications (teams came from different departments)
morale

$3 billion savings in US Navy, with a little help from the Royal Navy.

A very early exercise (1962) in creative problem-solving and international co-operation in creative problem-solving. After similar exercises in work-simplification in the British (Royal) Navy, the US Navy introduced brainstorming teams extensively to tackle serious inefficiencies in commissioning practices and operational readiness. Reported savings of up to 40 per cent on large budget projects led to the figure that deserves to find its way into the *Guinness Book of Records*. The result was fondly quoted by Alex Osborn, inventor of brainstorming, when people asked him what his technique had achieved.

Even these figures are small, if we consider 'second generation' use of brainstorming in Quality Circles all over the world, one of the standard ways of creating corporate change in job enrichment programmes, and value engineering projects.

Osborn's earliest brainstormings concentrated on commercial and educational problems. Later the technique was tested and modifications were developed on problems of a technical, military, financial and aesthetic nature by groups throughout the world. Today there are rent-a-brainstorming services in several countries, employing part-time participants from all walks of life.

In Denmark, in the 1960s, one successful inventor (Karl Kroyer) encouraged his staff to have at least one brainstorming session for new product ideas every week, as he believed that practising the technique increases an inventor's capacity to produce a regular stream of original ideas. In West Germany, the Battelle Institute among others published accounts of successful brainstorming sessions on commercial and technical problems. The technique diffused around the world, with enthusiasts spreading the word. In the UK, for example, Geoffrey Rawlinson, of the PA consultancy organization, gave hundreds of successful demonstrations of brainstorming to thousands of managers in the 1960s and 1970s.

From this enormous weight of evidence it is quite clear that Osborn's principle of postponement of judgement and his simple technique were helping groups to achieve creative outcomes from their meetings.

A GROWING FAMILY OF TECHNIQUES: THE SYNECTICS SYSTEM

Brainstorming developed in all sorts of ways. In his book Osborn had already suggested a range of idea-spurring techniques which could be applied in a practical way either as part of a group brainstorming, or by individuals. In time these developed into a family of approaches. Osborn's brainstorming also became a component of 'second generation' approaches such as value analysis, potential problem analysis, and more recently Quality Circles. Finally, other techniques for stimulating creativity arose which shared some operating procedures with brainstorming, another possible cause of confusion.

One family of techniques, known as synectics, is related to brainstorming and deserves particular mention because of its widespread use, and the research into the creative process that has contributed to the success of the system.

In 1961 an American psychologist, W.J. Gordon, summarized the results of over a decade of research into creative individuals and the creative process, mainly in the Arthur D. Little organization. He suggested that individual creativity was associated with certain psychological states which, if they could be induced, could increase the probability of creative breakthroughs. He transferred his attentions from individuals to groups of people partly because the communication process within a group could be recorded and studied for clues to the thinking which was going on. He also concentrated on technical problem-solving to provide more concrete criteria of success than might be obtained in artistic situations.

He reported his procedures for reproducing the psychological states systematically. In particular, he encouraged groups to attain a speculative mental state through the use of metaphoric and analogy procedures in a part of the meeting called 'the excursion'. In the next few years an important dimension was to be added to the technique by a colleague, George Prince, working initially very closely with Gordon. Prince recognized that, when people worked together in a group, powerful forces operated which neutralized any creativity-spurring value which simple metaphoric procedures might otherwise have. Consequently, synectics began to develop ways in which groups of people would work together more efficiently and productively. The elements of synectics today can be traced back to these two main inputs. Many of the elements can be found in other work on behavioural psychology and interpersonal skills. It is the assembly of a range of elements into a flexible system that gives synectics its place as a powerful problem-solving innovation.

The individual elements of synectics can be described as:

1 roles which should be adopted by the participants;
2 operational structures or procedures for running a meeting;
3 interpersonal skills reinforced by training and techniques to produce a positive and supportive environment.

Over time many of the elements have been modified, and we shall concentrate on aspects which illustrate the general principles, rather than itemize an exhaustive catalogue of operational steps.

Roles

A typical synectics session involves a small team (6–8 people) with a group leader who acts much like a skilled brainstorming facilitator, whose role is to look after the ideas and the group climate. The leader may also be the person who records ideas, although an 'ideas secretary' may be nominated for this. In addition, there is always someone present who is recognized as 'owning' the problem: the problem-owner or client. The careful distinction made between the roles of group leader and problem-owner is that the former attends to all the process needs of the meeting, while the latter has the first say in decisions regarding problem definitions and idea acceptabilities. The rest of the team is made up of people from as wide a range of backgrounds as possible, often unacquainted with the problem. Their role is to be open to ideas, and to accept the structures introduced by the group leader, and the decisions made by the problem-owner.

Operational structures

At the start of a meeting the client outlines the problem, what has been tried, what is wanted from the meeting. The team then carries out a brainstorming of the problem, using a 'how to' format. (The synectics research popularized the 'how to' structure for problem definitions.) Members also put into words any wishful statements of goals that they can think of.

The client selects some key problem statements. These are brainstormed to produce a range of ideas, and again the client selects those with the most perceived merit. In a final phase, the most promising ideas may have to be developed. Each can be assessed using a sophisticated version of 'yes and', which converts weaknesses into further starting points for problem-solving.

The basic structure can be thought of as three stages, each involving divergence and convergence. One consultant refers to these as the PIS sequence (problems, ideas, solutions). This apparently simple structure conceals many subtleties through which the team can develop more speculative and metaphoric ideas – particularly through the deliberate production of metaphors in an excursion. Timing of each stage calls for considerable skill on the part of the team leader, which can only be developed through serious study of each experience after the event. The serious student of team leadership has to become a creative analyst of group process.

Interpersonal skills

The synectics technique puts great emphasis on developing interpersonal skills, so that the meeting proceeds more effectively. Indeed the main difference between a successful and creative group and a poorly operating one is the degree to which the team members have acquired good interpersonal practices:

> We can avoid lapses of attention if we develop simple idea-trapping devices. The ubiquitous flipchart and sensitive team leader are needed to record all the information being produced. Each team member, furthermore, can improve attentiveness by using a note pad, and by jotting down key thoughts rapidly, in order to tune in to what is being said.
>
> We can reduce confrontational questions, and subsequent defensive discussions, by turning fact-seeking questions into speculative ideas or problem-statements. ('Have you tried mixing it with a different solvent? can be phrased as 'I wish we could find some different solvent that would do the trick'.)
>
> We can show process discipline by accepting the team leader's judgements, and by avoiding unfinished business, which is what happens when someone thinks his or her idea has been ignored, because a new item has been introduced without sufficient attention to the previous item.
>
> We can practise active listening by becoming more skilled at picking out the essence of what is being said. This can be aided by testing you have heard right, and whether your interpretation makes sense (feedback and paraphrase, respectively). One of the reasons why people talk in long monologues is that their main point is not being heard and understood. Justifications and repetitions are piled one on another in self-destructive profusion. Active listening helps reassure the speaker that the point is taken and, more significantly, that you are willing to develop the idea. It will also make you a better presenter of ideas. Just as negativity towards ideas breeds more negativity, active listening, feedback and paraphrase will lead to an overall improvement in attitudes and behaviour within a group, so that the climate becomes more favourable for creativity.

George Prince, summing up his view after twenty years of experimentation, wrote something that could be applied not just to synectics, but to creative problem-solving in general:

> Synectics® believes that nearly all of us have enormous potential for good thinking. Because most of us are in a constant competition with each other, we do not cooperate (as much as we could) . . . each of us, by systematically manipulating ourselves and the climate around us, can markedly increase the amount of that good thinking potential that we use. Not the least of the blessings that flow from wholehearted cooperation and support is that they make meetings more exciting and more fun.

NOMINAL GROUP TECHNIQUES: HOW TO BE ALONE IN A CROWD

A nominal group is a technical term to indicate that several people, though working together, are actually working alone for some portion of the meeting. The assorted ways of running nominal groups received a boost when it was discovered that under some conditions the arrangement led to more ideas in unit time than if the group had been allowed to interact under typical brainstorming conditions.

Not surprisingly, practitioners of creative problem-solving techniques find benefits in using nominal groups at some times, and interactive groups at other times. Nominal groups preserve anonymity and may suit teams where status differences are a problem. Interactive groups build more team spirit, and generate greater energy and motivation. In many situations a 'yes and' approach can be applied, and nominal and interactive periods can be combined during idea searches.

We shall look at three versions of nominal group brainstorming:

- Trigger sessions
- 6–3–5 method
- Delbecq and van de Ven's version

Trigger sessions

One of the earliest nominal group techniques, trigger sessions were developed for use in engineering and technical problems. A trigger session is a group idea-generation process in which members work independently for a period producing a list of ideas. At the end of a given time each person reads out his list, thus generating stimuli for the rest of the group to produce some ideas. The format is somewhat less threatening to more left-brain climates than interactive brainstorming, and has more immediate appeal to technical groups. This suggests that a warm-up (this time as individuals) is particularly important for a group concentrating on the trigger session method of idea generation.

One advocate of trigger sessions uses a series of different coloured cards for the different stages of the meeting. Ideas produced by each member independently are written on cards of one colour; ideas developed ('yes anded') subsequently by listening to the lists being read out are jotted down on cards of a different colour.

6-3-5 technique

A recent variation of the trigger session has developed in Europe and is particularly suited for rather smaller groups. Its name, 6-3-5 technique, refers to the practice of using teams of six people, each of whom generates three ideas, five times in succession, according to the following rules. Each member of the group receives three cards and is asked to think of three ideas and to write them down one on each of the cards. The cards are then passed to other members of the group in a sequence and a further idea, triggered from the one on the card, is added beneath it. These ideas in turn become stimuli for more ideas on the next exchange of cards. For six people it is possible to exchange the cards five time, with fresh ideas at each pass.

Although there was some enthusiasm for the 6-3-5 version in the 1970s, especially in Germany, it seems to have fallen out of use. This is a pity, as it does offer the brainstorming teamleader a chance to introduce some variety into his or her set of operating techniques.

Delbecq and van de Ven's technique

One further version of nominal group methodology deserves especial mention. It is the approach sometimes known as 'blocks and barriers' and has been extensively used, especially by its American co-inventors Professors Andre Delbecq and Andrew van de Ven, to brainstorm complicated socio-technical problems. In this technique, problems are tackled by individuals within a nominal group of up to a dozen members. (More members can be assembled into further groups of twelve or less.) The format is to ask each participant to brainstorm 'blocks or barriers' which contribute to the problem in hand. The statements are then collected anonymously, and a special voting procedure is followed involving each participant allocating ranks to each of the problem statements (the voting can also be anonymous).

The voting method has been specially designed to avoid the trap of over-quantifying the decision-making process, and can lead to identifying clusters of problems for subsequent attack. In a typical industrial application, a small contract research organization assembled its engineering designers, project managers, and administrative staff into three nominal groups. Each group assembled its own set of 'blocks and barriers' in what the director saw as the problem of poor project management. After the voting, it became clear that the groups had quite different perceptions of the problem. The managers believed the engineers lacked initiative and imagination. The engineers believed that one or two managers abused the system of production priorities, making scheduling a nightmare. The support staff believed they were poorly utilized, and deprived of information vital to their effective performance.

In the next stage of the exercise, these differences were challenged, and a strategy was agreed which made it more difficult for the senior project managers to distort the scheduling system. The nominal group technique was particularly effective as it overcame the reluctance of the junior staff to criticize dubious practices by senior managers.

HOW TO PLAN SUCCESSFUL BRAINSTORMINGS

If you want to run successful brainstorming sessions you have to plan successful brainstorming sessions. Expect to spend roughly twice as long in planning a brainstorming as in the event itself. (And roughly twice as long as the event in arranging and conducting the follow-up stages – of which more later.)

Planning a brainstorming is yet another process of creative analysis. You, as planner, have to analyse the what and why of some situation to arrive at a broad strategy for tackling a problem. Different people have very different ways of planning: you may be the methodical and systematic type of planner who likes long checklists. Or you may be the intuitive, more right-brain, person who prefers to rely on a feel for what's going on and what will be needed. That is a question of personal style. It is important to plan according to your style to enable you to carry out a detailed mental rehearsal of the brainstorming session.

In the long run you learn what are the important things to cover in your planning by conducting sessions and then by carrying out careful private post-mortems. The following tips from my own experience should be taken as starting points for such a process, rather than as a set of rules for all circumstances.

Is the situation suited for brainstorming?

A very early decision – to avoid time-wasting on anybody's part – is to make up your mind whether you can and want to help. It is dangerous to decide whether you can help according to whether you can see some potentially good ideas at the outset. The omens for a problem suited to brainstorming are to do with the nature of the problem, and the perceived needs of the would-be client. A good sign is when the client describes the problem in open-ended terms: 'We'd like a few new ideas to help our marketing/product quality/project review strategy/financial services/computerization...'. A less promising sign is if the client thinks that the problem requires a high level of technical knowledge from the participants. This mind set shows that the sort of ideas the client thinks important are likely to come from within the technical field. ('New natural chemicals to replace synthetic additives' would be a rather close-ended view of a problem, which would be reinforced if the proposed group was made up of PhDs in flavour chemistry.)

What timescales are involved?

Having decided to get involved, I have a series of points to check with the client. What timescale are we talking about? Usually the answer is unrealistically short, and without evidence of being part of a longer-term plan. It still gives useful information about the client's needs, commitment and management style. How much control does the client have over implementation? (Would you both be better off working to a different sponsor?) Which people are involved in the problem, and which of these should be involved in the brainstorming?

Who should be involved in the meetings? (the status issue)

Take the long term view, that those who are likely to be most affected by the ideas should be involved at some stage in the exercise. If (see below) this leads to too many complications for one meeting, consider a two-tier arrangement, with more senior people involved in broad goal-setting and strategic decision-making in reaction to ideas generated.

It is important to discuss with the sponsor the potential dangers of status, which are more often than not under-estimated. Companies with a formal style of operating and many symbols of status differences are likely to be troubled by status in brainstorming sessions.

What effect might 'volunteered' members have on a brainstorming?

There can be difficulties with individuals nominated but not consulted sufficiently. Beware of nominees who may feel their professional competence threatened. Some creative professionals such as designers, architects, and advertising executives have a deep suspicion of group creativity. Sometimes they honestly believe that creativity is too precious to be left to amateurs and anyway is a private, individual thing, not a public group activity. Such individuals can be involved, provided the focus of the session is more on the management of the problem than on the technical aspects they are paid to be creative about (so don't invite them to be clients).

Another problem may be the company's nominated creative genius. Such people may or may not be exceptionally talented, but if they are contemptuous of the creative abilities of others, they are better left to pursue their creative activities in isolation.

What sort of pre-briefing is needed?

This depends on practical factors such as timescale and level of prior experience of the process of brainstorming in the group. A face-to-face meeting beats any circulated information, and signals that the actual idea generation is only part of a longer-term process of problem-solving. However, this may not be possible, in which case a personalized letter to the participants should outline the objectives of the planned meeting, its background, and details of the people involved. One of the purposes of the pre-briefing is to help challenge unhelpful assumptions about what is going to happen, and it is important to emphasize the differences between brainstorming and conventional meetings.

What physical environment helps brainstorming?

Try to move the group into a fresh environment. The office reinforces office thinking and office mind sets. There is a genuine case for finding a convenient hotel – provided that it caters for commercial meetings. The room should be large enough for a work area, with comfortable chairs, plus additional space with a few small tables for accessories. Walls that accept plenty of large sheets of newsprint are desirable, as a good session will often end up with 20 or more sheets on which ideas are written.

A facilities checklist to discuss with the client would include the following:
- Suitable room (no telephone)
- Comfortable chairs to spare
- Several small tables
- Notepads and pencils
- Large stock of 30" × 33" newsprint sheets (or flipcharts, A1 Size)
- Rolls of masking tape or packs of Blue-tac
- 6 marker pens (3 coloured)

How do we record the meeting?

Some operators tape-record sessions, but since it is valuable to write up ideas at the time, where all can see them, this is really superfluous. It may also inhibit the session. Video recordings are, however, very useful to illustrate how a brainstorming session operates and to play back examples of verbal and non-verbal behaviours for training purposes.

How can we increase the chances of follow-up activities?

Far and away the best time to raise the question is at the very outset of the discussions with those who will be involved in getting the ideas into action. Try discussing the path that an idea from the brainstorming will follow. These are matters that do not occur to the person who has seen the brainstorming in isolation from implementation.

I have found from experience that the more attention I pay to such planning points, the more effective the subsequent brainstorming. Conversely, when I cut corners because of the urgency of the request, the more problems are encountered from things that could in part have been anticipated.

HOW TO LEAD A SUCCESSFUL BRAINSTORMING SESSION

The general principles of running a brainstorming are simple – encourage a team of people to postpone judgement, and see that all their ideas are collected and written up on flipcharts. Here are some practical points to assist in the process.

1 *Reward postponement of judgement*. The leader can send out reinforcing cues which help set the climate of the group. It is good practice to encourage successful postponement of judgement by the group, but dubious practice to single out specific ideas for praise. So, to comment along the lines of 'Now we are really beginning to move. Keep it going', is correct encouragement of process. To say 'That's a good idea, Sam' is indirectly to downgrade all the other ideas being produced.

2 *Avoid interpreting ideas*. Some leaders are compulsive tidy-uppers, modifying and interpreting ideas to suit their own mind sets. This again may influence the group, perhaps subconsciously, to produce ideas of the kind indicated by the leader. And in

addition, if the leader's interpretation is not in accord with the essential point of the original idea – 'that's not what I meant' – discussions can begin, interrupting the flow of ideas.

Even worse is the leader who strongly evaluates certain kinds of idea. The evaluation can be direct: 'I think that's straying from the problem we are supposed to be working on'; or indirect, as when a leader stops in the act of writing up ideas and looks incredulously at someone who may have produced a rather speculative idea. This is a right-brain version of 'yes butting', and strongly inhibits idea generation.

3 *Suppress your own solutions to the problem.* There are strong arguments that should discourage the leader from chipping in with ideas, because it breaks the implicit contract with the group – that he or she will concentrate above all on looking after the ideas from the other group members. It should be obvious why the leader should not put forward ideas before the other members have had a chance. But the practice is also undesirable even if the leader builds on someone else's ideas, for reasons already indicated.

4 *How to break a prolonged silence.* The best strategy is to let the group members break the silence. This shows that the leader is not there to put in ideas, even when the group is stuck. (This can produce dependency on the leader the next time there is a silence.) Try to convey the impression that you are sympathetic and that you recognize that the group will eventually come through the stuckness. Often this tactic leads to much richer ideas after the silence (all obvious ideas having been exhausted, the participants have to stretch their imaginations for further and more novel ideas.)

Another tactic is to check with the group whether they are 'drying up' and ask if they would like a break. This opens up the possibility of trying a different approach after the break – a metaphor is particularly effective for helping groups break out of stuckness. Note how the leader's creativity is always channelled into stimulating the group's creativity.

5 *Be firm but fair.* Try to be sensitive to the quiet group members. They may need extra encouragement (still concentrating on their success in the process of producing an idea, rather than on the merits of the actual idea.) It may be necessary to find a creative way of reducing the contributions from a dominant group member. This should be done privately during a break in the meeting. If the dominance is particularly bad, the leader may have to engineer a break by 'blowing a whistle' in order to make this intervention.

Suppose a group member believes the meeting has overlooked some important point? He needs a mechanism to 'blow a whistle' to stop play temporarily.

6 *The use of an ideas secretary.* Sometimes the leader may split the role into two, by inviting one of the group members to act as ideas secretary – that is, to write up all the ideas as they are produced. This makes the leader's job a little easier, although there are disadvantages in the strategy. Idea capture requires discipline – to avoid interpretation and evaluation. It takes practice to become a good ideas collector, and whenever possible the leader should keep the responsibility.

7 *When to stop.* Set a target and aim to go beyond that target. Fifty to a hundred ideas will usually be sufficient to collect the obvious thoughts of the participants, and also produce some unexpected new ideas. But be flexible, and remember that sometimes a group produces its best ideas after reaching the target, when a change of mood occurs, and the relaxation unblocks some members who find interactive brainstorming stressful.

How blowing a whistle helps groups to solve problems

A referee blows a whistle to indicate that the game (including all its rules) has been temporarily suspended. He wants the players to stop being defenders or attackers without having a goal scored against them.

Blowing a whistle is an absolutely necessary device when things seem to be going wrong – in games, industrial relations, and even in meetings. In sociological language, it allows people to 'step out of role'. If we try to change the rules of a game, while the game is going on, confusion and uproar can follow.

In a problem-solving meeting, the participants are following some agreed rules – e.g. someone is acting as a leader, someone else may be acting as a problem-owner, and so on. But suppose a group member believes that the meeting has overlooked some important point? He needs a mechanism for drawing attention to it without disruption. Hence, 'blowing a whistle'.

In a recent 'training the trainers' session with three consultants, one participant was slower than the others to understand the basic rules. By asking for 'time out', the unhappy participant can share his concerns. In his first few sessions he would blow the whistle on average about once every ten minutes, asking such questions as: 'Isn't that an idea disguised as a "how to"?' 'Shouldn't we still be brainstorming problems?' 'That's not what he said the problem was in the first place.' Over about half a dozen sessions his whistle stops became less. Eventually he accepted the process and became a valued member of the group.

I have no way of proving this, but my strong belief is that the whistle-blowing was an excellent way of bringing about his integration into the group. Without some such technique it is easy to ignore this type of group member – who, after all, is showing one characteristic of creative behaviour – sticking out for his own point of view.

How to have effective whistle-blowing

An excellent way to introduce constructive whistle blowing into everyday practice is to make it a recognized 'play' or 'signal'. For example, a team leader can say at the start of a problem-solving session:'One extra rule today. Because Andrew's new to our methods, he's going to think it a bit odd at times. Andrew, if you (or anyone else) get lost – just try to keep going – or "blow a whistle".'

Warm-up

Before many live comedy shows, the audience is given a warm-up session. It sets the atmosphere for the actual show. The same term is used in many other contexts. Before a tennis match the players warm up; athletes warm up before a race; even cars have a warm-up period before operating at their highest performance level.

Human relationships also require warm-up periods. We talk about the problems of 'cold calling' – attempts to sell without previous contact of the prospect. Among other examples where a warm-up seems to help considerably are:

1 in the development of confidence – in an idea or a person
2 in the workings of a creative problem-solving group – e.g. in a brainstorming

Psychologically speaking, the warm-up helps to establish a desired climate.

Some hints to assist the warm-up process

1   In general idea-proposing situations:

DO NOT be hasty in introducing any idea. The more challenging and unexpected the idea, the greater the need for preparation.

DO AVOID UNFINISHED BUSINESS – cutting across someone else's idea. That person is likely to become preoccupied with the threat to their idea.

DO SHOW YOU CAN RESPECT THE IDEA and find a bridge before introducing your own. Some people believe they should manipulate the situation so that the first person ends up believing he or she was the original inventor of the idea. This is not a total recipe for success. Better to work on the shared relationship so that you know that the idea will receive a warm reception.

If the idea is inevitably 'bad news', the warm-up may still be necessary – if only to establish that you are genuinely regretful about the bad news.

2   Before an ideas session (as facilitator or scribe)

DO explain (remind people of) the importance of a relaxed mood, and of postponing judgement.

DO invent some interesting speculative task for the group ('uses of a paperclip' is boring after a few such exercises).

DO keep an eye out for members who are by nature highly evaluative. You may have to enlist their conscious collaboration before asking them to write down their evaluative comments rather than interrupting the flow.

DO check when you think the group is nicely warmed up. Ask if they feel ready to 'have a go' at the real problem.

If all else fails, 'blow a whistle'. Call a time-out. Admit to the group that everything is a bit flat and check if there is some hidden reason for it. A break at such a time may help – a walk or a sauna.

Another valuable warm-up tip: try to encourage more right-brain behaviours. Metaphors are useful in this context. (But do not spend too much time on a warm-up metaphor, as the power of the metaphor may be reduced in the actual ideas session.)

What you are trying to achieve in the warm-up is a positive creative climate. You will have to work out the methods that suit you and your group. The more intellectual and 'buttoned-up' the group, the more delicate the challenge.

WHICH TECHNIQUES WHEN

If we look at types of problem that have 'turned out well' in brainstorming, and those that have not been so easy to make progress on, we start assembling selection rules. Broadly, a brainstorming type of technique 'works':

1. if there is a need to collect a large number of possibilities or ideas.
2. if the objective is to obtain a quick scan of relatively simple ideas rather than to obtain one or two particularly novel ideas.
3. for any problem requiring new ideas for improving a commercial system.
4. in improving the marketing of a product.
5. in improving the quality of a product or service to a customer.
6. in improving production methods (e.g. towards 'zero defeat' objectives).
7. in cost-reduction studies.
8. for anticipating potential problems during a planning operation, or a scale up of a pilot plant.
9. when looking for ideas for innovation. (brainstorming can help generate sets of attributes of a raw material or technology, and sets of consumer needs).

In contrast, brainstorming is not immediately applicable:

1. when a problem is posed in a close-ended way. (Who should be in charge of the new project?; Which chemical should we try out next to produce the desired effect? Where should we locate our sales and purchasing departments?)
2. where the nature of the problem signals a need for a team made up of specialists within a defined professional discipline. (A team of mathematicians who want a more elegant proof of a theorum; the team of computer programmers looking for a computing breakthrough; the geophysicists looking for an alternative theoretical explanation to a natural phenomenon.)
3. for problems framed in terms well outside the control of the participants. ('How to persuade the unions to be more reasonable'.)

As a rule of thumb, brainstorming is at its best as a simple technique for collecting relatively simple sets of ideas – i.e. when there are unlikely to be powerful mind sets producing stuckness. The benefits are greater if a team can be assembled bringing different perspectives to the problem. In almost any situation where ideas are required it will be possible to plan a brainstorming that will yield the ideas more effectively than a conventional business meeting would.

Why most brainstormings aren't

Most brainstormings aren't true to the principles of postponed judgement during idea generation. The reasons for this have to be understood if the techniques are to be applied in a more constructive way. First, brainstorming involves a special kind of process leader who knows how and why brainstorming works. Secondly, the leader and the rest of the group should be working together to bring about a climate in which judgement is postponed during an agreed stage of idea production. Thirdly, the creative climate should operate within a 'structure for freedom'.

Most brainstormings aren't because some of these conditions are ignored. It is not enough, for example, for a senior member of an organization to announce in the middle of a meeting that as new ideas are needed they will now move on to having a brainstorming session. Leadership is active, not passive; active in encouraging positivity, and minimizing the inhibitions produced by status and other climate-blocking factors.

Most brainstormings aren't because one or more of the members of the group is unable to avoid behaviours which kill speculation – in particular, evaluative comments on ideas. These quickly inhibit others and set a low-energy, low speculation norm.

Most brainstormings aren't because the individual members are able to postpone their inhibitions regarding evaluation of ideas by becoming totally self-centred – producing individual series of ideas without any regard for the ideas produced by anyone else. As a result, there is little in the way of developed ideas; each individual remains closed to the possibilities of 'yes anding' ideas. The session might just as well have been one of the 'nominal group' versions rather than an interactive version of brainstorming.

Most brainstormings aren't because brainstorming requires analysis as well as creativity. Like the best speeches, the most spontaneous brainstormings result from the greatest efforts in planning and subsequent creative leadership in the execution of the technique.

The irony is that brainstorming is not a difficult technique to use. The chapter provides enough guidelines to avoid the above pitfalls, and set up conditions for successful brainstorming sessions.

WHOLE BRAIN STORMING

Brainstorming can be criticized for being too 'left-brain'. It is a matter of common experience that some groups never escape from a mechanical production of ideas which are similar to those produced in a conventional meeting.

How can the technique be made more whole-brain? Some practitioners are experimenting with visual brainstorming – in which a group attempts to capture the essence of a problem through paints, drawings, or collages. Success has been claimed when organizational problems have been thought about in this way, and the method offers hope working with groups which find the intensely verbal nature of brainstorming too confining. For instance, consumer discussion groups might well benefit from visual brainstorming components; so might multicultural groupings.

A move in this direction would see further efforts by practitioners to introduce 'bunches of bananas' that trigger right-brain responses. Instead of turning to a dictionary to find random words, the group leader prepares a series of visual images. Some are evocative yet distant from the problem. Yet others are deliberately distorted or blurred, so that the group would be more likely to switch to a non-verbal, pattern-seeking mode of problem-solving.

A few workers are experimenting with a total environment that seeks to enhance whole-brain thinking. The brainstorming takes place in a specially designed room with restful colour schemes, and bean bags or soft floor areas for the participants. Restful music is played to reduce the dominating influence of the over-active left brain.

Already the work on deliberately stimulating metaphoric thinking has shown us how we can switch attention to more visual mental processes. These are directions which will take the venerable technique of brainstorming and produce a new series of 'dialects' that are more whole-brain in focus.

Structured brainstorming

This version of brainstorming has been found applicable in a wide range of organizations whenever there is a problem that requires fresh thinking.

1 Agree a problem that has a need for new ideas.
2 Obtain a willing team of people of different experiences.

3   Appoint a process leader to look after the idea collection. This person should not be the problem-owner.
4   Agree a general approach: this should include time constraints, and 'rules of the game' by the process leader. The group should be in a mood to try out new ideas. In other words the climate should be positive ('yes and'). It is a good idea to hold a 'warm-up' or practice session to reinforce the desired positive climate.
5   Invite the problem-owner to explain the problem, while other members try to think of differing perspectives ('how tos'). Uncertainties are better expressed as 'how tos' than as questions. (Too many questions means an evaluative climate.) Encourage the problem-owner to express needs and wishes.
6   Collect various perspectives or 'how tos'.
7   Take a break while the problem-owner inspects the 'how tos'.
8   Generate ideas without evaluating them ('postpone judgement') on a few key 'how tos' selected by the problem-owner.
9   Let the problem-owner select preferred ideas, encouraging 'yes ands' to strengthen promising ones.
10 If the session is 'stuck' (low level of imaginative ideas) look for a metaphoric way of tackling the problem, or liven things up with the unexpected statement ('bunch of bananas'). This will give new ideas and a more creative climate.
11 Develop and evaluate the ideas, trying to take account of success criteria ('must and wants'). Encourage people to take action responsibilities. Avoid broad generalisations without obvious implementation steps. Look for DBMs ('do by Monday' ideas).

SUMMARY

Brainstorming today is a large family of related techniques for idea generation, mainly in small teams, but always with some instructions to assist in the postponement of judgement during the idea generation stage.

Related families include synectics®, a powerful, well-researched approach for improving group interactions, and for deliberately seeking novel ideas through metaphors and other structures that encourage more right-brain thinking.

Nominal groups are versions of brainstorming in which the group members do not interact directly. Ideas are generated and collected, often with anonymous voting to deal with possible status problems. The methods are particularly sound for consensus seeking on complex social and organizational issues.

Successful brainstorming requires considerable planning, to establish the suitability of the problem, motivation and power to act of the person requesting the brainstorming, and selection and briefing of the team. Location should be also carefully considered to give a positive climate.

Leading a brainstorming well requires practice and sensitivity to small group behaviours to establish a climate of deferment of judgement.

Brainstorming (or one of its related techniques) is a good method of rapidly collecting a set of ideas, or beliefs. More complex strategies have to be incorporated (e.g. metaphor) to increase the chances of producing particularly novel ideas.

Much remains to be done to find ways of increasing right-brain thinking during brainstorming so that the technique overcomes a tendency to produce left-brain and verbal outputs.

7 Frameworks for thinking

To be creative we need frameworks to structure our thinking. As we have already seen, unstructured searches for ideas are too strongly influenced by experience and assumptions, and we overlook whole areas of potential importance. Therefore, there will be times when a technique is needed to avoid the biasing effect of personal mind sets.

This chapter describes three kinds of framework we can construct, each of which actually liberates our thinking, rather than confines it. The approaches, with variations within each, are:

Mind maps, e.g.
- Buzan diagrams
- Relevance trees
- Fishbone diagrams

Morphological methods, e.g.
- Grids
- Boxes
- Higher-dimensional morphologies

Checklists, e.g.
- Osborn's creative checklist (original long form)
- Scamper (a simplified version of Osborn's list)
- Kipling's checklist
- Critical examination (CE)

After looking at the individual techniques we consider why such structures actually provide freedom and enhance creativity.

MIND MAPS

I have used the term mind map to suggest techniques which help during mental explorations much as an ordinary map does during physical searches. The mind map can be a careful and detailed representation of the territory it deals with, or it can be a simple aid to memory. In other words, the family of mind map techniques will have assorted variations, each sharing with the others the property of representing some intellectual terrain, and permitting its exploration.

Several points are worth making about these structuring devices. The mind map is put together according to the particular mental mapping procedures of its owner, which differs in some ways from person to person. A personal map will be of more value to its owner than to others, although there are sufficient similarities to allow people from a shared culture to understand each other's maps. The map can be re-assembled into a preferred version after it has been drawn up. This is important, as it permits the creative process of going beyond the first idea or pattern to different ones, helping to break initial mind sets.

The British broadcaster and consultant Tony Buzan has been a leading advocate for the use of such maps, and his famous Buzan diagrams have been taught to thousands of people. Today you will come across students using the diagrams to assist revision in any library or for taking down the key points of a lecture. Among their industrial uses are organizing your thoughts before writing a complicated report, and summarizing your understanding of a meeting or of a presentation.

The basic notion is that each of us has a particular way of storing information, and of cross-referencing individual pieces of knowledge. We can assist the process of storage and recall if we make an effort to imitate our mental patterning in a visual representation or diagram. Buzan believes this is done through diagrams with 'memory hooks' of a right-brain kind. We might start with a few words or a sketch of a concept in the middle of a blank sheet of paper. Then we put related ideas around the basic concept, these growing outwards like a snowflake on a cold windowpane. The process continues with further sequences of ideas, which eventually occupy the whole sheet of paper.

Some users exercise their artistic talents, incorporating words, diagrams, and other visual effects, including selective use of colour to distinguish different aspects of the material.

Example of a Buzan diagram (framework for this chapter)

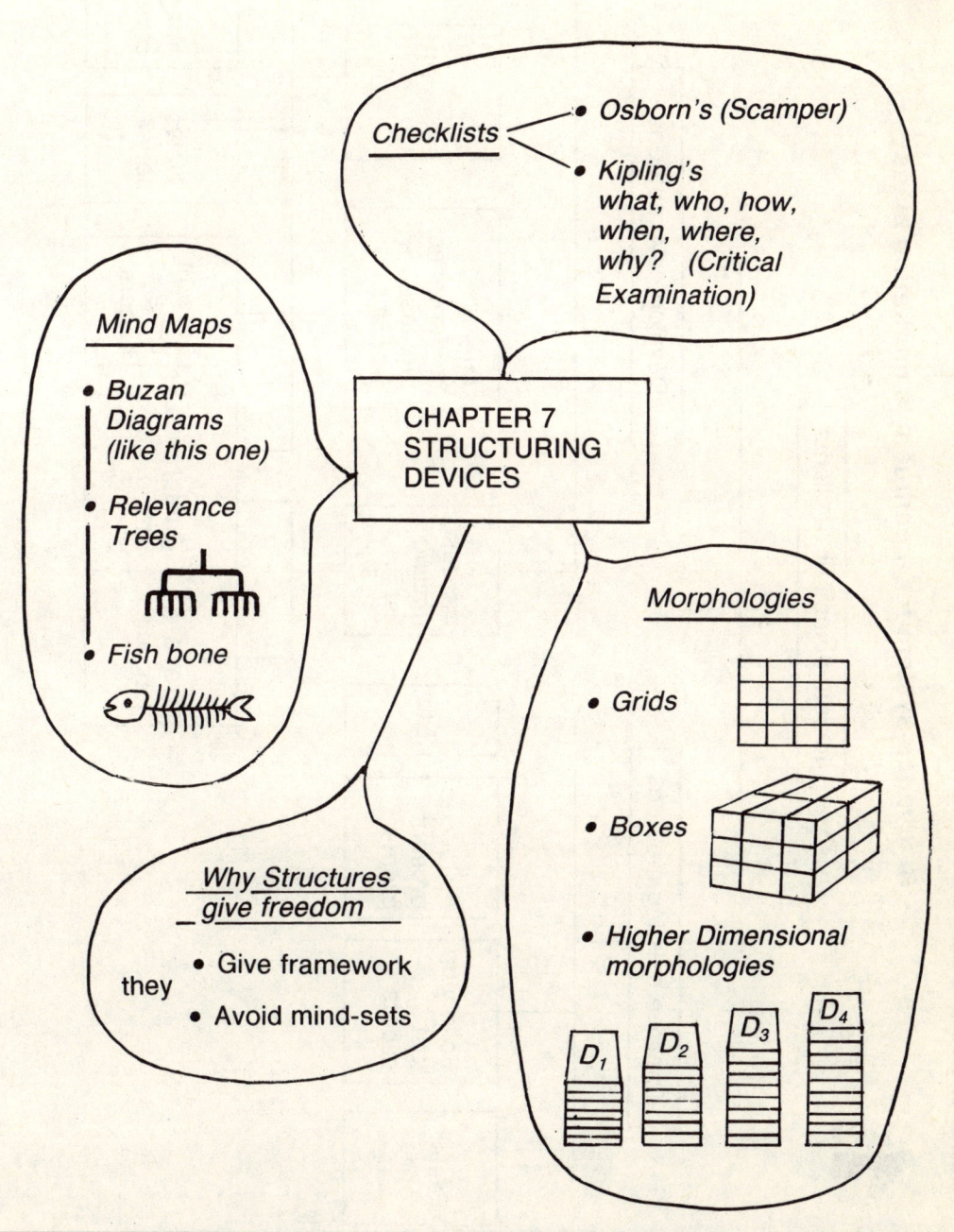

CHAPTER 7 STRUCTURING DEVICES

Checklists
- Osborn's (Scamper)
- Kipling's what, who, how, when, where, why? (Critical Examination)

Mind Maps
- Buzan Diagrams (like this one)
- Relevance Trees
- Fish bone

Morphologies
- Grids
- Boxes
- Higher Dimensional morphologies (D_1, D_2, D_3, D_4)

Why Structures give freedom
they
- Give framework
- Avoid mind-sets

118 PROCESS AND PROCEDURE

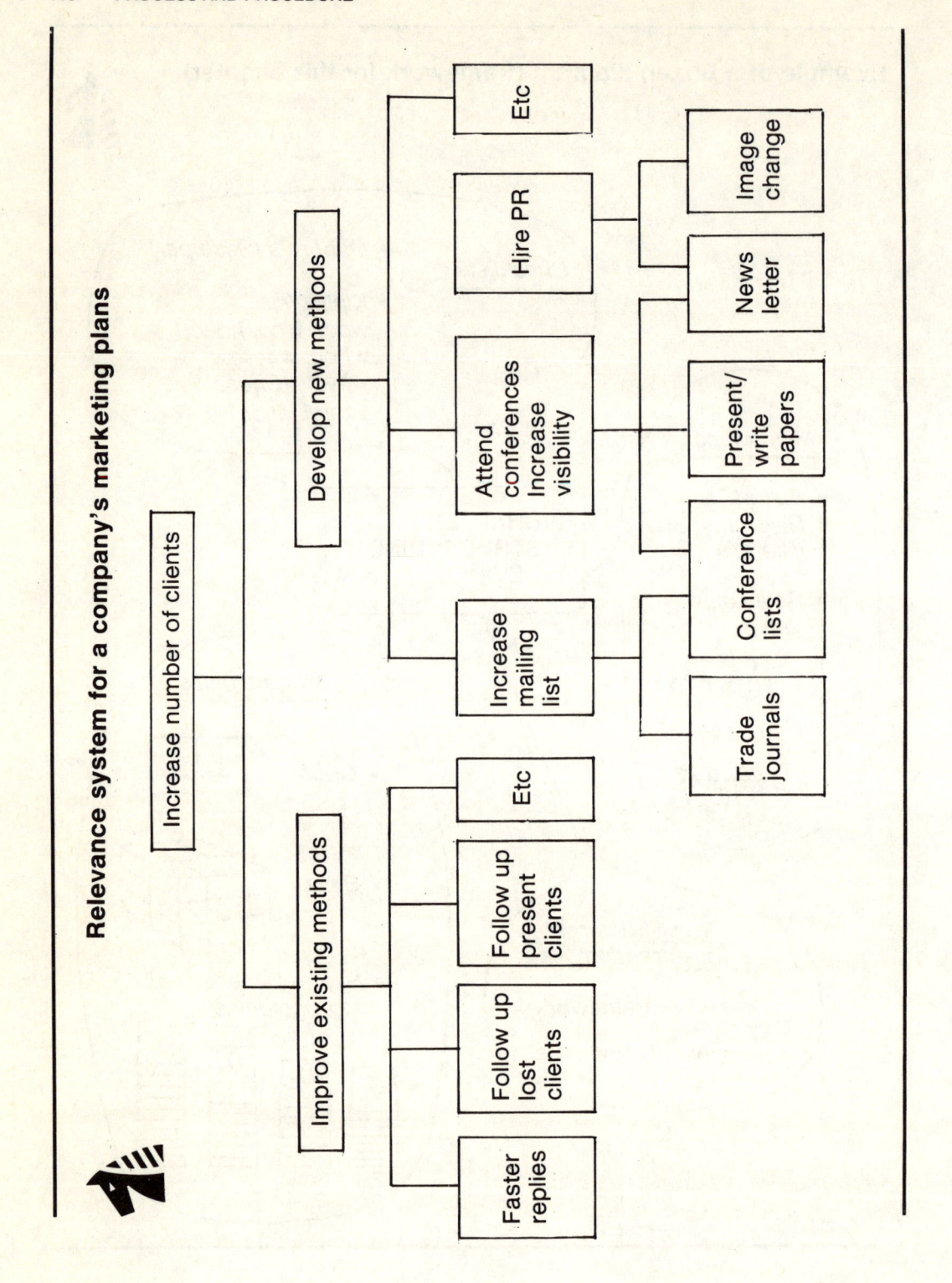

Relevance system for a company's marketing plans

- Increase number of clients
  - Improve existing methods
    - Faster replies
    - Follow up lost clients
    - Follow up present clients
    - Etc
  - Develop new methods
    - Increase mailing list
      - Trade journals
      - Conference lists
    - Attend conferences / Increase visibility
      - Present/write papers
      - News letter
    - Hire PR
      - Image change
    - Etc

FRAMEWORKS FOR THINKING   119

Another kind of mind map, known as a relevance tree, represents some dominant idea linked to a set of its own components, which can be further broken down into sets of subcomponents, as often as is convenient. Relevance trees illustrate the same basic idea at several levels of generality, and can be powerful tools for studying the nature of systems. A company organization chart is one well-known example, with 'the company' sitting proudly at the top of the chart,

Morphological analysis: a three-dimensional framework

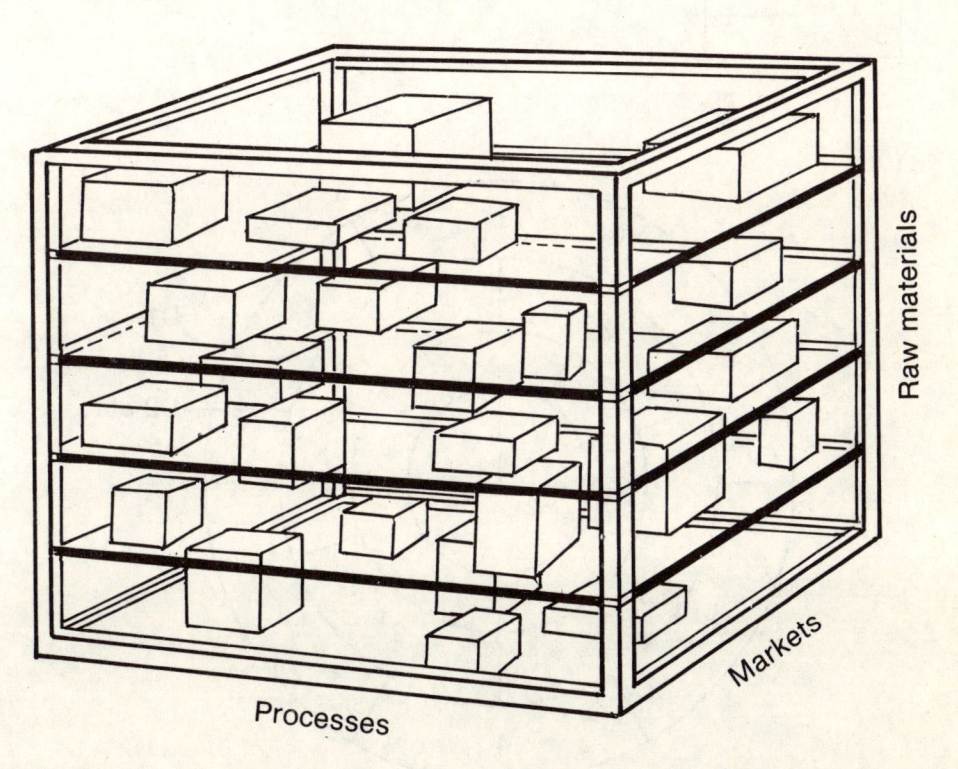

A physical display of a three-dimensional morphological analysis. The box represents a company. The filled-in cubes are existing products. Gaps represent opportunities for new products.

120 PROCESS AND PROCEDURE

Morphological analysis: four-dimensional representations

(a)

D1	D2	D3	D4
1	1	1	1
2	2	2	2
3	3	3	3
4	4		
5			
6			

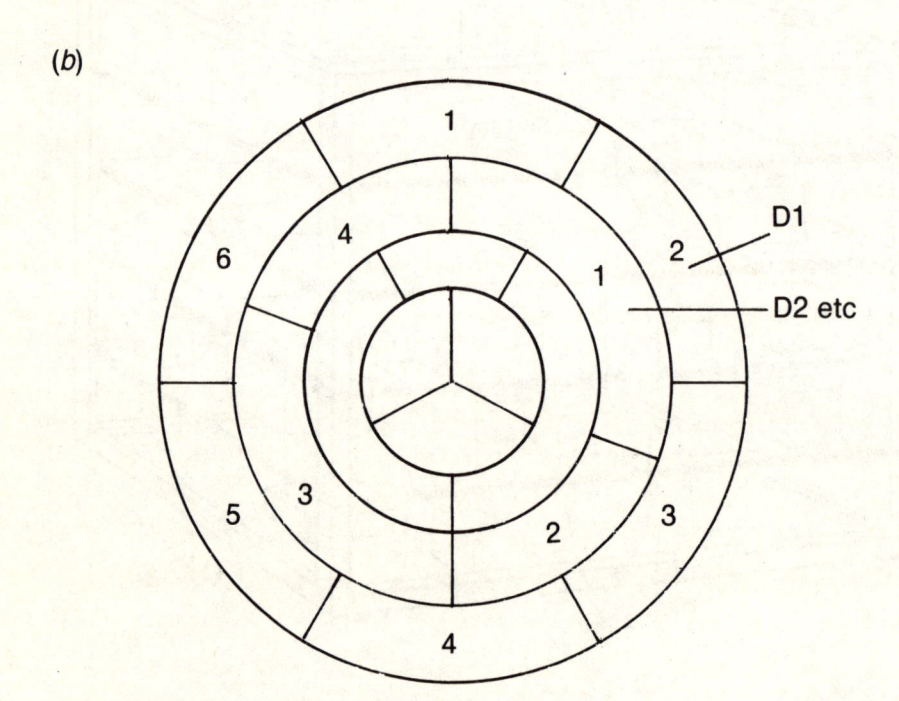

(b)

Here are two ways of visualizing four dimensions. The factors of each dimension are written in the spaces provided, on stiff cardboard.

Then the combinations of factors can be systemtically examined by moving the dimensions relative to one another.

then subdivided into its first layer of components, its divisions, which in turn are divided into departments, teams and so on. Used in this way the relevance tree serves as a visual illustration to aid understanding, although it can also be used more directly to stimulate ideas.

Working 'down' to greater levels of detail makes clear the practical first steps for putting the plan into operation. As the top-down approach encourages divergence, the construction of the framework offers opportunities for opening up thinking at every level of the tree.

Other examples of mind maps include a Japanese version known as the 'fishbone' technique – a splendidly descriptive term for the method, in which the central idea is like the backbone of a fish, with smaller 'bones' sticking out on each side.

A 'looser' mapping method is a version which involves decomposing a complicated problem into as many elements as can be thought of (brainstorming would be a suitable method to do this). Then the ideas are written on small filing cards – one statement per card. The basic notion here is to loosen our initial mental structures by deliberately breaking all connections previously assumed. Indeed, once a brainstormed set of cards is obtained, they should be left for a while, then extra ideas added on more cards, to give the incubation process a chance to work. Only then should provisional groupings or clusterings be set up.

The act of shuffling the cards around and building up larger groupings reveals the (creative) analyst's first and subsequent mind sets. When used in this way, the approach again helps the mind to structure and restructure complex issues.

GRIDS, BOXES AND CUBE CRAWLING

One of the most flexible categories of structuring technique comes with the ugly name 'morphological analysis', which just means studying the structure or shape of almost anything of interest from butterfly wings to business profitability and bridge building designs. A two-dimensional version is sometimes described as a grid or a matrix, and the most common ones are to be found on the walls of most offices and homes as year-planners or calendars. In business studies, it has become a profitable strategy for academics to study something, pick out two important aspects that are preferably independent, and reduce the complexity of the world to a two-dimensional grid. In the 1960s, we had Blake's grid of managerial styles (task orientation versus people orientation). Then there were product grids (technological versus market novelty), Boston Consulting Group grids, and many more besides.

Three-dimensional versions are also well-known. A famous one was proposed by the psychologist Guilford to study and understand 'the structure of intellect', to which he designated the dimensions of contents (types of thought) and processes.

A more industrial application of three-dimensional grids is the Scimitar approach to new product invention and implementation, originally applied in the Steetley Organisation by new products manager John Carson. His first three-dimensional models were made of perspex sheets supported by perspex rods. The model represented a company's raw materials, processes and Markets. Thus, each little box was an existing or potential combination of raw material, processed in a defined way, sold into a specified market and uniquely defined as a product or potential product.

Carson described the process of systematically examining the model for new products as 'cube crawling'. He and a team from the company looking for new products would take a 'slice' of the model (perhaps a market sector) and look at each box in turn – concentrating on the empty ones. Simple inspection of the boxes revealed instantly promising ideas, without any special idea-spurring techniques. These were augmented with brainstorming sessions in which metaphors and 'bunches of bananas' played regular parts.

In one exercise over a period of five years about 7000 ideas were obtained by cube crawling, and nearly 3000 more from the creativity techniques. Nearly a hundred ideas reached the marketplace, and of these the majority came from the cube crawling. However, most of the imaginative ideas came from creativity sessions, and these performed well in the marketplace. As might have been predicted, the first ideas discovered were relatively close to the experiences and mind sets of the searching team. It required further efforts to go beyond the obvious, to the new and relevant ones.

Which circumstances favour the use of morphological techniques? The methods are similar to mind maps, in that they represent or model complex idea systems which can then be valuable in understanding the system and in generating new ideas. In some instances they can be applied interchangeably to bring variety to idea searches – for example a group studying a business problem could brainstorm and assemble their ideas into a mind map. You could make out a good case for trying to set up a morphological analysis, or a relevance tree, while in Japan a group might choose the fishbone version.

Matrix methods are probably more widely used than the mapping approaches in idea generation and structuring activities. Perhaps that is because they are

1. more obviously systematic, thus appealing to those with a need for left-brain pigeonholing of ideas; and
2. more able to deal with extremely complex systems at considerable levels of detail.

CHECKLISTS AS STRUCTURING AIDS: CAN THEY STIMULATE CREATIVITY?

Most of us are familiar with checklists which serve the valuable purpose of itemizing a series of points – things we need to do or remember. Here we are concerned with checklists used to stimulate creativity.

Osborn's idea-spurring checklist (Scamper)

Various versions of this list have appeared in print. This one was shown me, on a grubby piece of paper, by a senior engineer. He kept it in his wallet when visiting sites all over the world, producing it at intervals to assist him in finding new ideas. He said it helped prime the pumps of his thinking.

Put to other uses? New ways to use as is? Other uses if modified?

Adapt? What else is like this? What other idea does this suggest? Does past offer parallel? What could I copy? Whom could I emulate?

Modify? New twist? Change meaning, colour, motion, odour, taste, form, shape? Other changes?

Magnify? What to add? More time? Greater frequency? Stronger? Higher? Larger? Longer? Thicker? Heavier? Extra value? Plus ingredient? Duplicate? Multiply? Exaggerate?

Minify? What to subtract? Smaller? Condensed? Miniature? Lower? Shorter? Narrower? Lighter? Omit? Streamline? Split up? Understate? Less frequent?

Substitute? Who else instead? What else instead? Other ingredient? Other material? Other process? Other power? Other place? Other approach? Other tone of voice? Other time?

Rearrange? Interchange components? Other pattern? Other layout? Other sequence? Transpose cause and effect? Change place? Change schedule? Earlier? Later?

Reverse? Transpose positive and negative? How about opposites? Turn it backward, upside down, inside out? Reverse roles? Change shoes? Turn tables? Turn other cheek?

> *Combine?* How about a blend, an alloy, an assortment, an ensemble? Combine units? Combine purposes? Combine appeals? Combine ideas?

The checklist is rather cumbersome, and, if you prefer, you can work with a simplified version which you can remember through the mnemonic Scamper:

Substitute (or Simplify)
Combine
Adapt
Modify
Put to other uses
Eliminate
Reverse

The Kipling checklist and critical examination

At school, we may have learned about Kipling's 'six honest serving men,' named:

Who
What
How
Why
Where
When.

Journalists and police officers are said to carry this checklist around in their notebooks to make sure they capture the essential details of the event they are covering. It is an excellent technique for checking that you have covered the main points of any topic when you are moving into a planning stage. Even in informal meetings, action plans are crisper if they are assisted by Kipling's six faithful retainers.

This framework for thinking in its essentials lies at the heart of a complex and systematic technique, critical examination, developed by a group of brilliant work study professionals in ICI in the 1960s. Important new projects, and particularly those with engineering design components, were carefully examined, sometimes in sessions that took days, by a team including a process leader skilled in the technique.

In essence the technique took the what question as the primary one, with the when, where, who, and how questions secondary to the what. (We shall come back to the why in a moment.) Stage one of the critical examination involved agreeing the what in a form which has been stripped of contamination by *when*, *where*, *who*, or *how* elements. In practice a major goal of the system became the *what* – in some such form as 'microchips are to be manufactured'.

This in turn threw light on the when, where, who, and how, and in the process some modification to the primary what statement may be seen as desirable. The why question gave this process further impetus. *Why* encourages challenge of the assumptions behind each of the checklisted components, at the level of the primary what, and at the secondary when, where, who and how level. 'Why microchips?' may lead to a discussion as to whether they should be manufacturing other components for the next generation of electronic products, leading to the amended what 'electronic components are to be manufactured', or perhaps, 'electronic components are to be produced'.

Used imaginatively, critical examination is a powerful blockbusting device at the design stage of complex engineering and organizational projects. Sadly, it was often used in the most mechanistic way, to the frustration of the engineers concerned. No technique can guarantee creative behaviour, and the chances of success are reduced by lack of understanding of the importance of climate setting, and other people skills.

WHY STRUCTURES GIVE FREEDOM TO CREATE

In this chapter we have looked at some widely used structuring aids. Some years ago the view was commonly expressed in books on problem-solving that there were things called analytical techniques and other things called creative techniques – which were by implication opposites. But this view oversimplifies the nature of creative problem-solving. Structuring techniques would be assumed to be analytical, although some gave the classifiers problems, and tended to be included in books and articles on creative problem-solving techniques. Morphological analysis is one of the most frequently quoted of these techniques, and Osborn actually called his checklist a creativity aid.

Let's look at the issue in a different way. Suppose the techniques are not creative or logical of themselves, but rather are devices which can be used in a creative or uncreative manner? At the simple level, a structure can at least help us to avoid overlooking the obvious in our thinking. At the level of a creativity-aid, greater freedom to create is gained.

Creativity can occur within the structure (e.g. in the cube crawling through a morphological analysis), or through changing the structure (by discovering a new perspective on the chief goal of a system during a critical analysis.) In either case, the structure has enabled the user to create more freely than would have been otherwise likely. This is because we can set up structures which have the potential to free us from the restricting influences of assumptions and mind sets.

We can even see this as a working principle for organizations. Each organization operates by establishing a series of routines, and then solving the problems of remaining competitive and generating new routines. A balance is needed between structures for maintaining the status quo, and structures which permit flexibility and creativity.

SUMMARY

Structuring devices play a part in creative problem-solving when there is a need to examine complicated and connected systems of ideas for deeper understanding – revising for an exam, preparing a technical report, considering design options, organizational restructures, etc.

Mind maps such as Buzan diagrams and relevance trees have been widely used in assembling information for writing reports, summarizing lectures, preparing notes for a public presentation.

Morphological systems have been applied in a range of graphical representations of data. Many new product ideas have emerged from two-dimensional grids and three-dimensional boxes by systematic and creative searching of the combinations displayed.

Creativity-spurring checklists help us widen our search area for ideas and serve to move us on from blinkers imposed by mind sets.

The techniques demonstrate that creativity requires both freedom and structure for new and valuable ideas to flourish.

8 Implementation

Most people find it easier to think of ideas than to make them work. In this chapter we look at how mind sets reduce our conscious ability to find implementation methods or strategies. Five rather different approaches are described, of which most people show a strong bias towards one or two, overlooking the others completely. Eight hints are offered to broaden your range of options for getting ideas into action.

HOW MIND SET REDUCES OUR IMPLEMENTATION EFFECTIVENESS

Implementation is a thoroughly approved of skill in the workplace. People who are good at making things happen catch the attention of their seniors and can expect promotion. This is not surprising, as management is largely a matter of getting things done with (and) through people. Once it was assumed that bosses gave orders which were carried out. In its famous pyramid-shape, an organization's commands originated at the top and were received by the compliant many. Maybe it never quite worked that way – there was always a Spartacus around to hamper the smooth implementation of top-down orders. And it is certainly not so today, which is why the whole question of implementation deserves close attention.

In our problem-solving seminars we ask participants to bring along important work problems. These can be technical, organizational or personal. By far the majority refer to the difficulties of implementation, often couched in such terms as:

> 'how to get a difficult client to accept my proposal'
> 'how to sell an idea to the board'
> 'how to obtain backing for an idea without losing control'.

In working through these problems a striking observation has emerged on how people go about implementing ideas:

> The majority of people at work have a powerful, dominant strategy which, while effective, sometimes can also produce stuckness and a failure to solve implementation problems.

In other words, automatic or habitual behaviour gets in the way of effective and creative problem-solving. And, as we have already seen, the key to becoming unstuck is creative analysis and the development of fresh approaches.

Dominant implementation strategies

Here are five strategies in roughly descending order of automatic use by people at work. We shall look at the strengths of the strategies and also consider how they can become part of a blocking mind set if circumstances do not justify their further application.

1. persistence
2. influencing people
3. 'Back to the drawing board'
4. 'I'm in charge'
5. taking a systems view

1 Persistence

An old song tells the story of a ram that kept hitting his head against a dam. In the song the strategy worked when the dam burst. Persistence can be a virtue, and many people give up too easily at the first sign of opposition, so that some dam-battering may be needed from time to time. Most entrepreneurs know that they have to knock on a great many doors in search of backing, and few succeed without persistence.

On the other hand... the obsessive personality is too persistent – persistently doomed to failure because there is something wrong somewhere that he has not been able to discover (dam-battering is not a process that goes easily with reviewing the situation). The successful implementer is persistent but able to recognize when to give up. At that stage he or she may switch to another strategy.

2 Influencing people

Dam-battering is rightly suspected as painful and with a low probability of pay-off. Another and quite different set of strategies is those in which the would-be influencer sets to work on persons of influence to gain their acceptance for an idea. Methods include bringing in the heavy boys, gentle persuasion, negotiation, sales presentations, logic, and so on. Within this enormous range of possibilities most of us have a very limited repertoire of strategies which we use regularly. One approach repeatedly raised in discussion is 'the only way to have my boss accept an idea is to make him believe he thought of it himself'. My suspicion is that the whole notion is over-rated, because (a) it is difficult to carry out, (b) its advocates are often crushingly insensitive to other people's motivations, (c) it is difficult to repeat, (d) human beings are differently motivated, very few being stereotyped idea-snatchers; and (e) as we shall see, there are far richer approaches, both within the general influencing strategy and outside it.

3 'Back to the drawing board'

Here the response to stuckness is to look for a different idea. Perhaps the emphasis will be on modifying the original idea, or on producing a totally different one. Consider an inventor who has hit upon a new board game and who sets out to interest games manufacturers. His game is repeatedly rejected, mainly because, he is told, the idea is too complicated. Having shown great persistence working his way through the list of manufacturers he does not fall into the trap of redoubling efforts on a failing strategy, but instead goes back to the drawing board. He might consider making the game simpler (a strategy that might also link with that of influencing the game manufacturers). Or he could opt for inventing a totally different game, or for returning to his job as a library assistant. Sadly, the very motivation that assists in keeping the inventor going often blocks him from accepting the need to return to the drawing board.

4 'I'm in charge' (taking personal control)

Good implementers, including a high proportion of successful inventors, switch their approach if the original strategy fails. In

The successful implementer is persistent and yet is able to switch to another strategy.

particular they look for some way of taking control without the direct support of powerful external agencies. The inventor of Monopoly, frustrated by the response of the leading game manufacturers, began manufacturing his game in the garage, and selling it to friends. The results were spectacular, and his decision to take control was justified. However, taking personal control can fail miserably, as we can see from instances of inventors and others who will never consider relinquishing control of any part of their idea, although that is the most likely way to progress.

5 Taking a systems view

We conclude by proposing a fifth strategy that is far from obvious, and yet worth careful study. The approaches already described tend to concentrate on one aspect of a more complicated system, be it the idea, or influential people, or getting started through personal control. By looking at the wider system we discover clues as to which of these or other approaches are most likely to be worth trying first. Strategies 1 to 4 occur because they have been discovered and rediscovered many times in practical endeavours. Taking a systems view requires a deeper understanding of the forces which operate within any system facing change, and which need to be taken into account for successful implementation. We shall be looking at those factors in some detail in this chapter through a technique known as Force-Field Analysis, but before doing so let us consider some ways in which we can become more effective in applying the relatively simple strategies already described.

IMPROVING EFFECTIVENESS OF SIMPLE IMPLEMENTATION STRATEGIES

If, as seems to happen, we have a single preferred strategy, it can become a mind set. We become sensitized to opportunities to deploy it, and less aware of the need to switch to other strategies. Developing sensitivity to stuckness will help us retain the balance between persisting in a strategy and trying something new. ('When stuck, challenge assumptions and try something different.') In addition there are techniques which can assist in specific circumstances which we shall now look at. The following list of tips has been assembled both from practical experience, and through relating the simple innovation strategies to relevant principles of creative problem-solving and human motivation theory. Once again readers are advised to study them and find those that until now would have fallen outside their normal set of procedures. In that way existing implementation mind sets can be identified, and the way opened to try out quite different approaches. Our list is:

'The eye buys'
Vision getting and giving
Getting started and maintaining momentum
Empathy ('Walk a mile in my shoes')
Thinking implementation earlier in problem-solving
Watching and testing for vicious problem-solving
Reducing the blocking forces
Respecting comfort zones

The eye buys – some simple window-dressing points

Logic may demonstrate the value of an idea, but the eye buys. Do you spend enough time considering the impact that your proposals have on other people? Professional influencers such as sales and marketing folk are highly aware of the importance of style in making presentations, and we do well to learn from the sales professions. (By the way, the professional mind set of salespeople is curiously specific, and they may be no better or worse than others in presenting ideas in general management discussions.)

A golden rule is : Do not try to sell an abstract concept if it is at all possible to back up the idea with a visual demonstration. Car salesmen know that even when a customer has made up his or her mind to buy a particular model there are psychological resistances to making the buying decision. An early critical step is to invite the prospect to try out the car. The psychology is the same with ideas. People find it easier to accept what they can see and touch.

It is a good strategy to look for a tangible prototype that can be demonstrated within any implementation exercise. In new product development this can be built in as one of the stages towards commercialization. Presentations will then centre around those ideas which have reached the demonstrable prototype stage, rather than abstract ideas.

> An excellent example of setting up a high-impact demonstration comes from Charles Kettering, who was an innovator of the highest calibre. Kettering liked to relate how during his distinguished career at General Motors he had been searching for a means of dealing with the most serious bottleneck in automobile manufacturing, the manual body painting process. After a wide-ranging search for solutions he hit on the idea of spraying instead of brushing on the paint. This in itself was a powerful creative leap,

but it was during the implementation stage that Kettering showed the importance of 'creativity past the goal-line'. For many months he could not persuade any of his colleagues in the various automobile plants to back the idea that he had developed in the laboratory. His reports claimed that enormous savings could be made from taking up his proposed spraying technology. Yet the people with the power to alter the production lines were slow to act. Kettering devised a daring and brilliant demonstration. He invited the manager of one unit to lunch and explained once again how paint spraying could substantially speed up the production rate. His colleague listened with amused tolerance to the idea. After lunch, they walked to the manager's car, which had been secretly given the new spray-paint treatment during lunch.

Its owner, knowing better than most people the time it takes for hand-painted car bodies to dry, was furious. It was only when Kettering grabbed hold of his hand and pushed it onto a newly painted but already dry surface that the mind set was broken. After recovering from the shock the unit manager became an enthusiastic champion of paint spraying technology, introduced it into his production lines, and contributed to the evolution of the automobile industry.

We know that Kettering was a good manager as well as a great innovator, and we can only speculate that the demonstration was designed with great care, bearing in mind the temperament of the powerful patron he was trying to influence. He had combined the persistence needed to succeed with an influencing strategy that smashed the mind set of the target manager. We can learn from such examples that the design of powerful presentations is a form of creative problem-solving which takes into account the proposed product and the motivations of the audience.

Vision getting and giving

There will be times when the influencing process requires acceptance of an idea or concept in non-tangible form. Then it becomes important to provide an evocative image for the inner eye to buy without an immediately visible external object. So the idea has to be presented in a way which captures the imagination and triggers off right-brain images. Skilful speakers know that one way this happens is through personalizing the message. As an illustration consider the following:

> *Tip 1.* Implementation can be improved if the message includes triggers to right-brain activity aimed at the recipient, and is

couched in terms which enable the recipient to identify with the idea.

Tip 2. Imagine you have just driven into work. The traffic was heavy and you are late. There is a pile of urgent messages to be dealt with. What you really want to do is to persuade your boss to give you more authority to do your job. Now imagine you are going into his office. He's on the telephone (he's always on the telephone). Instead of letting this raise your blood pressure you are going to wait calmly, pretending not to be listening, perhaps trying to read the letters on his desk, which will be upside down to you, of course (the letters, I mean.) Now he's put the phone down. It's time to start your vision-giving performance . . .

Now let's blow a whistle, as in a creative problem-solving session when we want to make a process observation. In Tip 2 I was trying to personalize Tip 1, to make it more visual and possibly attention-catching. If you found Tip 1 helpful at an intellectual level, but Tip 2 began to involve you more, the demonstration has served its purpose. To complete the story in Tip 2 you have to find some way of painting a word picture that involves your boss as the principal actor, engaged in a script which appeals to his interests and current concerns. The story will have little to do with you wanting more authority, but a lot to do with how much more enjoyable life will be once he has been relieved of the unnecessary responsibilities of defect rate monitoring (or whatever).

At a more general level, leadership involves finding a symbol which can become a shared vision for a group, or even a large corporation or social movement. Orators have successfully presented such images down the ages. Almost certainly the workers of the world found less inspiration in *Das Kapital* than in the images triggered by the invitation to 'unite, you have nothing to lose but your chains'. The development of a shared vision for a company is a powerful, perhaps essential, ingredient for mobilizing change.

Getting started and maintaining momentum

Sometimes there are blocks to implementing a strategy (or an idea) because you do not have a clear goal. So our old friend goal orientation can start the process of clarifying: 'what is it I really want to do and what's stopping me?'

It may be possible to convert the goal into a visual image which, even when put 'out of mind', continues to work for you.

In one exercise in conditioning the mind to be sensitive to opportunities, a student imagined himself discovering an important folder he had lost during a pub-crawl the night before. He set about retracing his steps. Approaching the fifth or sixth pub in his visualization, the image of the folder came back to mind, and he remembered stopping to make a telephone call at this particular pub, and leaving the folder by the telephone booth. To his relief, his visualization turned out to be accurate, and he recovered the folder.

But even the most powerful goal can lose its motivating force, if there are repeated failures with no sense of progress. So a tip for keeping motivation going is to set up much smaller subgoals. Reaching each target is a signal of progress, and an opportunity to feel good and reward yourself.

Setting goals that are bite-sized chunks is the method used to motivate people in many walks of life. Parish fund raisers display huge thermometers showing the rising level of contributions. Dieters plot weight losses. Many authors force themselves to a weekly word target, and perhaps a daily one before the first drink. Finding regularly attainable and measurable successes can be a creative and profitable exercise at work. Well-known examples are office displays of sales, production figures, accident-free weeks by department. Another worth mentioning is to encourage reporting of numbers of ideas produced in competitive units for suggestion schemes. Such initiatives assist motivation and increase sensitivity to opportunities for improved performance levels.

Empathy ('Walk a mile in my shoes')

Empathy is the gift of showing you understand and care for someone else's position. It is often a crucial factor in implementation strategies, e.g. when we are trying to decide just what the eye will buy, or what particular pattern of influencing behaviour has a high chance of success. If there were such a thing as a empathometer for measuring individual capacity for empathy it would show that some people have a generally low score, while others would maintain a generally high score. Like many other personality characteristics – including creativity – we can become consciously aware of our blocks to empathy, and improve on our previous standards, whatever our starting point on the empathometer.

In many implementation problems it is important to understand and respect the other person's viewpoint – get into his or her mind set and out of yours, if you like. Practice, and testing your hunches, both help improve performance. One salutary exercise is to take a report you have written, and rewrite it, trying to make it fit into your understanding of the needs and beliefs of the intended audience. If there is to be a wide audience, concentrate on a typical recipient, or an influential recipient. In time you will find it becoming automatic to think about this aspect of impact when writing anything for public scrutiny.

Practice in developing empathy deserves a user health warning. It is in essence a technique which helps people understand each other, and which leads to collaboration and 'win–win' problem-solving. Those who would like to influence people for ulterior motives will find there is a built-in self-destruct device. The best way of showing people that you care about their needs is to care about their needs.

Getting your implementation in first (thinking implementation earlier in problem-solving)

The simple model of implementation assumed by many people is:

    step one: discover an idea
    step two: do whatever is necessary to implement the idea.

'Whatever is necessary' very often turns out to be tortuous, so much so that the implementation process is widely considered the hardest part of problem-solving. And yet the process can be considerably eased if only we could carry around, lurking in the back of our minds, some pointers to the forces that will help implementation, and forces that hinder it. As these forces include people, it should become second nature to identify the most significant ones whose views will help or hinder the implementation.

As well as having to be aware of influencing strategies ('his point of view', 'the eye buys', etc), we can also extend a principle of creative problem-solving techniques regarding ownership of ideas. We have seen how motivation towards accepting new ideas is enhanced if the problem-owner is helped to discover new insights, but is given freedom to decide which one is important enough for further development. There is no need to persuade or coerce the problem-owner to accept an idea in a creativity session, and therefore the implementation strategy is relatively straightforward.

Translating this to more general situations provides a scheme for easier implementation: whenever possible work closely with the key people, identifying their most important needs (empathy helps here), until it becomes second nature to link your ideas and goals with the needs of those individuals critical for success of the project. There is a creative logic to this strategy. In negative organizational climates the pressures are for individuals to develop ideas in secret, delaying interaction with others for as long as possible, to avoid feared attacks on the idea 'before it is ready'. The trouble with such a strategy is that the deepest resistances to change can only be discovered through testing out the idea with those would-be idea killers. So we have every incentive to seek out participation, in order to defuse feelings of exclusion and build in acceptance-seeking aspects for new ideas.

To turn this general observation into some practical steps for reducing implementation problems, remember:

- It is never too early to start thinking about implementation – don't leave it until you have to.
- Look for ideas which have quality and acceptance.
- Pick out an idea-sponsor or powerful ally who will be able to support the implementation indirectly through his or her personal or organizational power.
- Seek ideas that fit in with the needs of influential allies, rather than ideas that require you to influence or change those needs.

This strategy is underutilized, but has a proven track record. It lies at the heart of the systems approach to implementation, about which we shall have much more to say later.

Implementation does not have to be the biggest and most difficult part of any work activity. Its difficulties can be reduced by intelligent and creative approaches which incorporate the views and needs of more than one stakeholder in the problem.

How to check for 'vicious' problem-solving

Vicious problem-solving occurs when 'solutions' are implemented and are found to create even bigger problems than had existed before. Most often we come across vicious problem-solving when those with power in a complicated situation think they can see a simple solution to a problem. There are rarely simple solutions to problems involving large numbers of human beings.

Here is a simple method to test for vicious problem-solving in your own thinking: during the process of problem-solving make a comparison between the control exercised over the problem and the proposed solution. Or, more succinctly, 'who owns the problem?'; 'who owns the solution?'

Vicious problem-solving arises when the ownership of the proposed solution (and, by implication, the power to implement it) has been broadened in the problem-solving in comparison to the ownership of the original problem.

> For example, suppose your managing director suffers from hay fever, and decides to relocate the plant to the Arctic, where there

are fewer allergy-producing pollen grains. This would very likely be a vicious piece of problem-solving, as the implications of this decision will cascade over all the other company employees who have to relocate to Baffin Bay; the suppliers to the company, who may have trouble communicating with the new location; the customers (who may decide to solve their problem by changing to a competitor); the shareholders; and assorted seals and polar bears, whose habitat has been violated. If the MD had decided only to move his own location to Greenland or preferably to a closer pollen-reduced zone, it would have been equally good for hay fever, and the action would not have had such vicious side effects.

In this example it is easy to see that 'who owned the problem' (as defined) was the MD. 'Who owned the solution' was a large and disparate number of other humans and innocent Arctic fauna. Hence, strong evidence for vicious problem-solving, which makes implementation so difficult.

Do not imagine, however, that vicious problem-solving is a rare phenomenon. The impulse is there in everyday behaviours, when we become fixated on one view or strategy which ignores some vital dimensions of the situation, especially the human ones. Many managerial actions during industrial disputes accidentally make things worse in this way. The chances of vicious consequences can be reduced by becoming more sensitive to other approaches, and by exploring the various factors that might influence the impact of any idea – i.e. through taking a systems view.

Reducing the blocking forces

One technique which helps us take a systems approach is known as force field analysis. It is another of those methods which can serve as an extensive group approach, or as a back-of-the-envelope aid to innovation planning. Readers should by now be able to construct their own versions of the team use from this brief summary of its principles.

We can imagine any human system such as an organization as being in a position of dynamic equilibrium at any time. This position gives it stability, and for this we have to assume the existence of a series of forces which balance each other out. Without balancing forces the system will be destroyed. A simple mechanical analogy is a ping-pong ball suspended on a jet of water at a fairground sideshow. The pull of gravity on the ball is balanced by the equal and opposing force of the water jet. In organizations the forces are more complex, but the principle is the same, and consideration of force field theory gives us very practical implementation advice.

Force field analysis

Force field analysis can be useful at the diagnostic stage of problem-solving in situations in which people's attitudes and reactions are important. Its basic model is that social systems such as organizations resist change because of a state of dynamic tension which exists between the needs, drives, aspirations, fears and other feelings of the people involved. The present state is an equilibrium between the forces for change and the forces resisting change. Force-field analysis involves the identification of these forces, their direction, and their strength, and suggests how the forces might be modified.

It can be used as a group problem-solving instrument or by individuals. It offers the advantages of relative simplicity and clarity of visual display. It makes possible a rough comparative measurement of the forces, leading to the development of key action steps for problem-solving.

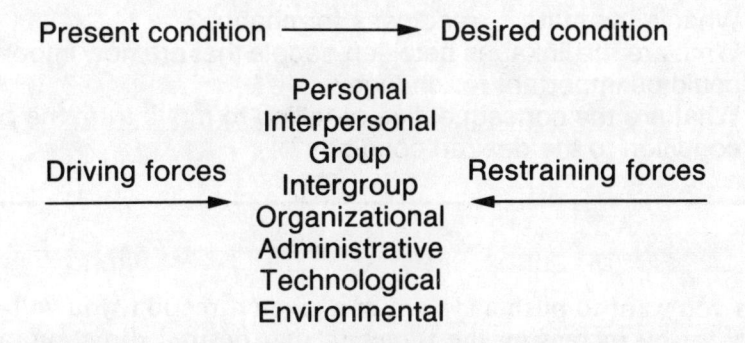

```
          Present condition ──────▶ Desired condition

                              Personal
                              Interpersonal
                              Group
    Driving forces ──▶        Intergroup        ◀── Restraining forces
                              Organizational
                              Administrative
                              Technological
                              Environmental
```

It is implicit in this model that movement in the desired direction can most readily be achieved by reducing or removing restraining forces. Intensifying driving forces increases reaction. Typical categories of driving/restraining force couples are indicated in the diagram.

To use this diagnostic tool effectively, it is essential to define the desired change as explicitly as possible and ensure full group understanding. Consider only forces at work and do not consider possible or likely or hoped-for additional forces.

The force field analysis is better used in trying to diagnose the present equilibrium state of a particular group of people (e.g. first line supervisors in works X), not people in general. It is important that one tries to understand the forces felt by this particular group and operate on them – not the group doing the analysis.

Some important questions to ask during a force field analysis are:

1. Do we have a general statement of the desired condition in terms of moving from one state to another?
2. Have we overlooked any of the important variables?
3. Do we have reasonably accurate information in terms of strength of the various forces?
4. How can we get additional data?
5. How do these forces interrelate?

In following up a force field analysis for purposes of action planning the following questions may be useful:

1. What is the relative importance or significance of the forces indicated?
2. To which people and about which forces do we have access – what is your point of entry?
3. Where do we have leverage or influence?
4. What is the state of readiness for change?
5. What are the linkages between people that are now important or could be important for change?
6. What are the consequences of failing to move from the present condition to the desired condition?

If you want to push a system in a given direction, you will not get very far by increasing the forces in that desired direction, as your actions will result in increased resistance from the opposing forces. For change you must look at mechanisms for reducing the opposing forces.

Some of the difficulties of a persistence strategy for implementation now become clear. The following illustration comes from a real case a few years ago.

> A company had been trying to keep better records of its weekly sales returns, the responsibility of its sales managers. The managers had been accustomed to preparing monthly returns, on which their own bonuses and those of their salespeople were calculated. A request by the general manager for weekly information was virtually ignored. A few weeks later the general

manager sent out another request. That was also ignored, so after another few weeks of waiting he sent out a memorandum to the same sales managers asking them to explain why they had not replied to his earlier request. One or two of his better managers passed back the message that they were having difficulties collecting the information, because their staff did not think it was important, and it got in the way of the selling.

Even the simplest of force field analyses would have suggested to the general manager that there were considerable forces opposing his request. To make progress he would have to work at reducing the potency of those resistances. An education programme was introduced, pointing out the benefits to the sales force of supplying up-to-date information, as a means of achieving good customer relationships, and eventually better sales bonuses. Acceptance of the idea of weekly returns was gradual, but eventually successful.

'But a manger's job is to manage', you may well say. 'Why all this pussyfooting around when all he had to do was make it clear that the weekly sales figures were an order, not a request?' Maybe, although possibilities for vicious problem-solving loom large when managers find no alternative but to impose a solution on a reluctant workforce. This particular company had a track record of confrontations and disputes in similar situations, so the circumstances were particularly ripe for a systems approach which aimed to reduce the suspicions of the employees.

Effective ways of reducing blocking forces can best emerge as creative problem-solving for the specific situation. Some broadly employed methods include:

- involving the communities likely to be affected in the change.
- letting people know what is going on.
- identifying the psychological costs of the change and dealing with these sensitively.
- operating with small scale trials to minimize fears of the unknown.

Respecting comfort zones

Most of us have limits to our acceptance of new ideas. These are our comfort zones, and may be partly founded on mind sets and value systems, partly on experience and knowledge. In creative problem-solving sessions some problem-owners, on reviewing the ideas produced, show enthusiasm only for those very close to their earlier thinking (and therefore ideas which do little to challenge mind sets).

These people have a 'too close for comfort' zone. Other problem-owners like middle-range uncertainty, ideas which challenge some conventions, but which are close to many of their core skill areas and knowledge. Finally, there are people who are intoxicated by novelty, regardless of any prospects of actualizing the idea. Their comfort zone is up in the clouds somewhere.

In presenting an idea it helps to form a view on the comfort zone of the person you are addressing. Is the managing director only concerned with ideas worth many millions of pounds? If so, don't waste his or her time unless you can talk those kinds of figures. Is the accountant concerned with the cash needed for a new venture? Find a way of presenting a stepping stone or actionable first step within his comfort zone.

Comfort zones are influenced by personal mind sets. Each individual is inclined to react positively to stimuli that fit within the mind set, and negatively to stimuli falling outside the mind set. Remember that mind sets are not always bad, but serve as mechanisms for coping with routine tasks, and for avoiding being overwhelmed with data. Unless there is clear evidence of a mind set having a malignant influence it should be respected and attended to when you are making a presentation. However, if there are signs of a rogue mind set, blocking an implementation strategy that deserves closer attention, there are mechanisms for change. It has been our contention that in order to challenge mind sets there is a need for consciousness-changing tricks, to bring about 'a whack on the head'. The creative thinking aids of Chapter 5 can play a particularly valuable part in such cases.

SOME FINAL THOUGHTS ON IMPLEMENTATION

It is likely that each reader of this book will be engaged on some implementation activity on a regular basis. It is also likely that most of the attempts to bring about change are being driven by powerful unchallenged strategy or mind set.

Most of the time that strategy works, but when it doesn't we find we need creative thinking to escape from stuckness. As a 'set to break set', begin to associate implementation with taking a systems view of what is going on. At least recognize the opportunities for strategies such as persistence, changing the idea, influencing other people, and taking more control over the implementation personally. Then, when you have decided on a strategy, ask yourself: 'Am I acting this way because the circumstances suggest it – or because this is one of my favourite ways of dealing with implementation problems?'

If you follow this simple advice you may find that implementation is not such a terribly difficult aspect of problem-solving after all.

SUMMARY

Five different basic strategies have been described for getting ideas into action: persisting until you succeed; modifying the idea; influencing key people to gain their acceptance and support; taking more personal control over the actions required; and developing a systems approach.

Most people have a dominant or preferred strategy from among the five, and few people consider all five before seeking to implement ideas.

When a dominant strategy is recognizably causing problems it is advisable to consider one of the others that has not been considered so seriously in the particular exercise.

A range of simple approaches can be practised to improve chances of getting ideas into action, including:

'The eye buys'
Vision getting and giving
Getting started and maintaining momentum
Empathy ('walking in another's shoes for a mile')
Thinking implementation earlier in problem-solving
Watching and testing for vicious problem-solving
Reducing the blocking forces
Respecting comfort zones

Part III
CREATIVITY IN ACTION

9 A tale of two projects

Records are available of practical experiences of stimulating creativity at work in the late 1960s and 1970s. The general creative problem-solving approach became the foundation on which the more recent developments have been established. Although insufficient attention was paid in the reports to interpersonal and organizational factors as they impacted on the change process, nevertheless reviewing the early work helps in making a bridge to subsequent creative problem-solving efforts.

In Case example 1 we look in some detail at a successful creative problem-solving exercise. In Case example 2, we study an exercise which had less successful results. This enables us to draw some conclusions about success and failure from the information available, and with the benefits of hindsight. (Each study involves entrepreneurial activities within an organization — hence the term 'intrapreneurs'.)

CASE EXAMPLE 1: A CREATIVE PROBLEM-SOLVING ACTIVITY WHICH SOLVED AN ENGINEERING PROBLEM

A large international company had established a small team of intrepreneurs to help in the discovery of new products and in the provision of new solutions to old problems. One session demonstrated how 'disguising' the problem could lead to practical and valuable results. An engineering section had been invited to submit currently important problems, on the understanding that the intrapreneurial group were 'catalysts', not suppliers of instant solutions. A young project engineer and a colleague came along to the group and outlined his problem.

His group had been commissioned to achieve a more precise monitoring of grease levels at a checkpoint of effluent flow from a manufacturing process of a local factory. The existing method of checking the levels of grease slurry released employed a simple dipcan: samples were removed from the effluent stream at regular intervals, and the levels of grease estimated. The grease particles varied considerably in composition and size from sample to sample, and analysis figures were suspect. None of the methods to hand seemed adequate and the team accepted that they would have to design a novel system for monitoring the grease.

A problem-solving team of six people was put together: three members of the ideas group, the engineer and a colleague, plus one outsider from a different division. The members had different background training and job responsibilities. The three members who were inexperienced in the problem-solving process received, before the meeting, a handout which was about two pages long and gave a general introduction to the principles and procedures of the proposed technique, and which drew heavily on the operating principles of synectics (as outlined in Chapter 6).

The engineer began by outlining the problem for about ten minutes. The rest of the group tried to understand it and redefine it in their own words, following the now famous 'how to' format. All redefinitions and possible solutions were recorded on flipcharts. At the start he defined the problem as 'How to take a representative sample from a large mass of fluid for grease analysis'. Typical redefinitions by the team were:

- How to meter the effluent without taking a sample.
- How to measure the density of the effluent.
- How to obtain a continuous representative sample and metering proportional to the flow rate.

During the redefinition stage, and within ten minutes of the start of the session, a possible solution had been suggested based on emulsifying the effluent and measuring turbidity. The client was asked to evaluate the idea. He said that it was a new approach as far as he was concerned, but that it could not be validated easily within the time at his disposal.

As there seemed a clear need for a more imaginative approach, the leader suggested that the turbidity idea be recorded as a fallback possibility, and invited the group to try some metaphoric thinking. One of the words from the original definition, 'sample', was taken as a starting point. The members of the group listed anything they could think of which might be considered samples from the world of astrophysics. Among the five or six ideas produced were:

- Moon-rock
- Urine
- Bacterial counts on astronauts

Then the group went into a second stage of the excursion, attempting to identify with part of the problem. The leader asked what it felt like to be a bacterium on an astronaut. The responses noted on the flipchart included the following:

- I've stopped multiplying.
- I'm aware for the first time that I am being observed.
- I'm still multiplying fast – I like the oxygen.
- I didn't ask to come. But now I've acquired an appetite for speed. I like the view.

After about five minutes, the group examined the material and tried to encapsulate it in an evocative and concise form. The following five statements were obtained:

- Flight of fancy
- Latent hunger
- Repulsive hero
- Passive pioneer
- Pioneering stowaway

'Passive pioneer' was then taken as a starting point for a further stage in the excursion. This time the leader requested examples of passive pioneers from the world of the Arctic, obtaining material such as:

- Husky dogs
- Penguins
- Spiders
- Rats
- Nuclear submarines
- Icebergs

The group was now nearing the end of the excursion, and as a last stage the members developed information about one of these examples – spiders. The following collection of both mundane and evocative facts was obtained:

They have eight legs, eat smaller insects, spin webs which are sticky to trap prey. Small harmless specimens generate fear. Ubiquitous symbols of perseverance, neglect and decay. They move in as soon as people leave. Their webs are horrible when dry, but beautiful when wet. In folklore, they have power to arrest bleeding. A spider can spin a silky lifeline to escape when you are cutting it with scissors.

At this stage the group returned to the original problem and linked it with the information about spiders. The concept of a spider's web seemed immediately relevant and the group descended to reality via an initially speculative statement. The steps in this force fitting process were as follows:

Step 1   Trap grease on a spider's web.
Step 2   Use a web or mesh of material that attracts grease.
Step 3   Use a strip of polyester fabric as the mesh to trap all the grease.

The client confirmed that this was a starting point for a possible solution, satisfying the criteria of novelty, feasibility and testability. The group was to return to the concept later in the meeting and develop it still further, so that in its final form it was stated as:

Remove all oil from a continuous sample by deposition on to a large lipophilic surface such as polythene, polyester or treated glass fibre. This could either collect all grease in the sample to give an integrated total over a given time-period, or the lipophilic surface could be in the form of a strip moving through the effluent sample to give a continuous record of the grease concentration.

Other possibilities were also derived from the material of the excursion. The final list of optional approaches provided by the group to the client included continuous centrifugation of the sample stream; colorimetric or radiometric monitoring of a tracer material which reacted with grease; and turbidity measurements after emulsifying the sample stream by mechanical, chemical or ultrasonic techniques.

The client accepted the 'spider's web' option as the most promising line of attack. Later, while examining the patent literature, he found a process from another country which was similar to the design that had been invented during the ideas session. Armed with evidence of its validity he was able to provide a specification which eventually solved the problem, thus avoiding very costly financial penalties and possible factory closure on environmental grounds.

We must beware of assuming that, because a creative problem session was successful, the process can be taken as a good one to follow uncritically. However, warts and all, we can see here how someone who had become stuck was able to escape from stuckness and obtain several satisfactory and imaginative ideas as a direct consequence of the structured ideas session, the salient features of which were:

1. the composition of the team – being quite naive concerning the technology involved, but mostly well-versed in the rituals of creative problem-solving and accepting the proposed procedures;
2. the process leader, directing proceedings as far as the group behaviour went – and to some degree helping break mind sets by judicious selection of metaphoric disguises for the problem;
3. the use of an extended and multi-stage metaphor which took the flow of ideas farther and farther away from the original problem, from which the group force fitted the final idea;
4. a problem-owner who was ready for new ideas – having tried and failed to solve his problem before approaching others for help;
5. a climate of acceptance of a procedure (perhaps because the group had taken pains to communicate their methods around the laboratory after earlier exercises)
6. an outcome which left the problem-owner with some work to do, so that he was not forced to accept a new solution in its entirety 'on the spot'
7. careful preparatory work by the creative problem-solving group. Notes made at the time by the process leader recorded that 'Serious public relations exercises in all major divisions had exposed a good cross-section of middle managers to (the creative problem-solving) techniques. Managers who had actually worked with the group tended to be ... favourably disposed, and often maintained regular contacts.'

CASE EXAMPLE TWO: A CREATIVE PROBLEM-SOLVING EXERCISE WHICH DID NOT LEAD TO IMPLEMENTED RESULTS

The background to the problem-solving session was similar to that in the previous example. The creative problem-solving team had been approached to give help on a problem requiring some new ideas. The clients were from the consumer research arm of the parent organization, which was engaged in a search for new products and concepts to be consumer-tested. Although their primary interest was in new concepts for personal washing and hygiene products, they did not exclude ideas in other consumer markets such as foodstuffs and disposables.

In addition to their stated goal of finding new product ideas, the clients wanted to evaluate the merits of the various idea-generation techniques to assess their scope and limitations within their consumer research activities. It was therefore proposed to test the outcomes of group meetings using brainstorming and morphological analysis, and to compare these with the results from a general discussion meeting to collect ideas (which is what the consumer researchers would have done under their normal operating methods). A panel was set up consisting of the four members of the intrapreneurial team, three members of the consumer research group (the project leader and two psychologists), and five additional participants, including members of the public who used the products, and a scientist from a different field altogether. The intention was to have available a wide range of different perspectives and experiences.

The first meeting to be held was the conventional one, with the most senior member of the consumer research group holding his customary role as chairman. In this capacity he prepared the group by circulating a summary shortlist of ideas already collected from various sources in and outside the company. During the meeting he combined the role of problem-owning client looking for ideas with that of idea generator (he was one of the most visible contributors). In addition, he acted as conventional chairman – directing and deciding on process and task issues.

Prior to the meeting the client/chairman had requested that those involved in the subsequent creativity groups should all attend to pool information and initial ideas. During the meeting (which was tape-recorded for comparison with the subsequent idea-generation meetings) some new ideas were noted that went beyond those on the circulated list. Additional ideas were discovered on the taped transcripts, and a list of 41 concepts was eventually drawn up.

There were mixed feelings about the meeting (which lasted for three and a half hours). The 'outsiders' and the consumer researchers, on being quizzed by one of the intrapreneurs, were generally pleased with what had happened, commenting that it was a very well-run meeting. By contrast, those who had prior training in creative problem-solving had been aware of the tendency of the chairman to filter out some ideas, failing to hear or appreciate them. They also felt that the atmosphere had been too evaluative and dismissive of unconventional suggestions. Without the evidence obtained from the tape recording far fewer ideas would have been collected for subsequent evaluation.

The first idea-generation session then took place a few weeks later. Three brainstorming types of meeting were held; two were of the extended metaphor kind, with smaller numbers of people involved – six and seven respectively; the third session was with non-metaphoric versions of brainstorming and with nine participants. Each session was tape-recorded, and subsequently carefully evaluated. Regardless of outcome, the group behaviours and attitudes to the experiences suggest that the events were not successful. The structure of the sessions – which included extended metaphors – was similar to the example quoted above. Each team comprised a spokesperson for the consumer research group, a skilled process leader and two other members of the intrapreneurial group, and two or three panellists. The mix of experience and variety of backgrounds corresponded quite closely with our previous example.

Indeed, in one of the sessions, the leader was the same person who directed the meeting on sampling effluent, and followed a quite similar format. The tape-recorded material revealed that a brief explanation of the structure of the session was given and clarified in a period of warm-up, including some practice at postponing judgement: 'Let's see how many ways we can dream up to make housework more enjoyable.'

The client's problem was then stated as 'How to find new concepts for consumer research' and a large number of redefinitions (approximately a hundred) were produced. The consumer panellists were increasingly disturbed by the strange proceedings, and one expressed her feelings of 'being lost' several times. The most senior representative of the consumer research team was equally uncomfortable, gradually retreating, metaphorically and physically, until he had almost disappeared under a piece of protruding wall furniture. Later in the session, when asked how he felt about being a villain pursued by Sherlock Holmes, he uttered the memorable statement, 'Feel? I feel bloody silly, that's how I feel. I don't know what all this is about.'

The group carried on doggedly with its pre-arranged procedure of looking for evocative metaphors for the problem. As a key theme seemed to be searching and finding, examples of searchers were studied from domains unrelated to personal washing products. 'Searches from the world of literature' were examined, including the search for the source of the Nile, Lancelot's quest for the Holy Grail, and Sherlock Holmes' battle with the evil Professor Moriarty. The flavour of the excursion is captured in the following extracts:

Leader: 'What does it feel like to be a villain pursued by Sherlock Holmes?'
Group responses:
  'Arrogant'
  'I'm OK, I'm in disguise'
  'Got to be careful, but I can give false clues.'
Leader: 'Can we sum up how we feel in some interesting book titles?'

Group: (after considerable confusion about the process from the inexperienced members)
Hidden Destiny
Living Signals
The Noisy Secret
Formidable Opponent

The group then looked for examples of formidable opponents in sport, which led inexorably to Liverpool football team, and thence to how a football scout searches for new talent.

> The search involves a lot of background knowledge; having to cover a lot of ground and having a lot of spies; avoiding influencing the prospect; going out to non-league grounds in the middle of winter.

This particular excursion led to one or two ideas for tactics for the consumer researchers, such as becoming more mobile, and recruiting more part-time interviewers. Then a different metaphor was tried. 'How to make housewives happy' became 'how to get a holiday feeling when washing up'. This excursion deteriorated into discussions as the panellists began to repeat some pet ideas which they had already mentioned in the formal session. Interestingly, at least one concept was generated which was later to re-emerge as a successful consumer product. Although it was consumer-tested and found to give very promising results, the idea was never taken any further within the particular project.

The other metaphor session (results not available) was reported as also being unsatisfactory in output and general climate. Again, the less experienced participants were particularly unhappy, constantly challenged the process and felt excluded from what was going on.

A week or so later saw another attempt at producing creative results – this time from a brainstorming session which included all five outside panellists, the entire intrapreneurial group and one of the consumer researchers. To add to the variety, Osborn-type idea-generation was followed by some individual brainstorming (called 'trigger sessions'), and a few selected idea-development sequences in which speculative ideas were force fitted back to reality.

Including some inevitable warm-up ('uses of a sugar cube') exercises, the brainstorming lasted an hour and a half. The contrast with the earlier session was marked, with the atmosphere extremely light-hearted – ('hysterical' was the term used by one of the experienced brainstormers present). The outsiders enjoyed it enormously, and on this occasion it was the intrapreneurs who were more critical. Specifically, the most experienced brainstormer present (who was not leading the group) commented afterwards that there was virtually no attempt at building on ideas of other people, the hilarity was excessive and if anything counterproductive, and the session had gone on at least half an hour too long. Another experienced brainstormer observed, before evaluating the ideas, that there seemed to be an 'above-average amount of rubbish' within the material produced. Interestingly, when the results of the normal and brainstorming sessions were combined, some 500 ideas emerged, 50 per cent of which derived from the brainstorming; 150 of these remained after eliminating 'wishful, vague, well-known, and non-implementable ones'. A shortlist of 40 concepts emerged from a stricter (weighting) method of filtering, and 5 'top concepts' subsequently resulted from consumer-testing – 3 from the brainstorming, 2 from the 'normal' session. Sadly, not one of the shortlisted ideas reached the market.

WHY DID THE ONE SESSION 'WORK' AND THE OTHER FAIL?

Can we learn anything from the two different exercises? What factors might have contributed to success with the effluent problem and rather unsatisfactory results with the consumer research group?

First, we can contrast the nature of the requests. In our engineering example, there was a client who arrived after all his attempts to solve the problem had failed. He had a genuine need for some way of getting unstuck. In the consumer research example, there was less evidence of motivation to act. Instead we had modest levels of shared interest from a group of professionals who indicated that the creative problem-solving techniques were very much under trial. The result was a deliberately 'scientific' design, with 'balanced' groups, and a range of techniques, rather than techniques selected for appropriateness for the problem.

Secondly, the problems were different. Or, to follow the terminology we have applied throughout the book, the focus of attention of the clients was different. Most people would describe the first as having a technical or engineering focus; the second as having a marketing or consumer product focus. We can't tell from the two case examples whether the nature of the problem was a critical factor in the outcome of the exercise. On other grounds, this seems unproven and rather unlikely. Both problems as stated provide scope for new and imaginative implementable solutions, and if anything we might find it more likely that the marketing problem would lead to practical and imaginative ideas. However, technical breakthroughs, although rare, can be screened against technical criteria, i.e. relatively hard data, whereas ideas with a strong human focus tend to be less susceptible to such validation. This means that technical focus problems may have a lower probability of yielding novel solutions, but lead to ideas which have an elegance and a perceived 'intrinsic rightness' which produce a higher probability of instant recognition when they do arrive.

Also, the composition of the groups differed. Although there were participants inexperienced in the creative problem-solving techniques in each session, the mix for the consumer research problem was particularly wide. This is not of itself a bad thing – indeed the greater the variety, the greater the potential for new perspectives. However, the wider the mix, the greater the technical problems for the process leader in designing and implementing the session.

Finally, and importantly, the procedures followed were different. The first problem was tackled by a set of procedures that the core team had developed almost to a point of standardization. The design of the sessions for the second problem was influenced by a desire to try out various techniques under semi-controlled conditions, rather than sticking to the one or two approaches which seemed appropriate to the problem.

WITH THE BENEFITS OF HINDSIGHT

Looking back over a decade later, the surprising aspect of the exercises is how little the actual creative problem-solving techniques have changed in the interim. As outlined in the earlier chapters of this book, practitioners are now reluctant to engage in such complex excursions (although it may be a matter of changing style rather than improved technique). Nevertheless, the broad principles and operational procedures are quite recognizable.

On first reading of the two examples it is easy to conclude that the first session was run correctly, and the second session was not. After all, the first client was satisfied with the outcome, and the second clients were eventually to find nothing emerging from the sessions. This view is challenged if we look more closely at the cases, using the priceless analytical technique of hindsight. Putting myself back in the shoes of someone involved in both sessions I would now want to spend far more time prior to the sessions in understanding the organizational context of each problem. Although this part of the exercise was skipped over, it turned out that it mattered less for the first problem than for the second. Almost certainly such an investigation would have suggested a less complicated design for the consumer researchers. Also, the potential dangers of overwhelming inexperienced participants with bizarre-appearing techniques would have been recognized, and averted by offering preliminary awareness-raising training for those involved for the first time.

I don't think I would criticize the techniques selected. Some form of 'right-brain' stimulation was a sensible method of challenging the mind sets of the young engineer. Brainstorming, morphological analysis and metaphoric excursions have been successfully applied to generate new product concepts in similar exercises. However, the complexity of the second design did increase the chances of confusion, and of failing to achieve a positive and creative climate. Pre-meeting briefings would have gone some way to overcoming the concerns of the inexperienced members of the group, and during the session the signals of frustration should have been dealt with.

One technique we have suggested for recovering from such process concerns is 'blowing a whistle', and spending as long as it takes to find out what is bothering people and to explain the procedures of the technique being used. Reading between the lines one suspects that the experienced practitioners were insensitive to the needs of the less experienced ones in both exercises. As it happened, in the first session the climate remained sufficiently positive, and the potential weakness in the procedure was masked. In the second case it was all too obviously intrusive.

Another similarity between the sessions was the lack of attention paid to implementation issues as part of the creative problem-solving process. Even in the 'successful' engineering project, no attempt was made to work with the young engineer to establish subsequent strategies for seeking acceptance of his new idea. Here we have one of the shifts in emphasis in the intervening years. Today it is recognized that 'getting new ideas' is generally much easier than 'getting ideas into action'.

'Well, that's all very well', you may be thinking, 'but the fact was the first session worked and the others didn't. So they must have been doing something right in the first that they didn't in the second.' Unfortunately it isn't as simple as that. The 'successful' session was much quoted within the company to illustrate how structured creativity can be applied to real work problems. At the time, the consumer research sessions were rather pointedly dismissed as an experiment which went wrong. It is true that not a single one of the ideas generated by the session reached the marketplace for the company whose employees organized the idea sessions. But we have additional information from a member of the team who continued to monitor new products appearing in the consumer markets studied. It turns out that, from the shortlist of forty new product concepts (all rejected by the host company), variants on three of the ideas have been developed and launched successfully by other companies, one of which has grown into a brand leader in the health food market.

This information is a salutary reminder of the dangers of assessing the usefulness of techniques, or even of idea generation sessions, simply on the basis of acceptability of the outcome to the client. To be sure, if a client finds that a session has helped to produce some forward motion, and fresh thinking, where things were becoming bogged down, the session has 'worked'. If there is no obvious positive outcome it should be remembered that 'remaining stuck' is not the same as 'failing'.

10 In search of diversification

David Sims and Sue Jones, working from the School of Management at the University of Bath, have developed an approach to industrial problem-solving which illustrates many of the key points of creative analysis. Their starting position was one of dissatisfaction with creativity techniques, which they resolved through the familiar cycle of developing approaches for opening up and closing down. Their sensitivity to the significance of personal experiences and wisdom, intuition and intuitive judgements gives a whole-brain flavour to their work which deserves close study. What follows is very much in the practitioners' own words and from their publications, particularly 'Mapping as an Aid to Creativity', which appeared in the *Journal of Management Development*, vol. 4, no. 1, in 1985.

WHY CREATIVITY TECHNIQUES ARE UNDER-USED

There is a veritable industry of producers of creativity techniques although the similarities among their advocated methods are more significant than the differences. Those who invent new 'aids to creativity' find ready markets for their products in consultancy, management training, and management development, all areas where vast amounts of time, effort and money are expended in the search for improvements to managers' problem-solving skills.

We believe that the hunger for new creativity techniques is partly because existing techniques do not work very satisfactorily. Certainly, brainstorming and related methods increase the numbers and the diversity of ideas brought to bear on the issue being examined. However, this very success poses new problems for those involved. How can ideas be weeded out without prematurely rejecting those which may be useful with a little modification? How do the different ideas relate one to another? If the idea generation group were part of an industrial project team how might its members make explicit and examine further the intuitive judgements and experience which would have strongly influenced the climate of the meetings, and the content of the ideas generated? And how might such a team effectively draw on the complex bodies of personal wisdom and experience of all its members? Reflecting on these personal bodies of knowledge is the key to effective learning and creativity, and it is only by sharing, negotiating, and building on these potential supplies of knowledge that the team's creative potential can be liberated.

Currently, most problem-solving techniques establish simplifying structures and procedures for 'right and proper' problem-solving which bear little relationship to people's own complicated ways of thinking. Not enough attention is paid to the rationale behind the procedures, nor are there means of getting to the intuitive behaviours of the problem-solvers.

JUMPING TRAMLINES

Yet it is important to escape from our own mental tramlines. Most of the time we avoid becoming overloaded with too many factors and possibilities by staying on these tramlines, and therefore some unconventional techniques are needed to assist our escape. We shall concentrate on one approach, cognitive mapping, which assists in the process of achieving appropriate action after the generation of new ideas. We have found the approach invaluable in a range of training and consultancy activities, but shall concentrate on one exercise to illustrate our methodology.

COGNITIVE MAPPING: A DIVERSIFICATION EXERCISE

A divisionalized construction company had sold off one of its less profitable subsidiaries, and the Managing Director was considering the possibilities of moving into tourism. The MD believed there to be considerable opportunities in the industry, and that there were reasons to think that the geographic base of the company would give

An example of an initial clustering of related ideas

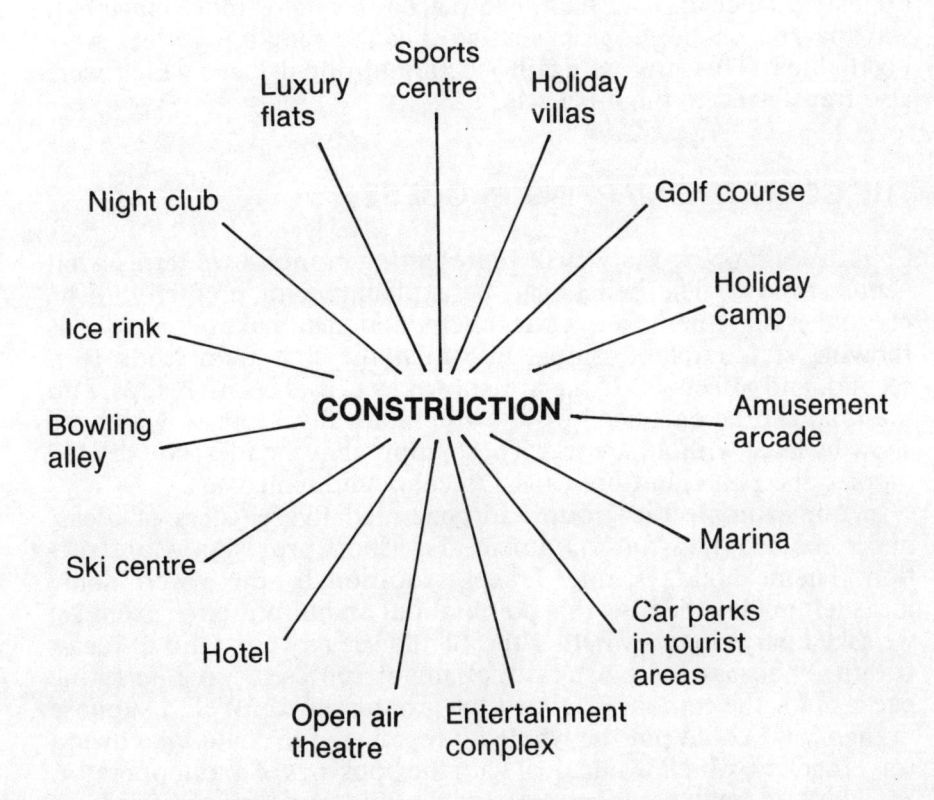

Centered on **CONSTRUCTION**:
- Luxury flats
- Sports centre
- Holiday villas
- Night club
- Golf course
- Ice rink
- Holiday camp
- Bowling alley
- Amusement arcade
- Ski centre
- Marina
- Hotel
- Car parks in tourist areas
- Open air theatre
- Entertainment complex

---

it competitive advantages through such a diversification. A team was assembled and asked to examine the concept in more detail. As well as commissioning necessary market research the team wanted to tap their own ideas, and we suggested they should try brainstorming.

We started the meeting by asking each member of the group to spend 15 minutes listing ideas independently. Then the ideas were read out on a round-robin basis and captured on flipcharts placed round the walls of the room. We discouraged evaluative reactions but encouraged the addition of ideas triggered off during the collection process. This gave us over 100 items to be managed. We asked if the group could see any broader concepts or themes that could be used to group the items. Each central theme was written in the middle of a sheet of flipchart paper and associated ideas assembled around it (see Buzan diagrams, Chapter 7). Ideas were placed in more than one category. This illustrated that the categories were not mutually exclusive. Once an idea had been placed in one or more clusters it was marked on the original list, so that the remaining ideas were highlighted. This process again led to additional ideas which were also transferred to the flipcharts.

THE COGNITIVE MAPPING PROCESS

Cognitive mapping is a way of representing in their own terms what people believe. The beliefs can be explanatory or predictive. The map takes statements and codes them, and also makes connections showing stated relationships, in which the first item leads to a second, and affects it. These are known as causal relationships, and the map can be enhanced by showing non-causal links – which we show by lines without arrows. These imply that the ideas are related (apples and pears) but not causal (alcohol and hangover).

In our example the group had generated five clusters of ideas, under the headings Entertainment, Transport provision, Construction, Theme holidays, and Travel. Additionally there were some ideas left unclassified. At this point (about an hour into the exercise) we asked participants whether they could see any portfolio of ideas, within or across the clusters, that might represent an interesting package for the company. One of the group replied: 'Well, I suppose in theory we could put the whole lot together. We could take over a travel agency, which would deal with the bookings of a tour operator, an entertainment complex and hotel chain and various kinds of holidays and so on. The trouble with that, though, is that it is probably too much in one go. It confronts us not only with financing problems but also with problems of whether we have the management skills. We need to be more selective.'

Another member of the group responded: 'Yes, I agree. We shouldn't be too ambitious. If we want to think about something more realistically within our capabilities, then the hotel idea is worth considering. It is something we can build ourselves and obviously that would fit with our current business instead of being completely unrelated.'

'Although,' added a third team member, 'just pursuing that idea, we probably shouldn't discount the possible advantages of just taking over existing facilities, whether hotels or anything else. For example, it may be cheaper, or it may be quicker, and we could use existing management.'

An example of part of a cognitive map

- Problems of whether we have the management skills
- Financing problems
- use existing management
- Being too ambitious ... something more realistically within our capabilities
- Cheaper
- Quicker
- Taking on too much in one go
- Fit with current business ... completely unrelated
- Take over existing facilities
- Putting whole lot together ... more selective
- Something we can build ourselves
- Hotel

eg. take over travel agency – bookings for tour operator, hotel chain, entertainment complex, holidays, etc.

The map comes from coding the person's statements. We listen for the belief constructs, coding the explicit contrasts where they have been stated, and for the expressed causality relationships between the constructs, which we represent by arrows. Sometimes we need to express a non-causal, connotative link, which we show by a simple line. Dots separate discrete opposite poles of bipolar constructs or indicate 'void' poles where an alternative has not been made explicit. Where the alternatives are not discrete but involve 'more' or 'less' of some state, the two opposite poles are inferred, as 'an increase'/'a decrease in'. A plus sign on an arrow between constructs A1–A2 and B1–B2 indicates a relationship between similar-sided poles (A1 leads to B1, A2 leads to B2); a minus sign indicates a relationship across poles (A1 leads to B2, A2 leads to B1).

As the group continued to discuss the ideas we mapped their statements, sometimes asking for elaboration of the consequences of a particular idea. We also tried to bring the quieter team members into the discussion, especially if the more dominant members seemed to be denying them 'airtime'. The walls became papered over with sheets of flipchart, and the mapping ended on completing the examination of the five themes.

After the meeting we tidied up the maps, and examined them in order to set up an agenda for the next meeting. The ideas were restructured into the decision areas that had emerged, such as financial, marketing and organizational decisions. The group had signalled their particular interest in construction within the leisure field (an idea now expanded to include other than the building of hotels). They were also interested in the provision of various transport facilities, whereas the theme holidays concept had been rejected, although the possible takeover of a regional travel agency was still under discussion.

At the next meeting, one week later, we re-presented the maps and also the isolated ideas still remaining. We advised the group to start with these. The mapping followed the process already described. The outcome was another couple of options for consideration, after which we went back to the areas that had been identified as needing further work. This meeting lasted about two hours, and at the end of it the group had arrived at an agreed set of diversification possibilities which they were prepared to research more formally, e.g. through market research, or financial advisers. The process had shown the gaps in their knowledge which needed to be filled, and where there was already enough existing knowledge.

The members of the group then shared responsibility for initiating these investigations and brought the findings back to a third meeting, nearly four weeks later, which reviewed progress and contrasted the group's initial position with its present one. At the end of the meeting the group was ready to present its findings and recommendations to the Managing Director.

IMPLICATIONS OF THE CASE EXPERIENCE

Our approach is strongly influenced by our belief that it is not helpful to manage the output from a creativity session by simply testing the ideas against a set of pre-established criteria. To do so is to fail to make full use of the rich and complex experience, wisdom, judgements and intuition of the persons concerned. Nevertheless, because of the dangers of thinking in tramlines, some different kind of aid is needed which goes beyond mere idea generation.

The mapping approach can help because, through the model, the group members are able to grasp each other's views which would otherwise very likely be lost in the inefficient listening that is a characteristic of many business meetings. The process makes differing views more explicit, and makes the creative resolution of potential conflicts easier. As individuals examine their own thinking and that of their team associates they are also able to access components of their own experience which they might have otherwise forgotten, thus finding new connections.

The power of this process is particularly enhanced through the interactions of team members. When an individual or group has become experienced in the practice of the mapping technique it can increase the variety and fluency of ideas generated in brainstorming. It appears that knowing that there is a technique for using the output of a creative idea generation meeting helps to establish a positive and self-confident climate in the group, which is an important feature for successful creative behaviours. Participants are able to bring more energy and motivation to the exercise through the knowledge that further development of the ideas is possible through the mapping procedures.

Many managers on our development programmes had attended courses on creative problem-solving but had failed to put the techniques into practice. Afterwards they frequently reported that they were able to use previously learned techniques, because mapping helped them to make sense of the generated material. The approach works because it does not try to manage complexity by simplification. Instead it offers a device through which additional, deepening insight can be made explicit. We consider the provision of such a facility a fundamental issue for the development of problem-solving skills, and it can be used by individuals or in teams as described here.

11 The Magnolite story

In what follows, the application of creative problem-solving techniques in an engineering firm is described from the viewpoint of two external innovative consultants. They draw on earlier experiences in other companies to throw light on their own decisions. Some details of the company and of the ideas produced have been modified to preserve confidentiality. Many of the details that we would like to know about the company were not made available at the time. Some information was kindly provided later by the company, and the case is described through the reconstructed perceptions of the consultants, Trefor Little and Kevin Large, operating from the department of management studies of a British university.

INTRODUCTION TO MAGNOLITE (KEVIN'S ACCOUNT)

I seem to have drifted into a role as Trefor Little's bag carrier from time to time. I think he picked me because I'm a bit older than his other graduate students, and I'm used to dealing with people (I was in the police force before returning to university). What usually happens is that I get some enquiry from a company wanting help. Perhaps it's for a brainstorming, or some creativity training. I try to find out as quickly as possible if we can help, and if it is a serious enquiry. I've learnt to be wary of certain companies which have a deserved reputation as time-wasters. One very large company has a replenishable stock of internal consultants and trainers who must spend a lot of time going around finding out what's on offer, writing reports, but hardly ever commissioning work.

Anyway, someone in Magnolite had been on a creative problem-solving course that Trefor had been involved with, and asked would we 'run a brainstorming' for them. That was last February. Most requests of this kind turn into something different. Some fail to get the go-ahead from someone in authority; other firms have a change of heart for various reasons. With the minority who turn out to be serious we like to be given access to the company for a diagnosis of their problem or need. I would usually make the diagnostic visit, although in this instance Trefor visited the premises because they were close to his family in Wales. Magnolite turned out to be a medium-sized engineering company which had been attracted to the principality because of generous development grants.

This was going to be particularly interesting for me as it would be the first time that I had accompanied TL on a consultancy assignment of this kind. I'd had a fair amount of experience working with him on creativity training exercises, especially around the University, and on idea generating sessions for local 'customers', e.g. one person businesses; local charters; sheltered workshops, etc. The subject matter for these modest ventures ranged from generating ideas for products which could be manufactured commercially by mentally and physically handicapped people to new uses for a disused cotton mill.

But this work with Magnolite was to be, for me, of a different order. They had put money up front and undoubtedly wanted 'results'. I was interested to see how the problem-solving techniques would be received in the 'real world', i.e. in a hard-nosed commercial enterprise.

THE PRELIMINARY VISIT (TREFOR'S ACCOUNT)

'You can't miss us. We're just off the M4,' they said. I did miss them. The first meeting was during the miners' strike of 1984, and the motorway was intermittently blocked by convoys of strike-breaking trucks moving coal to the power stations of West Wales. As well as losing my way I was temporarily pulled up by a policeman who must have thought I was a flying picket.

Magnolite has nice new premises not far from the Welsh coast. Before that they had a very old site in London. I am met by Alan Prothero, a large, friendly man, job title – engineering manager, who has an open-plan office in the laboratory occupied by the technical development unit. He's been put in charge of an innovation team – a part-time arrangement led by David Baldwin, the technical director, who has control of £1–2m budget for new product innovation. Even Baldwin is only concerned with innovation part-time, and he answers to Jamie MacKinnon, the works manager. Lots of scope for expansion and new products here.

David offers me the inevitable tour of the factory. I'm never sure how to get the best out of these visits. If you go in with a checklist you risk overlooking some important point not on the list. If you wander around planlessly, the impressions fade rapidly afterwards. I try hard to avoid getting ideas too quickly about the key issues. This is probably contrary to what an expert consultant would do, but it would almost certainly make it harder for me to operate as a process consultant – when it is actually a handicap if you think you know what's best for the company. More important is to get as near as you can to 'talking in their language', trying to capture the mysterious thing called corporate culture, as well as picking up general information; the condition of the plant; the attitudes of the operatives and their reactions to unexpected visitors in their space.

Like most engineering units, it's a jumble of activities and locations. Even in a newish location the layouts always emerge over time and are quickly accepted, perhaps because 'we've always done it this way'. They have some modern and expensive equipment; and rather sophisticated tolerance engineering. The production manager may describe the firm as metal-bashers, but this is a term designed to trap non-engineers into misunderstanding just how sophisticated the processes can be, and the levels of skill needed by the operatives.

After the site visit, we set off to meet as many of the firm's executives as are available. This means there's someone you are expected to impress, to ensure that the project is in good odour. Maybe your contact needs as much legitimization as you do. Not surprisingly, Jamie MacKinnon, the works manager, is top of our visiting list as the person for me to convince how a brainstorming might help Morganite. He can spare me ten minutes ('although you can expect this to be extended if he doesn't take an instant dislike to you').

Jamie has an office to himself, and is very preoccupied – he spends some of the time telling me how busy he is, and the rest answering phone calls. I counted four during our meeting, and although it probably was ten minutes' discussion, it lasted over half an hour. He emerged as one of the 'let's not waste time' school of managers, who nevertheless wastes a lot of his own time, and those around him. We had hardly been interrupted by a phone call or completed the introductory courtesies when he gave me a fierce glare and asked aggressively, 'What have you done with companies like ours?'

Some years ago I would have said that the nature of the company doesn't really matter. Or I might have been riled and become aggressive myself. In time you learn more constructive replies. 'In some ways you are no different from many of the companies we've helped,' I say. During the telephone calls I realize he doesn't seem to be looking for a reason to veto the proposed idea, but is going through the motions of being a no nonsense manager. The next step is to suggest that we move towards a longer session than a brainstorming. Alan had already accepted the benefits of a two-day event, off-site, and mentions the subject again.

'Up to you,' Jamie replies briskly. 'We've been living off our Ceramite patents for twenty years. It's your responsibility to find us some new products.' Magnolite produces hundreds of components, for electric power stations and car batteries alike, but most of them are variations of this Ceramite discovery, a technical development inside the company in the 1960s. We agreed that I should put a proposal to David, who would go ahead and arrange a venue, and a time to suit his innovation team. I drove back up the motorway listening to West Indian bowlers destroying the flower of England's batting for the umpteenth time, half my attention carrying out a preview of the shape of the innovation workshop: what, who, when, where, how and, of course, why. The West Indies finish off their problems long before I have worked out mine.

THE TWO-DAY WORKSHOP (TREFOR'S VIEW)

Summer has gone. The earliest date we could fix is the last week of September. Kevin and Alan dealt with the logistics between them. We are to meet for an evening meal in a Cotswold hotel (Alan's choice). We couldn't get Jamie along. Can't remember the reasons, but not a good sign. Managers often think it is best to let the troops get on with it. Usually the troops prefer top-level involvement, and it speeds up decision-making as well. Foul weather on drive down; inevitable that hotel is tucked away from everywhere. Kevin can't get down until after dinner, but the Magnolite group drove up after work and are relaxing in front of a log fire. We seem to be the only occupants of the place.

First impressions over dinner are favourable. At this stage we are mainly on the look-out for warning signs from one or more participants who may make it difficult for everyone else to free up and relax. No one obviously hostile to the prospect of giving up time from a busy schedule to bother with what may be considered an expensive waste of company resources. There are some enquiries about what's going to happen, but the general trend is to wait for the

General search scheme for Magnolite

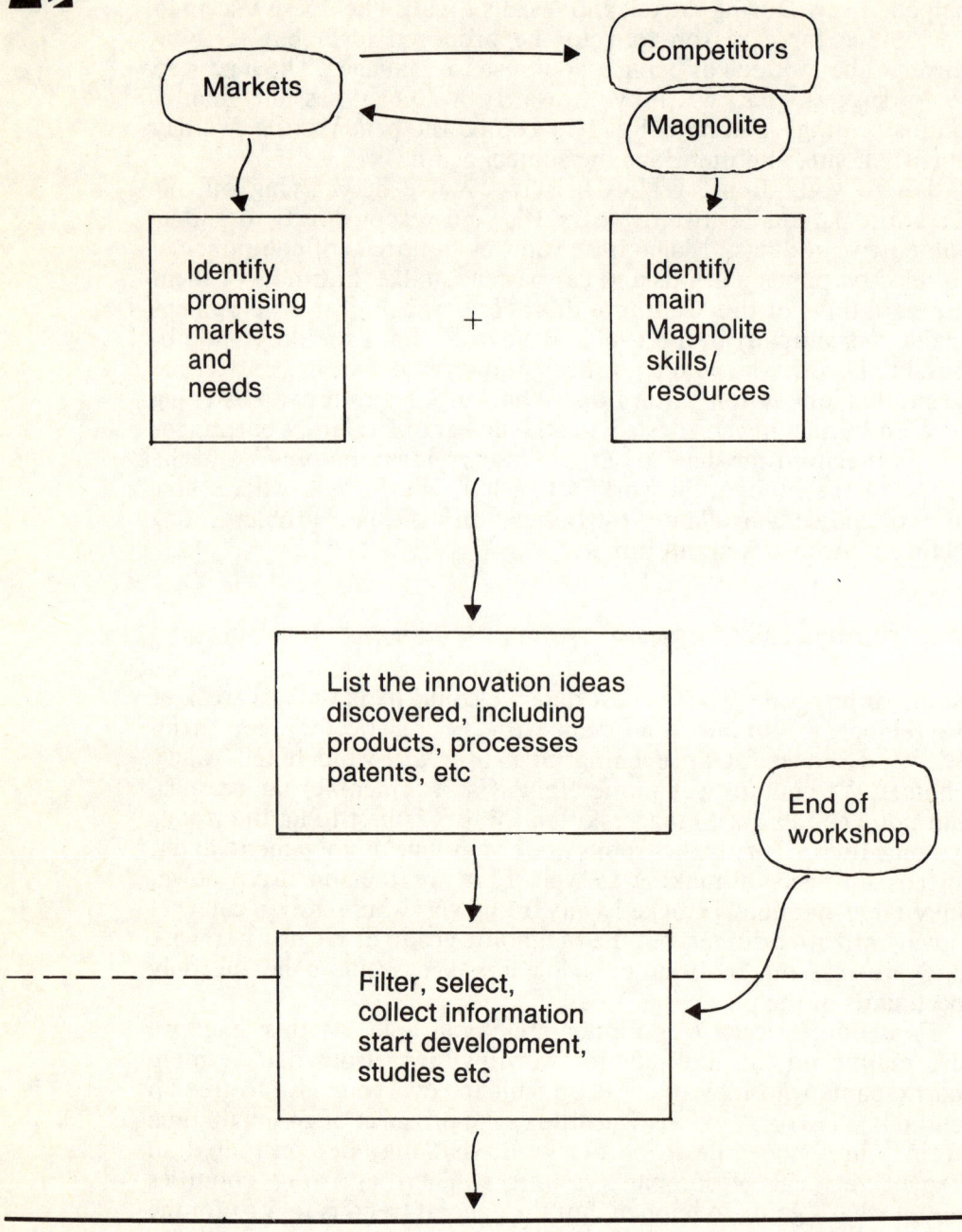

```
      Markets  ──────►  Competitors
         │       ◄──────  Magnolite
         ▼                    ▼
  ┌──────────────┐      ┌──────────────┐
  │ Identify     │      │ Identify     │
  │ promising    │  +   │ main         │
  │ markets      │      │ Magnolite    │
  │ and          │      │ skills/      │
  │ needs        │      │ resources    │
  └──────────────┘      └──────────────┘
                 │
                 ▼
       ┌─────────────────────────┐
       │ List the innovation ideas│
       │ discovered, including    │
       │ products, processes      │
       │ patents, etc             │
       └─────────────────────────┘
                 │
                 ▼
       ┌─────────────────────────┐      ╭─────────╮
       │ Filter, select,          │◄─────│ End of  │
       │ collect information      │      │ workshop│
       │ start development,       │      ╰─────────╯
       │ studies etc              │
       └─────────────────────────┘
                 │
                 ▼
```

first session in the morning. The meal is excellent and very leisurely. We have arranged a light buffet lunch without too much booze. It is a myth that alcohol in quantity enhances creative performance, and we may be in a reasonably 'warmed-up' state by lunch tomorrow anyway.

I leave them in the bar, talking shop, at about 11.30 pm. At this stage I have no clear plan of the workshop session by session, although my mental run-throughs have continued – as Kevin and I prepared for the event and on the three-hour drive today. Sometimes in the last meeting with your client some new and vital piece of jigsaw might fall into place, and the whole programme needs adjusting. Also, location and room atmosphere and facilities influence decisions about the structure of the event, as does your 'feel' for the group that has been assembled.

The group of eight people is a good size for some brainstorming work, although its numbers were mainly dictated by the membership of the innovation team. My broad plan is to spend the morning in some training, raising awareness of the importance of a constructive climate for a successful innovation team, and to introduce some techniques for idea generation within a positive climate. We shall have a shade over a day for idea searches and starting the implementation action plans. We have found it good to keep the group away from tackling the problem until towards the end of the first day, and then to stop after some progress has been made, e.g. after a single session of reformulating the problem. Although it can be emotionally harrowing to the process consultant and to the company person who set up the event, a general feeling of mild disappointment at dinner after the first full day of the workshop will be no bad thing. After a good night's sleep the first sessions in the morning seem to convert these emotions into high energy commitment to solving the problem.

Lunch: the introductory sessions went well. The room is a typical hotel conference venue – green baize on a horseshoe of tables; overhead projector and a king-sized flipchart: its sheets must be a metre wide and over half a metre long. Plenty of space for sticking up the fruits of our deliberations if we include the windows which make up one long wall to the left of the leader's position. People are relaxing and entering into the spirit of the creativity exercises.

Notes at the end of day 1: We have ended the day on a dull rather than a high note. The 'real' business began with a recap by Alan of why we are here: the company needs some new products. The discussion was summarized as:

1 How to find new (for us) markets for monitoring products;
2 How to find and cast out 'motes in our own eyes' in our process systems;

3   How to exploit our skills with special materials, especially in hostile environments;
4   How to invent/design versatility into our processes;
5   How to find new outlets/collaborators for our materials;
6   How to find overseas opportunities in patents and licensing;
7   How to find new applications for our existing products;
8   How to sell solutions to costly industrial shut downs;
9   How to examine our own production systems as trials of new product/process innovations.

The consensus was to go for items 1 and 4. Alan was reluctant to exercise a right as a specific and individual client to make the choice and instead invited suggestions. Is this good collaborative leadership, or is it evidence of some lack of confidence? I suspect the latter.

At this stage, the Magnolite team's selection of 'how to find new markets' helped me decide which techniques to use. The choice had always been between some kind of brainstorming and a systematic search through a new-product matrix. The matrix approach had seemed most appropriate. This method generally involves linking markets with company skills. I would have liked the group to produce a large list of markets, and reduce the list in number. One or two of the team could not accept that such a list would be any good without 'agreeing what the criteria are'. What does a process leader do when the group does not want to follow the proposed structure? I pointed out to the group that it is hard to know in advance which structure is best, and the important thing is to become more confident in the general process. I also agreed to the proposed modification – if they remain bogged down we can have a process review and I can put the boot in about them sticking to their job of supplying knowledge about the company and its markets, and letting us stick to our jobs as architects of a structure for creative thinking.

We agreed to list markets with above-average growth; with evidence of some features giving Magnolite a competitive edge; with lower entry barriers for Magnolite than for its closest skill competitors; and without the dangerous complication of finding themselves competing with major current customers. Not surprisingly, the group then continued in a rather evaluative way, taking about half an hour to produce a list of markets ranging from energy conversion, chemicals, agriculture, metal refining, paper and print, mining, food and drinks, leisure, civil engineering and aerospace. Discussing and checking the industries against the criteria continued in the evaluative mode and gave me the strong impression that the group, left to its own devices, would be very left-brain. Kevin made one or two attempts to loosen up the atmosphere, but wisely did not throw in too many hand grenades.

I had vetoed late evening work as counter-productive for the next day's creativity. By dinner, a shortlist of market areas had been drawn up, and individuals allocated to work in each area. In some instances, this was based on specific knowledge of the market – but some group members had to take pot luck. Overnight, the participants have been asked to come up with a few promising ideas in their allocated market area. The whole process is poised on a knife edge. If the first session tomorrow goes well, we shall have a success on our hands.

KEVIN'S NOTES

I arrive after TL on my motorbike – it's rained all the way so that I look like a cross between Captain Ahab and Tarka the Otter. Conscious of the need to project a professional image I quickly change into smart (and dry!) clothes and join TL and about half a dozen Magnolite people.

During the initial encounter over dinner and drinks everyone is making polite small talk and staying on 'safe ground' – talking about their work. Most, including TL, have a science/engineering background. I feel a bit uneasy, for being a non-scientist it's a little difficult to follow some of the conversation. So the tack is not to 'read the words' but to 'listen to the music'; what is the mood/attitude of the group? Well, some are sceptical as to the value of the exercise; others aren't sure what to expect but appear willing (at this stage) to see how things develop. TL is very good at talking their language – the properties of carbon; latest technological developments in the chemical industry. I'm impressed. I can see why he's so keen to meet the client group the evening before the first full day – it gets the introductions out of the way and allows some sort of rapport to be established.

Next morning: The first session deals with the creative problem-solving process. TL is doing his explanatory and justificatory bit. He seems to have a built in tape-recorder he switches on. I've heard it all before so I can concentrate on how the group reacts to it. Some are more enthusiastic and positive than others. One in particular (Brummie) has arms folded, leans back, and radiates dismissiveness and doubt from every pore. Could he be a spanner in the works? (I'm rather pleased with that engineering analogy . . .)

There is some 'points scoring' off each other as well. Each trying to impress with knowledge of engineering and science – the company personnel manager gets a rough ride here, being a social science graduate. (I find in him a kindred soul.) TL explains the creativity techniques and tries a few examples. One of them is to have some of the group role-playing being negative to an idea, effectively destroying it, and others working on its weaknesses, demonstrating that it has considerable merits that could easily be destroyed by premature criticism. I chip in with a few solutions. Some join in without being directly asked, while others remain sceptical and on the sidelines.

Gradually the group pick up the rules of the game we are asking them to play. They then move into a self-regulatory phase, e.g. 'Stop being judgemental ... just write that idea down, we'll evaluate it later.'

TL is working well; the group climate is gradually becoming more positive and participatory, but still one or two doubting Thomases. The problem definition session goes well. I think people are beginning to see the relevance of such techniques. Some appear to be impressed with the variety of ways in which the project can be approached. At the end of the day we have long lists of 'how tos', production processes, and of markets. After dinner and copious draughts of wine TL retires with the lists of processes and markets, and a flipchart and pen. I wonder how he is going to make sense of this for first thing tomorrow morning? (I guess others are thinking the same thing.)

Day 2: TL reappears at breakfast with a matrix which is displayed and examined in the first session. (He tells me it took about 30 minutes last night – I'm even more impressed.) His credibility is high and getting higher as the event progresses. The group climate is very positive. Even Brummie is becoming more vocal and committed. Ideas are being generated thick and fast, the atmosphere is optimistic. A shortlist of DBMs (Do by Monday) is drawn up. Some are really hooked on the process and want to carry on (especially Brummie). Enthusiasm is high. Towards the end of the final session a little doubt begins creeping into my mind. How are these ideas to be progressed 'back at the ranch'? I think Alan had nominated one person to act as collator and organizer of the next step. Certainly no one stepped forward volunteering to progress any one particular idea. The final atmosphere is a mixture of jubilation within the group (at having generated hitherto unthought of ideas) and frustration at how to best progress further. There's going to be a lot more hard work for someone to do.

THE SECOND DAY (TREFOR'S VIEW)

Ten minutes into the day and I knew it was going to be a positive climate with a good chance of a satisfied client. We started by taking a matrix of needs in the selected markets and a set of processes that the company could quickly bring to bear on the needs, for example, a particularly expensive kind of metal fatigue caused by vibration in the engineering plant was linked with a wear identification process currently in use in a quite different context.

Each participant stayed with a given market and worked his way through the checklist of needs, initially in isolation from the other team members. Two reasons for this: it built up an extra tension through the silence and it was a way of heading off any evaluative comments from the one or two particularly convergent team members. Kevin was to act as a back up idea generator, switching roles with me as needed, thereby giving me a chance to put in some ideas. I don't particularly like doing this, but by becoming a contributor you can reinforce the point about postponing judgement – by putting in your own not particularly elegant ideas. (I do still try to avoid becoming hooked on any particular idea, however.) It is usually easier to influence the mood on the second day, and the intervention is accepted more readily from me – it reminds them of the admonitions in the training – 'if it's worth thinking, it's worth sharing.'

The idea flow was impressive. About two hundred ideas were collected, some being greeted with clear enthusiasm – 'instant winners'. In our original plan there was time scheduled for a deliberate 'excursion'. In practice, the matrix activity took on a momentum that was not interrupted. So we kept going. The main job Kevin and I had was to keep an eye on the clock to make sure the whole matrix was covered, and that the psychological sense of a good job done more or less coincided with lunch. In practice, this meant cutting short discussions and evaluation which did tend to break out. But there was a growing willingness to accept that the discipline of limiting judgement (if not actually postponing it) was helpful. The group was beginning to act more like a co-operating unit.

It's not much use having a fixed technique ready for the closing down stage until you are well into the final idea search activity. The group may want to spend the residual time sorting out an action plan for one uniquely acclaimed idea. Or there may now be a feeling that the closing down process requires different people to be present. In this instance, one unexpected event helped in making the decision. Just before lunch Alan received a telephone call from his wife, who was about to have a baby. A moment or two of uncertainty. Should the whole evaluation process be called off? While Alan waited for a taxi, we had at most a few minutes of his time, and it was used to good effect. He quickly ran through the ideas, making a shortlist he would particularly want included in the next stage. None of the 'I'll leave it all to you today,' but crisp and decisive leadership accepted by the others.

Alan's taxi arrived and he was whisked away, still outlining his own requirements for a meeting on Monday morning. Another good sign. Over lunch I checked whether the others would like to leave the rest of the evaluation to a later date when Alan could be present. But the general view was that the team should carry on to have a series of action proposals for their first meeting on his return. We could have made a list of criteria again – as was done for the market sectors. But the group was now in a far more intuitive frame of mind. The procedure of choice was to check the list for other items to be added to Alan's. This gave us about eighty starting ideas from the 200+ written down from the morning's work. As we went through the list, individuals were asked to volunteer as idea champions for developing each idea further. No volunteer and the idea was dropped. (Alan had already indicated his favoured few in this respect.)

In my interview with the works manager he had commented that the company was slow to implement change. This was a piece of information the team had agreed about – so now they were challenged to do something about it. Kevin would write up the entire set of ideas. (He had nearly completed this during the morning session.) But they should not wait even a week for a typewritten record of events. Instead, the winning ideas were to be sorted once more into DBMs and others. A DBM needed the qualities of novelty, originality and a clear first step that the volunteer champion could set in motion by the next week's meeting. Some thirty DBMs were publicly announced. As far as I could tell, these were well spread around the group.

In any kind of sensible world, we would meet again on a regular basis to continue to progress the ideas. As typically happens, however, the customer finds it increasingly tempting to carry on without the expense of outside help. Will anything come of the exercise? The team has given itself a very powerful starting point to begin the commercialization process. The drop off among promising ideas is high, and 90 per cent or more of even the short listed ideas will never reach commercialization. What happens to the handful of potential innovations that do get through to the market place will depend on decisions yet to be made. There is no obvious way of proving this, but in my own mind this kind of creative search increases the company's chances of subsequent innovation – if only because without it Magnolite would have no new approaches at all worth mentioning.

POSTSCRIPT: KEVIN'S ACCOUNT

I felt a little bit embarrassed ringing the client so long after the workshop (18 months) to ask what progress had been made. Alan's reply was a bit frosty.

'Not a lot,' he said. 'We didn't know what to do with the ideas list generated. When we did the market research we realized the ideas couldn't be put into operation.' It appears that they called in another set of commercial consultants to assist in implementation. Of our ideas, one diversification theme had been accepted, but this contribution was considered negligible compared with the product development work provided by the other consultants, who had even suggested that they start with a brainstorming, not unlike our own. I'm sure it would have been more satisfactory from both the client's and our point of view if there had been continued collaboration on the 'first steps' phase of new product process development. It was clear that Alan evaluated our workshop according to only one criterion, i.e. what came out of it in terms of new products/markets/processes. It may well have been that the experience of the workshop gave them an insight into their 'mind sets' about their business and fostered greater willingness in Magnolite towards new initiatives.

LEARNING POINTS

It has been said that dealing with complex management problems is the art of muddling through – of avoiding taking decisions that commit one unnecessarily early to a course of action. Trefor repeatedly changed his plans for the event, trying to achieve, through creative analysis, a process that could be adjusted to the needs of the group from moment to moment.

It may well have been that more time spent in advance could have reduced some of the uncertainties. Interviews with prospective participants, for example, would have revealed that there might be some convergent group members. We could have pursued this to the extent of arguing that the possibility of Alan's wife going into labour could have been anticipated. On balance, however, we concluded that some uncertainties will always remain, and that there will always be the need for flexibility inside such innovation-seeking exercises.

The composition of the group raised other questions: should the works manager have been invited along? He seemed to want no part in the exercise, but this may have created a further problem of problem-ownership. Alan, on day 1 at least, did not show a great deal of confidence in his own responsibility as a product champion. One outcome of these conjectures was the difficulty of getting change implemented. At least Trefor and Kevin could have explored these issues before the event. Another potential weakness in the ideas search as it developed was the absence of information on some of the market sectors. It might have been more effective to have focused on markets well-known to the company, and to have set up market investigators in the others, to bring in more specific needs data.

The relatively untrained nature of the group meant hard work to overcome negative attitudes. More training and a greater mix of experienced practitioners of creative problem-solving would possibly have helped – maybe in two subgroups with three Magnolite team members and three innovation-trained outsiders in each.

However, it is instructive to note that even under these circumstances the structure of the event played a positive role in producing a range of new and potentially valuable ideas.

Was the event a failure or a success? We left a group of apparently motivated innovators ready to go back and start work on Monday on a range of ideas. Two years later their recollection of the session is, to say the least, lukewarm. The experience confirms the problems of treating innovation as a two-step process of 'getting ideas' and 'getting ideas implemented'. The organization did reveal signs that it was weak at following ideas through, and it would have been a good strategy for the consultant as well as the company to have reached agreement for collaboration that went beyond initial idea generation. Creativity regarding the management of innovation would have focused on the whole organization, and the mechanisms for empowering the innovation team.

Such experiences demonstrate that the technology of idea search is now reasonably well established, following principles outlined in this book. To convert insights into profits requires creativity past the goal line, and changes in working practices, as well as two-day workshops.

Trefor, in his enthusiasm to meet the request for a two-day workshop, may have reinforced the unreasonably high expectations of the managers of what might come out of such an event. The process might have been better explained as a first step towards establishing on a routine basis an improved means of managing innovation within Magnolite.

12 Introducing new technology

This case example describes the contribution which creative problem-solving methodology has made to a complex project involving design and implementation of new technology educational systems. It shows that, while useful, the actual techniques make up a very small proportion of the total effort, a perspective that can sometimes be lost in a book whose primary focus is creative problem-solving and techniques for assisting it.

THE IBM PROJECT AT MANCHESTER BUSINESS SCHOOL

In 1985, Manchester Business School won a major award to be directed towards introducing new technology into business education. The award included support through programmes and systems applications specialists; hardware comprising a mainframe computer and a generous number of workstations; and software as applications systems and other business packages. The scale of the project made it one of the largest undertaken by the School, and it was generally considered to be extremely ambitious in view of the need to integrate the work with existing academic responsibilities. Additionally, the declared intention was to achieve workable results within two academic years. A project team was assembled which had the challenging task of introducing new training methods and materials to result in improved education for business graduates.

In effect there were several overlapping projects, and we shall concentrate here on the one in which most deliberate use was made of creative problem-solving methodologies as a conscious contribution to the design and development work.

The team leader, Hugh, had played a big part in winning the award, through his proposal of an innovative way of thinking about management education. He suggested that with emerging computer technology it should be possible to provide a realistic learning experience, as if the students were actually running a company. The 'devices' to help bring this about would include making available the kinds of information needed to run a company, including production, financial, strategic and distribution components. The innovative features of the new educational approach were identified as:

1. Information simulating a flow of events as in a real company;
2. The student/managers having access to different information, again as in real life;
3. The management educationalists using the system having the facility to modify the company environment and its information, but in ways which do not encourage students to spend all their time trying to beat the system (as can happen in current management games);
4. The essence of the system being an architecture which enables users to design more specific projects according to their teaching needs;
5. A practical implication of the first four points – the system having to simulate the physical environment of running a company, which suggests the need for multiple terminals linked to a mainframe computer, offering scope for distance learning methods of operating.

A friendly company offered to become the model for the project, and released an abundance of information about its operations and management. The company acquired the code name of the project, Proteus plc, with its subsidiary (Proteus Rainware) the first division studied. The exercise had become known as project Proteus, after the mythical creature with a capacity of assuming a whole range of different forms.

The Proteus team was a little like Proteus itself, with people joining and leaving from time to time. In its early months the regular participants included Pat, an IBM systems manager seconded to help the Business School implement the award; Andrew, the School's most senior computer specialist; and representatives of business streams thought important to the final project: Ali and Gerry (L), finance; Peter, production; and later, Rick and Gerry (J), strategy. In addition Andrew, a senior systems manager from ICI, attended as a source of disinterested but expert knowledge of design and implementation of computer-based systems. Six months into the project Tony was recruited to carry out the day-to-day development of the systems architecture, which involved him in learning a range of programming languages, writing software and assembling into working prototypes the structures required, including data for the various facets of Proteus.

Some time during that period I became interested in the possibilities of using the new technology to overcome a problem within the introductory MBA programme. This project was aimed at providing the new intake of graduates with a few skills that would help them when working in small teams. Over a period of a few days at the start of term, with some follow-up sessions on assigned tasks, the students were encouraged to try out the brainstorming and blockbusting techniques outlined in the early parts of the book.

Because of increased numbers of students, we feared we would not be giving teams the attention needed to monitor and improve their creative problem-solving behaviours. The multiple terminals being installed around the School suggested themselves as a means of improved communications in the introductory project, and I began to consider 'how to use the Proteus project within the MBA introductory sessions on creative problem-solving'. I became a more regular attender of the meetings.

ACCEPTANCE SEEKING FOR A CREATIVE PROBLEM-SOLVING APPROACH

For many months there appeared to be no movement on the Proteus project. In fact there were many and varied things going on that were indirectly needed, mainly through the computer department. Hardware was arriving and being installed. Software was being acquired, tested, and modified. Within the Proteus group meetings followed a pattern of discussions and disagreements about what was to be done. As team leader, Hugh had been living with the project over longer periods between meetings. He tended to rattle on with great enthusiasm and technical knowledge about the new technology that had arrived or was arriving shortly. Other group members would intervene with issues that were troubling them, typically of the 'I can't get started until someone gives me the machines/software/go-ahead' kind. Andrew, as the outsider, tended to become the guardian of educational goals that were not being addressed. I gave up asking for clarification of acronyms and concentrated on getting a view of why the group was so stuck.

After a few meetings the signs of stuckness were clearer to me. We were going through a long and painful group formation stage during which people were having to put their efforts into sorting out their own roles. Attempts to take decisions or actions were being delayed, as there would always be someone ready to say 'we can't do that until we've done such and such'. 'Such and such' included winning approval from colleagues, clarifying some technical matter, sorting out our relationship with IBM, and getting more control over our budgets and time available for the project. I had come across similar patterns of behaviour in groups that had been assembled to look for new products for organizations. Some of the uncertainties come from the nature of starting such projects, and I quickly became convinced that a creative problem-solving approach would help to reduce the stuckness, and perhaps produce a few steps forward.

There was one potential problem that did worry me. In most successful creative problem-solving exercises there is a client or group of people with 'felt needs'. The consultant needs to establish a psychological contract which gives permission to involve (rather than to be seen as interfering, not intervening). This is easiest if you have been approached in the first instance. Failing that, the would-be consultant needs to find a strategy for his or her acceptance at a personal level, as well as acceptance of methods and philosophy. In this instance there was the 'cobblers' children' effect to consider. Cobblers' children are said to be the worst shod. In professional organizations there is a wariness of offering (and of requesting) internally the professional services made available to outside clients. As a result the internal services are sometimes impoverished of skills that are close to hand. Those involved in the Proteus project had had little exposure to creative problem-solving techniques, although the parent institute had been associated with a considerable body of work in the field over a lengthy period.

I enlisted some of the Proteus team to help in the introductory project for the MBA graduate programme. This was a non-threatening way of raising awareness of the techniques. One key figure was obviously Hugh, the project leader, but it looked as if an even better approach would be to involve him indirectly. Peter, who had been developing the production management side of the work, had already taken part in some brainstorming sessions, and seemed a better person to start the process of diffusing the ideas of creative problem-solving. I did genuinely need someone to help me get ideas at this time – an important point for me. Life seems to be getting fuller of people who want to involve other people in schemes, perhaps with conscious or unconscious motives similar to my own. If the whole exercise seems primarily to be a crude influencing strategy, the initiator quickly acquires a reputation for being manipulative.

Peter's office was next to my own. I asked his help in a brainstorming for ways of linking the introductory project with the Proteus work. Hugh was also invited, partly as a group member, but partly 'to see if we could carry out more brainstormings on other aspects of Proteus'. In my own mind I had no doubt that it could help, but felt that to show such certainty might be counterproductive at this stage. Two other invited participants did not arrive, and the three of us settled in Peter's office (not mine, deliberately).

On several scores the conditions went against some 'preferred practice' for creative problem-solving. Hugh had been given the impression it was a trial. Usually trials involve evaluating what is going on, which cuts across the important climate-setting principle of postponing judgement. The group was too small to give many guidelines for sessions with the much larger Proteus team. As problem-owner and the only experienced brainstorming leader my own roles would be distorted. I had run sessions with three people and with similar role conflicts during regular meetings of another group, and it was my experience that such 'minibrainstormings' can be dominated by the leader, who finds it harder to remain divorced from personal goals. Yet there is considerable merit in that the interactions are rather lower-key and less artificial, the meeting falling somewhere between a 'proper' brainstorming and an informal ideas discussion with a positive and trained group.

A minibrainstorming (as used in the innovation Proteus project)

During the innovation Proteus project a minibrainstorming was held by a group of three people, all involved in the project. The technique is somewhere in between a 'fullblooded' brainstorming, and an informal but positive discussion of ideas. A dozen or so problem redefinitions can be listed on a blackboard or flipchart, and used to trigger discussion and ideas. The format was selected because of the small number of participants, time constraints (about half an hour of free time), and because of possible role conflicts which would reduce the impartiality of the process leader in the accepted method of brainstorming. The ideas are more controlled than from a full brainstorming, and 'only' ten were obtained. We can contrast that favourably, however, with the likely outcome of a half-hour discussion on an agenda item in a conventional meeting.

Problem statements

1. How to improve the introductory Innovation project
2. How to achieve in twenty hours results that require a term
3. How to teach problem-solving to 140 students
4. How to find an interesting innovation case for them
5. How to enable the students to teach themselves
6. How to find rooms for the extra groups this year
7. How to deal with a sudden rush of refugees
8. How to be in 140 places at the same time
9. How to be in 20 places (groups of 7) at the same time
10. How to find 20 assistants
11. How to use Proteus to help the innovation project
12. How to use the innovation project to help Proteus
13. yes and . . . How to bring both projects closer together
14. How to computerize the innovation project

Ideas generated

1. Use case material collected for Proteus Rainware for the innovation project.
2. Set the MBAs the task of inventing a logo for the Proteus Rainware product lines
3. Appoint a team observer to monitor process issues
4. yes and . . . rotate the observer roles to keep everyone happy
5. yes and . . . put the observers in groups other than their own
6. Split the teaching into two streams of 70
7. yes and . . . run one set a.m., one set p.m.
8. Arrange for the actual case work to continue during the term, to reinforce the teaching
9. Ask for individual reports on progress, demonstrating understanding of creativity techniques
10. Involve Proteus team members as tutors

In about half an hour we had begun to develop a few good ideas for helping the graduate course. My own thinking had changed from 'how to improve the introductory project', to 'how to link the introductory project with the Proteus work'. The meeting had given me some food for thought, and I wanted to see if it had also made an impression on Hugh.

'Do you think this sort of session might work with the whole Proteus group?'

'Let's give it a try.' Hugh's enthusiasm was genuine. The idea of an innovation Proteus had found a product champion, and it would now be possible to consider further implementation steps.

THE PROTEUS TEAM BRAINSTORMING SESSIONS

There were strong arguments for setting up a one- or even a two-day problem-solving workshop with members of the Proteus team plus other relevant people around the School. However, we had already found it was virtually impossible to set up such meetings, especially at short notice, and so we settled for three lunchtime meetings at two-week intervals, to progress through the stages of problem seeking, idea production, and action planning.

The first meeting took place in a smallish private dining room. As well as the core members of the team we had included a supportive faculty member, and a potential recruit to the team. There were nearly a dozen people present, and after a brief meal we went through an even briefer review of brainstorming and a warm-up reinforcement. Sheets of paper had been pinned around a conveniently corkboarded wall. The group showed unusual willingness to accept the process instructions, and the result was a wide-ranging output of over a hundred different perspectives expressed as 'how to' statements. Within a week Hugh and I had grouped these into categories.

At the next meeting each member of the group was invited to nominate the most important statements on the basis of urgency and importance. In addition the participants were asked to indicate any which they saw as falling into their specific areas of responsibility. This was a strategy intended to gain commitment for action by group members, and was one suited to the circumstances – the group leader had very little position power or leverage for more directive approaches.

The most urgent and important areas were brainstormed at the third meeting, and winning ideas were identified by the prospective action champions (i.e. the volunteers from the previous session). The levels of uncertainty and problems remaining made it clear, however, that the group had taken only the first few steps down a long road towards implementing the new technology.

NETWORK BUILDING: SPREADING THE USE OF THE NEW TECHNOLOGY

As the spring of 1986 went by it became clear that Proteus was even more ambitious than it had appeared at the outset. The team meetings settled into more conventional reports of progress (usually of delays to planned milestones of installation of technology or recruitment of staff). The action plans from the brainstorming were not being progressed directly, although with hindsight some of the concerns were being resolved: we began to get better intelligence about current trends in information technology. We stopped worrying about finding what software was available as we realized we could do all we wanted to do with our available systems.

Although it was not put into words at the time, the big problem was how to make more people committed to the project. One moment of creative realization took place in a discussion about which groupings we had to involve. The grant had been provided primarily to give the kind of learning which would equip MBA students for their roles in a high-technology world. Although our thinking had tended to focus on the graduates, the more we took a systems view the more we saw the benefits of designing tasks that would involve as many other groupings within the School as possible.

At this stage we had a shared vision of where we wanted to go, expressed by someone on the project as 'putting a terminal on every desk in the School'. This is a powerful factor assisting change, which could be augmented if there was general dissatisfaction with the status quo, and if we could identify actionable first steps towards achieving our vision. Not surprisingly we encountered considerable resistance on quantifiable cost and psychological cost grounds.

It became an important part of our strategy to let people know what we were doing, and involve them so that they could share our vision of a terminal on every desk, thus creating a supportive environment in which networking took place naturally, because of the requirements of participants in the culture. We envisaged a network in which communications took place between students, faculty, administrators, and support staff especially secretaries. There was plenty of dissatisfaction with the status quo, especially among faculty members who had not been first in line to obtain a terminal for themselves. This helped Hugh gather a certain amount of support for the project among the faculty, who had worked out that it was a fast track to receiving a terminal. Actionable first steps began to emerge from the lunchtime meetings of the Proteus project, including a host of ideas for the introductory innovation project.

As for resistances due to the cost factors, we were relatively well placed financially through the generous sponsorship of IBM, although even in times of the best harvest some farmers are known to complain. Even the IBM support did not satisfy the 'ideal case' of putting a terminal on each desk. However, the psychological costs were to provide the greater challenges. To cite one example, one professor had built up a whole range of computer-aided education packages. When he began to express vehement opposition to the project we could at least see the problem from his point of view, and take every possible opportunity to avoid reinforcing what we suspected were his worries about having much of his work become obsolete.

An even more important resistance came from some of the secretaries, who were reluctant to give up their trusty typewriters and did not want to 'go back to class'. It took an enormous amount of patience by the computing department and members of the Proteus team to deal with repeated outbursts against what the secretaries saw as stupidities being inflicted on them, as we cut corners on training to meet deadlines.

THE INTRODUCTORY PROJECT

The Proteus team had spent some time designing the introductory innovation project that had been the subject of the minibrainstorming earlier in the year. With the summer approaching it was clear that all our ideas were far too complicated. We were actually trying to accelerate the implementation of the full Proteus concept by a year, and produce a prototype. This was a mind set which trapped us all, for several months, until after we received the long-awaited terminals and accompanying professional office system (PROFS). At this point my own computer illiteracy became a blessing. I found PROFS enormously powerful for dealing rapidly with large numbers of messages. It now made it possible to handle the day's administrative matters far more efficiently than had previously been the case. More significantly, it was established that dozens of items could be dealt with in less than half an hour. This began to suggest a method of dealing with the problems of communicating with the increased numbers of students in the introductory project.

The idea was to use the PROFS system as a means of rapid communication with graduate groups. The project would centre around the graduates applying the creativity methods to the Proteus company – presented in case study and video form. Then, at the different stages in the project when faculty process intervention was desirable, the groups could interact with tutors via the PROFS system. This had provision for storing all messages – an essential benefit for improved monitoring of the student idea generation sessions, in the short term, and research in the longer term. From this idea the new design emerged.

Day 1 was to be as close as possible to the format of the 1985 project, an introduction to the principles and practice of creative problem-solving, with some provision for introducing the graduates to the PROFS system, and allowing them to practise sending messages on progress during one of the creative problem-solving exercises. Day 2 would again be the start of a large-scale problem-solving activity, this year using the Proteus case, and with assistance from the new technology to help the faculty monitor progress and intervene as appropriate.

For this, a surrogate board of the Proteus company had been assembled from among faculty members, each member allocated an electronic mail address within the PROFS system. Thus the ideas from the student groups could be channelled to faculty with specific areas of expertise. (It was also seen as a decision which would speed up the education of the faculty in using the electronic mailing system.)

IMPLEMENTATION OF THE COMPUTER-AIDED TRAINING

The first day of term, and of the introductory project, arrived. The demands on the newly acquired mainframe computer were high, as it was receiving all the School records from the older machine. This meant that it was only available for the first hour or so of the first day of the project, although it was free for the second day's main PROFS exercise. It also emerged that, because of last-minute changes to the graduate course lists, the names and user addresses of the students were still being coded into the electronic mail system. All this required last-minute adjustments to the introductory training programme.

Even as the increased number of students began to fill the lecture theatre to overflowing, the final modifications to the programme were being made. The computer department was given the first hour to present a demonstration of logging on to the PROFS system, coverting a supplied password to a personalized one, and sending and receiving messages. The demonstration, using a large screen, appeared to the observing faculty team to be too complex to be taken in by a group of people who were still suffering from culture shock at entering an alien environment. Unfortunately there was no time available for the hands-on approach we would all have favoured for reinforcing the messages.

The rest of day 1 followed the general format of the non-computerized event of the previous year. (It had to, as we had used up our allotted computer time for the day.) Despite extra numbers of participants the involving nature of group work, and non-threatening puzzles, once again generated a good deal of energy and interest that was to be valuable currency invested towards a good day 2.

Nevertheless, the faculty approached the uncharted waters of day 2 with some trepidation. The first task was for the twenty-three groups – each now with access to a terminal and the electronic office networking system – to study an introductory document to the Proteus Company and to report to the tutors via the PROFS system. The computer department instructor expected that the time allotted to introducing the technology would have been inadequate (one hour on day 1) and that much of the morning would be spent giving further hands-on experience. Some idea of the speed of events can be gained from the following recorded sequence of activities.

The twenty-three student teams dispersed from the main briefing theatre at approximately 10 a.m. Hugh and I returned to Hugh's office, which was equipped with a terminal for receiving the messages, while Pat, the computer manager, made himself available as a technical back-up in the computing area with the largest concentration of terminals. By 11 a.m. a great deal was happening at once. Groups were logging on, and sending messages via the system, at what seemed to us to be an increasingly rapid rate. For a while it was unclear whether the system would work as intended. Would we be able to deal with the twenty-three teams in time for the afternoon session? At 11.30 the backlog of unanswered messages reached its peak (12 in all). However, by 12.15 p.m. the backlog had been cleared, and we were able to deal with the last few group messages rapidly and with relative ease as they came in. By 1 p.m. the task had been completed successfully by all the teams, and all messages had been replied to. The general tone of the messages was enthusiastic and at times triumphant and creative.

We had a small number of prepared messages which were used to deal with the two main types of information request: 'The answer to your question will become clear later in the project' and 'Make whatever assumption you like about that – we have no information at present.' In addition we needed a message that confirmed that the case study did have a paragraph missing, and that again it did not really matter at this stage of the project.

After lunch the project moved to the stage of using the brainstorming methodology to create a range of perspectives on the problems of the Proteus company mentioned above. The groups had already been provided with case material (an outline of the company, its product areas, and general information, in about 1500 words). Additionally a video of the actual MD of the company was shown, briefly giving his view of the company. After that the groups were left to manage their own time in completing their brainstorming, being given the option of finishing the exercise before the end of the day, or fitting in a team meeting before the deadline for returning their report via the electronic mail system in two weeks' time.

In the previous year some groups failed to complete the first brainstorming on a big business problem, providing very poor reports indeed. Because we had failed to monitor these poorly-performing groups, we now hoped that an improvement in monitoring could be achieved by examining the brainstorming outputs to give clues to those groups that were performing well, and those which needed personal attention. As it turned out, all the groups presented satisfactory outputs for their level of experience with brainstorming, and the 'fine tuning' to their group processes was made via the electronic mail system. As an example: some teams were providing material that read as if it emerged from a conventional meeting. They had been asked not to eliminate the more speculative material. Those teams with more mundane outputs were reminded, through the electronic mail system, of the advantage of building on each other's ideas, and of 'throwing in a bunch of bananas' to intervene during a session which had failed to escape from routine and conventional ideas.

Once the reports had been received they were assessed in the first instance for evidence that the teams had acquired the routines leading to successful brainstorming, and especially evidence of postponed judgement, and 'yes anding' (building on each other's ideas). On this count it was estimated that five teams had produced outstanding reports that would have done credit to teams that had received extensive training and practice in brainstorming, and that all the other teams had been able to produce substantial numbers of ideas, albeit rather conventional ones that might have emerged from extended discussions under more traditional meeting conditions.

These results compared very favourably with the brainstormed outputs of the previous year, and were later compiled and passed on to the MD of the 'real' Proteus company, who has begun the process of evaluating them with his colleagues.

INTERIM CONCLUSIONS

The project has shown how creativity training and introduction of new technology can be mutually reinforcing. The planned application of creative problem-solving techniques contributed to learning and problem-solving around the Proteus project. There are increasing signs that faculty and students are using some version of brainstorming during projects requiring new ideas, including consultancy assignments for clients. The knowledge has diffused and led to a change of working procedures. Similarly, the introduction of the new technology has assisted in the training of large groups of students, and also led to new communication habits, as faculty, support staff, and increasing numbers of students routinely turn to the PROFS system for rapid conveying of information.

It is interesting to consider the time spent in dealing with the 'political' side of acceptance seeking of ideas in this project. If an external brainstorming expert had been called in for one session on designing the introductory project, and a second session on the Proteus project, the chances of the sessions making a significant impact would have been greatly reduced. Here we have an alternative to the simplistic notion that a problem can be solved by the discovery of one bright idea. From a starting point of improving educational practice, only a small number of ideas from the actual brainstormings have made much impact on the project. This is as might be expected – perhaps one novel idea in a hundred turns from a promising concept to one which succeeds in bringing about change. However, the process of stimulating creativity in a deliberate way has somehow helped set up an environment in which ideas have been produced regularly – for example, during the Proteus team meetings, long after the brainstorming sessions. It should come as no surprise if the creativity has come about in unexpected, and perhaps unintended, ways. Implementation has not been a logical step-by-step progression, but a gradual change of position, appearing sometimes to advance, sometimes to retreat, as unexpected events make demands on the creative problem-solvers.

13 Changing corporate culture

The material for this case study has been generously provided by Les Jones, who acted as principal consultant and trainer to the company in the exercise. Les has been active for many years in creative problem-solving and the management of change during his career as a management consultant.

BACKGROUND TO CHIMCO PLC

Chimco plc is one of the largest chemical companies in the UK. In the past Chimco has been a commodity chemical company with a fairly narrow range of products. It has built up a reputation in its niche in the market and has much expertise and a good trade record of product development in this branch of chemistry.

In recent years the company has taken a decision to diversify into the speciality chemical field. It has done this by a mixture of acquisitions and internal attempts at innovation. Many of the acquisitions have been small companies with no R & D effort of their own and covering fields as diverse as electronics, building materials, metal finishing and biocides. The common factor is that all the areas have good growth prospects over the next few years. However, it was recognized that to produce this growth R & D support would be necessary in the new areas of expertise. This would mean that the company's Research and Development department, which was oriented towards the commodity end of the business, would have to provide an additional service to the new special chemical businesses. Furthermore the department would need to combine an ability to get close to the marketplace with the establishment of longer-term basic research work.

STIMULATING CREATIVITY IN THE RESEARCH DEPARTMENT

The demands for change were felt within the company's UK-based research laboratory in 1984. At senior corporate level, and within the directorate of the laboratory, it was recognized that the scientific professionals would require help if they were to develop technical breakthroughs in areas outside their traditional field of knowhow. A senior management innovation team had been instituted, and had begun operations aimed at collecting and evaluating new ideas from the scientific staff. However, the contributions were meagre in numbers, and far too close to the traditional areas of the company's expertise.

Following discussions with outside consultants, a two-day training session was arranged at the request of the senior management for twenty of the scientific staff of the laboratory. The participants chosen were those most likely to play leading roles in future innovation activities (assessed by their track records and general potential as perceived by the senior technical management). They represented a spread of seniorities within the laboratory.

On the first day of the programme the participants were introduced to the principles of creative problem-solving and some of the techniques for increasing effectiveness of such problem-solving especially in groups. Particular emphasis was given to brainstorming (including brainstorming of the problem) as a powerful means of working in groups. Warm-up exercises and psychological inventories were also administered. On the second day issues of interest with potential for innovative ideas were generated and three were selected to be worked on, each with a product champion. (The selection process had been made with careful attention to the commitment of the problem-owner.) Under these circumstances it was possible to extend the creative problem-solving beyond the time limits of the training. During the day each problem was examined, ranges of new perspectives were generated, and starting ideas were produced for some of the more promising perspectives. Additionally an action plan was drawn up, including 'immediate first steps' by the product champion and any other team members who had been co-opted to the implementation effort.

OUTCOME OF THE TRAINING PROGRAMME

At a follow-up session some months later the three projects were reviewed, and a progress report was given.

> *Project A 'Applications for Chimoxides'* This group had chosen to stay close to existing expertise (the chemical oxides which were the company's mainstream business), but to seek applications in new market niches. Some progress had been made, although the group considered that the techniques had had more obvious impact when they had applied them to other areas (not specified).
>
> *Project B 'Rod manufacture from molten oxides'* The project, to produce various gauge rods from molten non-metallic oxide mixes, had been running for four years. The first set of ideas from the brainstorming did not lead to any breakthroughs. Just when all seemed lost a slightly different requirement arose from one of the markets, and one of the proposed solutions fitted the need very well.
>
> *Project C 'Low energy detergency'* The sessions generated a range of ideas, some of which challenged conventional technological wisdom and were considered new and potentially valuable at the time. The project was a victim of the 'champion's' success, as a promotion deprived him of the chance to continue his involvement. As so often happens, the achievement of one corporate goal (promoting a good manager) cut across other corporate goals (successful implementation of innovative ideas). Once the champion moved on, interests in the project waned.

The manager of the innovation team evaluated the exercise as demonstrating the potential for creativity rather than having achieved tangible new product results. The groups felt that the much-desired creative climate did not follow from the training, and that such a climate would not be achieved without reinforcement and practice in using the techniques. The groups were too homogeneous, and could beneficially incorporate non-specialists. The different levels of status within the groups seemed to produce inhibitions which could not easily be overcome (a classic block to creativity which participants related to the need to build up a climate of trust). It was also felt that structures were needed to routinize the operation of creative problem-solving groups and to assist in communicating and sharing good ideas.

THE NEXT STAGE

The general consensus was interpreted positively by the management, who proposed that more staff should undergo training in creativity techniques. However, this posed a problem for the consultants, who were not convinced that the problem was 'how to train up more staff in creativity techniques'. In fact, they were not at that stage sure of the nature of the core problem beyond 'How to help the Research Laboratory achieve more innovative results for the company'. The consultants recommended a diagnostic survey, a proposal which was accepted.

The innovation consultant (LJ) interviewed the management team and samples of other staff grades and sat in on a meeting of the innovation committee. At his meeting with the research manager the problem was initially stated as 'how to achieve an enhanced level of creative problem-solving by whatever means possible'. Following the familiar creative problem-stating and restating procedure, this was taken as a starting point in subsequent interviews, from which other viewpoints were produced.

Reviewing these interviews, the consultant concluded that the majority of staff were positive in their approach to innovation, that the quality of technical development work carried out was of a high standard, and that there was no evidence that they were uncreative. He began to see that improvements would be obtained, not in focusing on the deficiencies of the staff, but by removing or reducing barriers to creativity in their working environment. Five groups of blocks were identified as follows:

1 *Conflicting work objectives.* Long-term development work required to develop new products or significantly new applications was being regularly squeezed out by urgent demands from production and business departments. These demands were of a routine nature. There was also a feeling that the pressures of such bread-and butter work meant there was no time available for thinking. In some instances there was a feeling of guilt about sitting down 'just trying to get new ideas' when a workload was beginning to build up. Technical staff tended to think of longer-term issues only when away from the workplace – travelling, or at home.

2 *Inefficient use of (human) resources.* There was almost universal concern about the rewarding of creative effort. It was widely stated that the job evaluation system does not adequately recognize the intrinsic nature of the research scientist's work, leading to pressure to succeed through the only available route – out of research into general management. A few projects were recognized as high-profile and advantageous for those involved, and this demotivated those working on other, less glamorous, projects. It was also felt that the research staff did not always present themselves and their ideas very effectively outside the depart-

ment, failing to think about and present research as a business function.

3 *The organizational climate.* There was clear evidence of creative track record and an acknowledgement of successful past performance. Yet there were also reported feelings that creativity was undervalued. Besides the inadequate reward system, the scientists believed there to be insufficient internal encouragement to produce new ideas and share them with others. The consultant was reminded of a football team full of highly skilled players who are not achieving their potential because they do not really believe in themselves. That is not to say there was lack of confidence in the department's managers, who were seen as strongly influenced by external pressures over which they had insufficient control.

4 *Communications.* There was widespread concern that poor information sharing was limiting the department's creativity. Circulating masses of data was not seen as the solution (it would add to the workload problems), but there was frustration about not knowing what was going on in other areas, and about the possibility that individuals had contributions that could help others, but that were being largely ignored.

5 *Problem-solving techniques.* Perhaps influenced by the training emphasis, those staff interviewed displayed a constructive discontent about the way individuals went about tackling problems. (During the two-day event several people said their main goal was finding some systematic way of approaching problems.)

THE IMPLICATIONS OF THE INVESTIGATION

The consultant suggested that the key to many of the concerns was not 'how to make the staff more creative', but 'how to play a more effective role in the business'. The following recommendations come from his concluding report to the management of the divison, with modifications only in the interests of confidentiality.

1 The objectives of the research department and the strategies for achieving them need to be set out more clearly in terms of the company's business objectives, endorsed at the highest levels in the company. Once endorsed they should be communicated to all departmental staff and departments likely to be affected. Each work group within the department should be involved in determining what its role is relating to the wider goals. Where possible

targets should be agreed. Such strategies should recognize the relevant balance between long-term and short-term work, provision being made to ensure that long-term work does not suffer.

2. Rewards should be instituted for innovators. These need not be entirely financial: for maintained high performance promotion or merit bonuses are appropriate. Where promotion is not a good option technical posts at comparable levels can be introduced. Such persons would typically lead a small team of assistants on specific specialist areas of research but would have no other managerial responsibilities. In some cases this would lead to individuals becoming company or industry-wide experts in special topics. For outstanding performance on a particular project a special bonus would be more appropriate.

    Psychological rewards could include the encouragement of staff to make visible their contributions in written form or as presentations. At the junior level this is likely to be internal to the company and with more experience they could represent Chimco externally. Contributions to professional journals should also be encouraged and rewarded. Although these activities already occur, I suggest that they could be routinized and extended to a much wider grouping of staff.

3. The department needs to sell itself more effectively to the rest of the company. While the foregoing measures would help in this process, there needs to be an active publicity campaign to make other people aware that the research department is a young, dynamic and innovative department which has clearly identified itself with the business objectives of the company. For this to succeed everyone in the department has a part to play. Hence, in setting targets and assessing and rewarding performance, business awareness and influencing skills will need to be considered as well as technical ability. Where training is needed there are good reasons for giving it to entire work groups, rather than singling out individuals for external courses.

4. There are some major gains to be made in morale by visibly attending to the communications needs of the department. A small, but broadly based, group could be set up to investigate ways of improving communications without incurring large costs in terms of money or time. If the group were to invite all members of the staff to submit suggestions, the commitment to the outcome would outweigh the costs of time involved. Improvements to communications would be a bonus to the gains in staff morale.

5 There is a perceived need for some form of training in problem-solving which again could be carried out within workgroups. Group leaders should be encouraged to train their own staff, in conjunction with an external trainer when needed.

Ideas into action: a systems approach

We can learn more about getting ideas into action by studying driving forces and restraining forces, the technique known as force field analysis. A second approach is to consider factors which assist the change, and the resistances produced by costs. This method follows Beckhard's change equation. By putting the two methods together we arrive at a particularly powerful technique for analysing change, and for deciding on the most suitable first steps.

1 Identify the 'what' that is undergoing change, and define the problem in terms of the change or achievement to the system ('How to introduce new technology to our department')
2 Look deeply (postpone judgement) to find key needs, that the change will meet. These are sometimes seen as dissatisfactions. The more shared dissatisfactions you find the better.
3 Look more deeply for a description of the goal that will be achieved that represents a shared view. This is sometimes called the shared vision of where the people involved want to get to. The more evocative you can make this, the better. ('When those difficult customers call, we'll be able to keep them happy by giving them fast service, without hassle to ourselves'.)
4 Recognize the financial costs of change, but be prepared to accept that the cost/benefit estimates may not be quantifiable yet. This is therefore a check that your proposed idea is broadly financially acceptable.
5 Look for the psychological costs of your proposals. Again use your knowledge of the system and its personalities ('short-term views, sacred cows, avoidance of decision taking . . .').
6 Consider the psychological blocks (resistances) that have to be dealt with. These will influence your action plan.
7 Now you can begin to develop short- and long-term actions. It helps to have a satisfactory first step. Again, you cannot be absolutely sure, but you can usually find one that gets you moving.

IMPLEMENTATION

The consultant's proposals were accepted as a blueprint for stimulating innovation within the research department. Items 1 and 3 were seen as requiring most immediate attention.

Ideas into action planner

1. **What is the need?**
   (Dissatisfaction)
   _____
   _____
   _____

2. **What is the goal?**
   (Shared vision)
   _____
   _____
   _____

Immediate first steps
(High control, short timescale)
_____
_____
_____

3. **What actual costs**
   (Assess general viability)
   _____
   _____
   _____

4. **What psychological costs?**
   (List as 'how to reduce')
   _____
   _____
   _____

Meetings have been held between departmental managers and section managers to examine the company's objectives and those of the department. These meetings helped clarify understanding of roles, and problems of individual groupings. Section managers then began the process of sharing the information with their sections, and of redefining their own objectives. It was felt prudent to approach the matter of upgrading influencing skills with care. All staff whose work involves influencing and motivating others were selected for training, starting with the management group. Two-day events for six people at a time are being held, and part of the action plan for managers is to return and persuade their own staff of the advantages of participating in such programmes.

The 'creative problem-solving' within the influencing training centred on implementation, and on developing richer perceptions of the factors influencing change, such as the needs and objectives of the people whom the change is affecting. Attention was paid to the resisting forces to change, the importance of a clear vision or goal to be achieved, and also to identifying actionable first steps.

There is growing evidence that members of the research department are operating in a more confident and innovation-oriented way, liaising comfortably with other business groups. Already the indirect impact of the training is showing itself as communication improves across groupings. The work has also provided a non-threatening forum in which personal viewpoints and concerns have been raised.

CONCLUSIONS

This example illustrates how important it is to test out the starting point of problems with those involved. The senior management began with a view that the problem was uncreative staff. This is an understandable interpretation of events where a group is failing to produce new and needed ideas. However, investigation often reveals a range of factors that may be producing the problem. Indeed, it is very likely that there are blocking factors in the environment, as few business problems have simple and obvious cause. Here we have a salutary lesson for those of us who become involved in creative problem-solving. However skilfully the techniques are carried out within the ideas sessions, the impact will be minimal if there are organizational factors blocking implementaion of ideas, and it is not a case of merely coming up with previously undiscovered novelties.

Under such circumstances the consultant has to work carefully at the pace at which the clients are willing to have their preconceived views challenged. In this instance the clients were receptive enough to accept the consultant's suggestions (who, incidentally, displayed considerable skills in those subjects he was providing, problem-solving and influencing). Here we have the recurring theme of creative analysis, summed up by LJ as: 'It now appears that the next step forward should be to work on improving relationships with other departments. But as we have already seen, creative analysis of problems leads to completely different insights into what the problems are, and what solutions might be envisaged. Who knows where the problem-solving process will take us next?'

14 Some long-term applications

Creative problem-solving techniques have been the subject of industrial interest since Alex Osborn introduced brainstorming over thirty years ago, but it has been the last decade that has seen the development of important initiatives, in literally hundreds of organizations, in which the techniques have been applied in the creative and analytical ways advocated in this book. We can compare some of the most recent practices with earlier work in a range of different situations in order to draw some conclusions for further exercises.

EARLY CREATIVE PROBLEM-SOLVING EXPERIENCES (1969–72)

These examples include the two described in depth in Chapter 9. The work concerned an innovation team within the Research and Development division of a large international organization, using an approach for stimulating creativity which had been strongly influenced by the synectics version of group problem-solving.

The team acted as an internal idea generation service for other groups within the organization. Most of its clients tended to have technical projects which required some imaginative step that was not immediately obvious. Success was measured in terms of the client gaining new insights enabling progress to be made towards project goals.

A record was kept of the outcomes of the idea sessions, and as many as possible were followed up within a few months. At the level of gaining new innovative insights for the client, the approach was successful in roughly half of the large number of sessions that took place. However, there seemed to be a much smaller number of sessions after which the clients actually were able to convert insights into innovations.

In retrospect, it is clear that the innovation-seeking team considered its main task to be technical problem-solving. Any failure in implementation was put down to 'bloody-mindedness', stupidity of senior management, technical ignorance of marketing groups and so on. The team worked on the assumption that innovation was a two-step process of discovery followed by implementation. Failure to gain acceptance for invention was put down to problems 'downstream' of the technological problem-solving. Little consideration was given to the possible resolution of managerial or interface problems with other departments.

In some respects the experiences were to have considerable long term consequences. Several participants retained their enthusiasm for the techniques in long and distinguished careers inside the organization. An early initiative by a young Lever Brothers development chemist, Richard Duggan, involved a systematic search for new cleaning products (using morphological analysis) and resulted among other innovations in the successful cleaner plus polisher Dual. Contributions to the technologies of enzyme detergency, and solvent plus detergent products, were also made through group creative problem-solving sessions. Although not reported at the time, these were among the first examples of practical results from deliberate attempts to stimulate innovation through creative problem-solving techniques.

THE SCIMITAR SYSTEM OF INDUSTRIAL NEW-PRODUCT DEVELOPMENT

Scimitar stands for Systematic Creativity and Integrative Modelling of Industrial Technology and Research. Its origins were described by John Carson and myself in an earlier Gower publication (*Industrial New Product Development*,) covering the period 1973–79. The system was originated by John Carson, whose experiences as a new products manager in Europe and America had convinced him of the possibility of reducing the uncertainties in the discovery and implementation of new products. He found that a powerful mechanism for this was to model the company as a three-dimensional matrix. Such modelling provided a matrix which could be systematically examined cell by cell for new business opportunities, but which also permitted imaginative efforts within each cell. In the first exercise emphasis was placed on finding rapid, easy to implement, ideas, within the existing company 'box'. However, in later exercises the power of exploring outside the box to reveal important diversificational options was realized.

The system incorporated further procedures aimed at simplifying and enhancing the stages in implementation of new product ideas: the importance of cross-functional representation in the venture team and strong, regular contact with the decision-making levels of the organization to negotiate and re-negotiate resources (terms of reference, commercialization decisions, and funding). A very important criterion for continued attention to developing any idea was evidence of consumer interest in the potential outcome. This could lead to modifications – either to the original product concept, or to the perceptions of the client. The essence of this strategy was captured in the 'equation', needs + means = innovation. The customer's contribution to new product development was also recognized and actively sought. The process was neither technology push, nor consumer pull, but an iterative one of harmonizing both components within the innovation team's efforts.

As originally conceived and executed, Scimitar divided up the innovation process into three stages: idea searches; idea development; and commercialization. The first stage involved building the three-dimensional model; establishing a small venture team; carrying out market research for market needs; and setting up an administrative function. The second stage covered the development of the new products into tangible form through experimentation and optimization. The third stage took the successful prototype products through pre-launch activities to launch, commercial development and transfer of responsibilities to the appropriate part of the organization. By 1979, the process had been applied in a large number of projects within the sponsoring company, and regularities had been observed in the outcomes as new products. Providing decisions were controlled within the new venture team, the flow of ideas, to projects and then to commercializable products, took on a recognizable pattern. Approximately ten thousand ideas had been systematically generated and evaluated, out of which nearly one hundred achieved commercially acceptable returns, and broadly speaking about 100 ideas were needed in a specific exercise to yield one commercial product which eventually returned profits for the organization.

From the first trials (which took place within a large chemicals organization), Carson showed considerable awareness of the importance of creative management of the non-technological components of innovation. As I had the good fortune to work with him throughout some of these activities I was able to study his particular brand of creative problem-solving.

Significant differences were apparent in his methods of operating, from situation to situation. When working as leader of a group looking for ideas, his approach was essentially that of a facilitator or 'process leader'. Outside 'idea sessions', however, many of his behaviours and value systems were close to those of a small-company entrepreneur – a role model he admitted admiring. The switch from a facilitative manager to a more directive one was observed regularly – and might occur several times within a single stage of a single project. This flexibility seemed intuitive, rather than consciously engineered.

The morale and motivation of his team-members were generally high, and did not seem adversely influenced by these role switches. The benefits from flexible leadership seemed to outweigh the advantages of maintaining a consistent process-oriented leadership style.

Later the system was applied to twenty-four different companies mainly within the manufacturing sector of industry, and of large divisionalized scale. Clients were mostly UK-based with some US, other European, and Indian contributors. Its impact in four areas was assessed: establishing corporate venture capabilities; idea generation; idea development; and commercialization.

Eighteen of the twenty-four companies accepted the need for some restructuring of their operations. Ten allocated some full-time resources (six of which were venture teams). Eight set up part-time committee-type structures; while eight retained their existing structures. According to Carson the part-time structures are more prone to organizational problems, and have a higher attendant risk.

> In particular the need for high level support, preferably at chief executive or at least board level, has been proven. A clear remit or definition of the aims and targets of the new business group have also been proved to be vital. Several attempts in large companies failed because these preconditions were not met. ...once established and running, the need for product champions arising out of the group becomes crucial, and the ultimate success of even the most exciting, relevant, and actionable ideas depends on the dedicated leadership of the product champion.

The use of a three-dimensional model was found successful by virtually all the clients (only one of the twenty-four failed to benefit, and even in that case there was some reasonable doubt about the viability of the current company model). Approximately 250 ideas can be obtained in a search process involving the company venture team members in a full session over two to four days. The cubes within the model are systematically examined (a process that requires a trained and decisive leader, as there may be many hundreds of cubes to examine in turn for links between company means and identified market needs).

> These yield the most obvious, most relevant and most actionable new business ideas for the client but they frequently contain shocks regarding what has been previously missed. . . . out of all the ideas that will eventually be placed in the portfolio, some 70% will be discovered by these purely logical approaches.
>
> Of the various creative problem-solving techniques applied to new business idea generation within the scimitar system, by far the most successful has been Synectics. A version of the analogy method has produced almost a thousand new ideas (out of about 9000 ideas recorded during the exercises). Many of them have been truly novel and yet, because of the focusing effect of the model, they have subsequently been proved to be actionable by the client company.

The idea standardization, development, and assessment system offered within the Scimitar approach follows the 'closing down' strategies of Chapter 3. In particular, the hurdles, and weighting procedures are put to work. From the 250–300 ideas, some 50 or 60 survive the screening, and move towards consumer trials. About 20 of these ideas reach the launch stage, in a flow of 3–6 in year one, with the remainder in years two and three, for those companies that have made figures available. (This appears to conflict with the '100 ideas to one success' ratio until it is realized that the portfolio of 250 was itself a second stage after the elimination of large quantities of unusable concepts.)

Eleven of the twenty-four companies followed the Scimitar recommendations for product launches, five of them comprehensively. The approach emphasizes low-cost advertising, and incremental or 'net-spreading' strategies in response to trade enquiries. In 1983 a financial evaluation was made of the results.

> Rapid market penetration has been achieved at low cost, and no venture has floundered after launch. The most successful product is now selling at the rate of £6 million p.a. Other successes amount to new sales of a further £3 million p.a. In all, over 100 new business ventures have been successfully launched, and their combined turnover at maturity will exceed £25 million p.a. . . . Overall, one in every 88 ideas produced has become a successful new venture for a client.

THE PII PROJECT, HOLLAND

At roughly the time of the Scimitar work another ambitious scheme for stimulating innovation was taking place in Holland, again involving a combination of creative problem-solving approaches. The project, PII (Project Industriele Innovation) was the brainchild of Jan Buijs of the TNO, the Netherlands Organization for Applied Scientific Research. The scheme involved new-technology-based firms (NTBFs) and small to medium-sized enterprises (SMEs). The NTBFs tended to need 'expert' consultancy advice, on specific commercial issues. In contrast, the SMEs in mature industries required a process-consultancy approach that was not available at the time in Holland. It was suggested that NTBFs tend to have a core idea and are looking for means of commercializing or implementing it, whereas the SMEs have an existing structure, often in declining markets, and need assistance in 'learning to learn' so that new products can be obtained in a systematic manner.

The five elements of the original approach were summarized as:

1 A step-by-step model of the innovation process based on strategic planning approaches, management of innovation theories and organizational learning.
2 A team approach which involves all functional departments of the company, including the participation of management.
3 A strong external orientation, conditioned by the fact that the reason for most innovation is to be found outside the company and depends on the acquisition of relevant information.
4 The intensive use of appropriate creativity techniques to provide intervention methods for the consultant.
5 A process-oriented consulting role.

The programme defined the main strategy of PII, not as finding innovations for the firms, but as teaching them how to become innovative. At the end of one set of trials in 1982, about two-thirds of the seventy-nine firms involved had reported innovative changes arising from the project. Many of these also considered that a learning process had ensued which would better equip them for future innovation initiatives. Only about 20 per cent considered they had gained nothing from the project. Another criterion of success was that after the subsidized phase of the project over 90 per cent of the companies were found to be continuing the processes of innovation seeking and exploitation. In about 30 per cent of cases the original consultants were invited back to continue their work.

The PII team had decided against giving their process consultants a predetermined package for stimulating innovation. The most successful consultants were those who had assimilated the principles of process consultancy, but who nevertheless operated in a flexible style providing expert technical advice, or process support, according to circumstances. Less successful were consultants (e.g. financial experts) purveying expert advice regardless of circumstances. The Dutch group experimented with brainstorming, and to some degree with the Scimitar approach, but decided to introduce only a few components into their own work. This was because they wished to emphasize the freedom of their consultants to proceed using whatever techniques seemed most appropriate.

With experience it was found important to improve communications, especially to the smallest potential participants, with more briefing in advance about the opportunities and the possible problems and responsibilities of becoming involved. The selection and training of the consultants were also given more attention, with those types unable to escape from an expert mode weeded out at the selection stage. It was also found that companies with grave problems and management weaknesses did not benefit from the project, and were unable to escape from their short term problems.

All those points presumed to increase the effectiveness of the innovation consultancy were found to be statistically significant: the step-by-step framework was an effective way of structuring the process, yet another example of how structure assists creativity. The success of the process consultancy role was of particular interest, 'surprising the Netherlands consulting world', according to Jan Buijs, because beforehand most consultants considered this role only applicable for "soft" organizational issues like communication, but not for such a "hard" process as technological innovation. Of particular interest was the finding that creativity techniques were essential for achieving divergent thinking, and an important correlated factor with concrete innovations emerging from an exercise. The results could not be explained by factors such as industry sector, turnover, etc. of the participating companies.

In follow-up studies it was found that a majority of the companies continued their commitment to innovation after the project ended. At that stage (1984) twenty-one innovations had reached the market, representing an increase in sales of 10 per cent to the innovating companies. A typical creative leap was illustrated by the manufacturers of electric fences, who redefined their business as being 'expert modulating of electric current'. This was to lead to an electric meat tenderizer now marketed through slaughterhouses. By the end of 1985 forty-three innovations had reached commercialization, with sales contributions of 17 per cent for the organizations concerned.

The expectations for 1986 were for 150 commercialized products as the final outcome of the exercise.

The results of the PII work have encouraged other schemes to be developed elsewhere. In 1986 two schemes began which were strongly influenced by it, one in Norway, and one in the Manchester region of the UK (the Mico scheme, which is described later in this chapter).

THE ETHICS SYSTEM

Ethics stands for Effective Technical and Human Implementation of Computer-based work Systems. It was developed at Manchester Business School by Professor Enid Mumford and co-workers and has been applied extensively in Europe and America over the last ten years.

Conceptually, Ethics is simple. In designing new-technology-based systems the creative problem-solving is largely a matching of technical and social needs. Ethics provides a series of procedures for this which can be summarized as:

1 Diagnosis of business and social needs and problems
2 Setting efficiency and social objectives
3 Choosing a strategy which best achieves both sets of objectives
4 Designing this in detail
5 Implementing the new system
6 Evaluating the new system

The most important principle of Ethics is that those who do a particular job are best suited to designing the improvements to it. Although the implementation of information technology is the crux of the methodology, the basic principles can be applied to any work design procedure. Ethics is a set of techniques whereby a group of individuals can work together to analyse and design their own work systems. The problem-solving team will be joined by technically able designers, but any expertise status given to that designer in making decisions is balanced by the expertise of the users. The individuals concerned work together to design a useful, feasible system which can be implemented, to give acceptability and effectiveness in improving the job. To do this, job satisfaction is given a high priority in the procedure of design.

Ethics starts by getting the users to describe the objectives of their system. This is encouraged by a facilitator who can create an atmosphere which is non-threatening to the users. This atmosphere is important as the users may not feel confident enough that their own knowledge is credible. It is just this knowledge which is needed for effective design, and for which an open and creative environment is required. In such a climate the objectives which emerge include those associated with job satisfaction needs.

The generation of alternatives leads to a requirement for closing down or convergence mechanisms. Checklists have been developed for both financial and user acceptability factors, and these are incorporated into a cost–benefit analysis. The recommendations are then developed by the technical designers, who follow the requirements expressed, and are encouraged to keep in touch with the users of the system. An organizationally useful and psychologically acceptable product results, and it has been found that there are substantial spin-off gains. User attitudes are positive because people feel more committed to a design they have helped create, and when they learn more about their job, how others see it, and how it fits into the wider organizational picture.

SETTING UP AN INNOVATION SUPPORT COMPANY FOR SMALL FIRMS

Case examples are, by tradition, factual, objective, and essentially left-brain. This may be why they present a picture of a world in which logic triumphs over the forces of uncertainty and ignorance. By way of a change I would like to offer a different picture; one that includes more of the emotional and right-brain component in some recent work that has been attempting to apply the principles of creative analysis. But first, let's stay with the more descriptive format of the other case examples: Mico stands for The Manchester Innovation Company. It was formed in 1986 to help small firms in the Manchester region of the UK to create new products and processes.

It has been funded by grants from regional authorities, and additional non-financial support has come from representatives of public and private sector bodies. As a pilot trial eight small firms have been invited to take part in the scheme for a nominal fee (£200), for which they receive the equivalent of £1200 of process consultancy help. The (part-time) consultants have all been trained in creative problem-solving approaches, and understand that their role is to help the small-firm owners to discover new perspectives on their medium-term innovation needs.

An administrative officer has been provided to coordinate the scheme, and there is also a project manager who liaises closely with a steering group representing potential supporting bodies, and a small board of directors. The project manager was responsible for designing the framework for the work, and (as an experienced innovation consultant and academic) for providing support training for the consultants and managers. The training centres on problem diagnosing, and idea generation techniques, and modelling using a version of the Scimitar approach.

A stage-by-stage sequence of activities was proposed as follows:

1. Local companies are surveyed.
2. Companies are approached.
3. An initial appraisal is made of their innovative potential.
4. A process consultant is selected.
5. The consultant helps the firm clarify its innovation goals.
6. Idea searches are carried out.
7. The firm draws up a business plan for implementation.
8. First implementation steps are carried out.

What actually happened?

Yes, well, that's the sort of 'factual' account that management scientists learn how to write. But I can remember a different kind of reality that is rarely included in such accounts. For instance, Mico didn't just spring into life in early 1986 as a completely worked out plan. As early as 1974 I had been very impressed by John Carson's Scimitar approach for systematically generating new products, and we had talked about its benefits for regenerating British industry, if it were to be applied widely enough. We had a mutual acquaintance in Jan Buijs, who was at the time working on the PII project in Holland, and the idea gradually emerged that Scimitar could be an all-purpose technique for a process-consultancy approach.

Our efforts to interest the British government reached ministerial levels, after which nothing happened. Then in 1983 I had an opportunity of presenting the ideas to a forum of regional government officials and managers out of which a product champion emerged, in the shape of Roger Taylor, the then Deputy Town Clerk of the City of Manchester. In the meeting I explained how Scimitar could always produce hundreds of potentially valuable ideas for a company, and demonstrated this with audience participation. The group 'invented' a few dozen ideas, some quite novel, for a local firm of builders' merchants. The discussion was politely sceptical ('yes, but it's different with my kind of firm . . .'). However, Taylor, who was chairman of the meeting, made a positive summing up, and my guess is that it was the practical demonstration which resulted in his putting his considerable influence behind further developments.

The starting idea was to use process consultants with back-up help from John Carson to introduce Scimitar into the small firms of the region to generate innovation, and therefore subsequently employment. Possible sponsors were invited to lunchtime meetings at the town hall, where time and again I went over the story. I became aware of serious difficulties in explaining what we were trying to do. Sometimes people related the idea to an existing scheme for supporting small firms (It's being done already; there are too many things going on at the moment, etc). For others I was talking in academic jargon. The word 'innovation' was replaced by 'new business ideas'; process consultants became 'our business school helpers', with no appreciable gain in understanding. Other would-be sponsors wanted on the one hand evidence that it was a new scheme, and on the other hand evidence that it would 'work'. This became a frustrating double-bind. We needed money to demonstrate that the scheme would work, and we were being promised money only after we had proved it could work.

The meetings were seen as building up support prior to a public meeting of relevant regional figures from small-firm advisory bodies, banks and industrial companies, government departments, university representatives and so on. This was supported by the Town Hall, with some topping up from a small research budget to which I had access at Manchester Business School. The main speakers were to be Jan Buijs and John Carson, as advocates for the approach now to be proposed from Manchester. As would-be project leader I had the role of explaining for the umpteenth time what we proposed to do, and the Deputy Town Clerk ended the meeting with an invitation for support for such a scheme.

The upshot was a steering committee selected from those groups we hoped would play a part in supporting the scheme. Numbers varied from half a dozen to a dozen people, and the project lapsed into a nightmarish stage out of which there was no obvious escape. Delegates delegated to delegates who had to be brought into the picture. Two of the potential sponsors repeatedly returned to the 'prove it works' or the 'how will you be able to prove it has worked when you've finished' lines. The Deputy Town Clerk began to send apologies for unavoidable absence (he was preparing for his apotheosis as Town Clerk and Chief Officer of the City). One or two delegates were determinedly present to protect existing schemes which they believed might be harmed by any new project. When I failed to explain what the scheme was trying to do I was asked to 'put it in writing to make it understandable to our people'. From time to time someone in the meeting would explode in frustration at the lack of progress and call for action – only we never seemed able to pin down what the actions should be.

After many such meetings (I would estimate at least a dozen, spread over a year), morale was non-existent. One of the potential sponsors had dropped out, resigning with a chilly letter about lack of progress. (As he purported to hold the pursestrings that might have started some progress if he'd opened them, this was not as rational a step as it appeared.)

Only now can I see that for all the pain, something was happening during this stage. A small number of the steering group had somehow sustained a mix of increasing frustration with determination not to give up. Of particular importance, Caroline Jones, the City's industrial liaison officer and the new Town Clerk's representative, and Roy Hatton, a technical director of an international company based locally, persisted. Behind the scenes Caroline had been finding funds for an administrative officer to do many of the essential steps within the project – if we could only get it started. Roy Hatton had been experimenting with the Scimitar system in his own company, and had become emphatic that what could work with large companies could be translated to smaller ones.

I began presenting the salient details as a case example to business people attending courses at Manchester Business School. Almost invariably they were astonished at the tale, which was in their eyes a clear example of the bureaucratic idiocies of the public sector. They could not understand why I had had so much difficulty – especially with the top level support forthcoming from the Town Hall. I must have been insufficiently prepared – hence my communications problems. By implication, a competent manager could have sorted it out in next to no time. However, when I asked for practical first steps, it was clear that the managers had as little of value to offer in the way of implementable solutions as I had myself.

Nevertheless, the process did lead to action. The more the managers brainstormed what we should be doing ('get rid of the steering group; ask Prince Charles to help', etc.) the more I developed a conviction that the answer was to get started somehow without waiting for the money ('how to take a second step before the first one').

Additionally there were spin-off activities arising through the contacts made during the Mico start up. A new scheme for putting redundant executives into companies to generate business opportunities was launched at Manchester Business School after discussions with the Manpower Services Commission. This enabled us to introduce some of the creative problem-solving approaches we had in mind for Mico. The scheme in turn provided us with a few firms to try out our methods with more experienced expert consultants.

The first chance to do this arose in the summer of 1985 when we found our first volunteer firm, a manufacturer of textile machinery. This was a little time-window of opportunity, for if we failed to act then we would have to wait for the arrival of the promised administrative help, or for the next available student projects, the following spring. As we were about to start, the Managing Director of the company broke his leg playing tennis. The time window slammed shut, and Mico implementation was as remote as ever.

By the spring of 1986 my own feelings were fatalistic. If money came through we would proceed. If it didn't then the project would sink lower and lower in everyone's priorities – not least my own. Meetings of the steering group had mercifully dropped in frequency, and we had promised to convene the next one only when we had something to report. We were even finding it a far lengthier process than imagined to bring Mico into existence as a legally constituted entity. Caroline Jones had obtained funds for an administrative assistant, part-time, for the project, to start in the summer, but I had severe doubts whether anybody would still be interested if nothing happened until after he or she was in post. The reality was that the idea was limping along with little real effort being expended, but without anyone wanting to call it off either.

During the spring of 1986, a student was co-opted to have one more try at making the elusive 'second step first' by doing some work before there were any funds available to pay him. Our mechanism for this was the availability of his services as part of an innovation project at the Manchester Business School. He in turn was able to draw on several teams of Business School graduates in search of companies where they could practise their creative problem-solving skills. Using the School's network of regional contacts he was able to pick out five promising candidate firms and prepare a report describing them.

The effect of this report on the steering group was a startling boost to morale. Something was actually happening at long last. In addition we were able to announce that Garry, the administrative officer, had been appointed and would be starting work and visiting the firms within the next few months. We seemed to have bought some time to keep interest in the project alive.

The summer of 1986 offered us another brief time-window. Peter, the innovation student, was available to work with Garry, and introduce him to the companies and to the broad background to the Mico concept. There were also other students available to widen our search for companies. Perhaps we could even start helping the companies.

But we had still not really solved the problem of getting started. We couldn't wait for the formation of the company, as this now threatened to run into the autumn, and technically I could not hire any students without a budget with money in it. In the end I asked three students to do the work on the understanding that they would be paid eventually. As the preliminary stages began we became aware of the transient nature of our shortlist of interested companies. Over a period of a few months we might find we had found two and lost one candidate firm. We felt that a pilot study with less than six firms would carry little impact, and were therefore hoping to start with eight firms to allow for drop-outs, which was also the estimated limit of available funds (still awaiting release when the company was formed).

In the autumn of 1986, two and a half years after the idea was first proposed, a group of representatives of six small firms met with six process consultants and the core members of the steering committee who had remained faithful to launch the scheme. Mico had recently become a legal entity, and was able legitimately to offer the firms creative problem-solving support. Within three months we were learning of very positive results inside all the companies. The project was gaining momentum from the numbers of committed people now getting involved.

The pilot project began in the autumn of 1986. By spring 1987 one firm was developing a new product arising out of the problem-definition stage. Three other firms had made progress towards commercializing ideas.

Interim reflections on the project

What can be learned from this anecdotal account? Was the managing of the project as inept as those Business School students seemed to think? Plenty of things could have been done more efficiently. In the becalmed days of the steering group we might all have been better off 'doing' instead of 'talking about doing', for instance, by visiting firms and inviting them to joint meetings. And repeatedly our estimates of time were hopelessly optimistic. And yet, the perceptions of those to whom we told the case details seem to be unrealistic in another way. The project had a pattern to it that is recognizable to those who become involved in the creative problem-solving process. It never was (as the managers implied) something that could have progressed neatly from a planning stage to an implementation of the plan step by step. Rather it was having repeatedly to cope with the unexpected as best as we were able, sometimes doing so imaginatively, other times less adequately. When the goalposts changed in the middle of the game we had to start looking for the new locations of the posts. Furthermore, the whole messy business reflects the kind of problems that our innovating firms are encountering, and which will inevitably require the skills of creative problem-solving. Again, and again and again.

After six months, the results from the first six companies were assessed through consultant and client feedback and a questionnaire.

Four of the six companies had created jobs (19 in the six months of the project). In half these instances, respondents considered that involvement with Mico contributed to the job gain.

More directly linked with the project was the information that five of the six companies considered they had developed improved problem-solving skills and new perspectives on their innovation needs. Four of the six reported gains in marketing skills, three finding benefit from networking with a large business school.

The exercise confirms the experiences of the PII project, Scimitar, and Ethics – namely that creativity at work can be released through the systematic application of the principles of creative problem-solving as they have been outlined in this book.

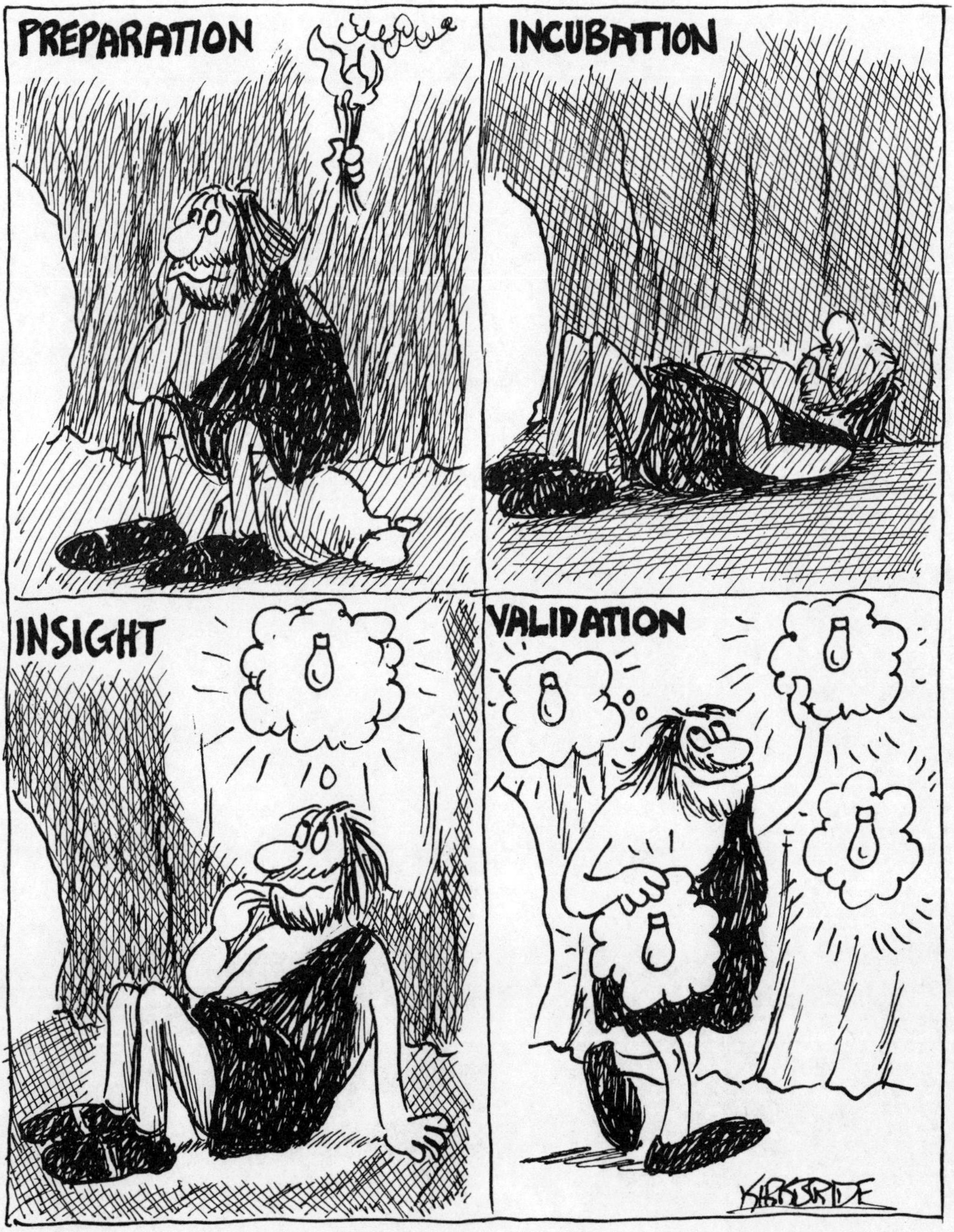
PREPARATION
INCUBATION
INSIGHT
VALIDATION

APPENDIX: Computer-aided creativity

The subject of computer-aided creativity is of growing interest, as computer experts and programmers turn their attention to problems of a kind we have called open-ended in this book.

Networks are emerging whose members share an enthusiasm for such applications, communicating through electronic mail, disks etc. In Europe at least one company has completed a pilot investigation into the introduction of computer-aided creativity for personal and small group applications within its Research Department.

It has been known for some years that a computer can act as a kind of problem-solving adviser. One famous program called Eliza, which dates back to the 1960s, provides convincing responses to enquiries from humans. A well-known incident involved a vice-president of a company who, unwittingly engaged in exchanges with Eliza on a teletype machine, was convinced he was communicating with one of his colleagues. Other accounts tell of a secretary who knew she was talking through her problems to 'just a machine', but who nevertheless acted as if the machine was a kindly human being, and found consolation and help in the interchange.

The program's inventor admitted that the reflective psychiatry model is an easy one for computers to emulate, because the psychiatrist makes no claims to any prior knowledge of the subject's problems. The similarity to a brainstorming leader, or someone seeking to set up and maintain a supportive climate for creative insights, is clear.

Design engineers have found their jobs revolutionized, and their creative potential enhanced, through a range of computer simulations. Computer-aided design is now established as an effective way of promoting engineering creativity.

More recently, in the 1980s programs have been written for personal computers which claim to stimulate creativity. It is now relatively simple to write programs which help you arrange and rearrange your ideas, thus acting as an electronic structuring aid. There are several commercially available programs which help in clustering ideas, and in setting up morphological matrices. Again, the programs are acting as non-directive facilitators, leaving to the users the decisions of what the clusters should be, or what the dimensions of the matrix should be.

There have also been attempts to produce instructions according to the mind sets of the users. At the start of the computer interaction information is collected about the user's learning and problem-solving styles, and subsequently the material generated by the computer is presented so as to be compatible with the user's information processing bias.

Another program invites the users to produce metaphors as aids to creative problem-solving. Once again, the computer program acts in a facilitative mode, although there is scope for designing an expert system version that will give considerable guidance in selecting a metaphor.

Two programs were developed at Manchester Business School over the period 1985–7 as demonstrators of more advanced modes of computer-aided creativity. Their inventor, Tony Proctor, designed one, Oracle, along the lines of the Eliza program. The other, Brain, attempted to provide stimuli for new ideas through unexpected word associations.

Results to date are interesting. Oracle and Brain have been tested on real problems provided by groups of industrial executives, as well as on model problems supplied to Business School graduate students. Different people have completely different reactions to programs. Establishing what factors contribute to acceptance or rejection will be an important next step in the work. There is a parallel with applying creative problem-solving techniques: an approach which works for some people will not be acceptable to others.

Success was measured in terms of the proportion of users claiming that they arrived at new and valuable ideas while working with the programs. Success rates were found to increase

1. when the program incorporates warm-up materials;
2. if opportunities are provided for users to challenge their assumptions and mind sets; and
3. if there were redefinitional stages involving the 'how to' format.

INTERIM CONCLUSIONS

There is already widespread acceptance of computers as thinking aids, through the power of their data storage, manipulation, and retrieval capabilities.

As fourth and fifth generation computing methods become available we shall see exciting advances for users working with fuzzy problems for which there is great scope for creative thinking.

At the time of writing, however, programs of the kind described are harbingers of future promise, rather than effective aids to stimulating creativity. They are already providing research ideas and insights, however. For the future, mind sets need to be broken – not least among designers of software for computer-aided functions. One of the big challenges is to attend to the subtle interactions between a successful creative leader and participants in a creative problem-solving activity. More attention will have to be paid to the 'chemistry' of the interaction between computer and users. What cues will assist in achieving a willingness in the users to loosen up on assumptions and blocking mind sets? How can the climate for creativity be set and maintained?

We know that computers can induce emotions of playfulness and creativity – but mainly when they purvey adventure games. For work applications they seem to induce a highly serious and analytic climate. This is one possible direction for research: the business user as adventure gamester, with the technology helping learning about, and escape from, the dungeons and dragons of inner space. Some obvious design points suggest themselves. There should be powerful cues to indicate that the computer is not operating in its traditional binary, logical mode. The hardware and software should be incorporated unobtrusively into a total creativity-spurring environment. Perhaps the system should have a range of electronic and non-electronic elements which challenge the mind sets of the users. The interaction should refine the existing attempts to reflect user mind sets and user thinking patterns.

Glossary

Practitioners of creative problem-solving techniques have evolved their own vocabulary when referring to various aspects of their work. Although most of the following terms are explained in the text, they are collected together here for easy reference.

Some terms have additional information provided. For example: Brainstorming (BS; CPST). This means that brainstorming is often abbreviated to BS, and that it is a creative problem-solving technique.

Although I have tried to keep cross-referencing to a minimum, some descriptions contain other glossary terms. These are indicated by bold type.

Attribute listing (CPST): A process of brainstorming the attributes of a system in order to uncover opportunities. E.g.: in looking for cost-savings, the attributes of a waste product are listed, and systematically examined, perhaps as part of a team problem-solving effort.

Blockbusting techniques (CPSTs): Deliberate attempts to help individuals or groups to escape from mental blocks. The best known individual methods internationally are the various versions of lateral thinking (but see also **knight's move**).

'Blowing a whistle' (metaphorical, during a meeting): A pre-arranged agreement, especially useful in creative problem-solving meetings, which allows any member of the group to stop the process by announcing a wish to 'blow a whistle'. Without such a signal many meetings deteriorate into general confusion. With it, an individual's uncertainties can be dealt with, and the meeting swiftly put back on course.

Brainstorming (BS; CPST): The most widely known and used family of group CPSTs. Although popularly considered to mean any meeting where ideas are needed, the term technically refers to a structured meeting during which ideas are generated in quantity under conditions of deferred judgement.

Building (on an idea): A deliberate effort to improve an idea – usually within a group. The process helps in setting and maintaining a positive group climate.

Bunch of bananas (CPST): Introducing an unexpected and deliberately irrelevant idea into a group meeting or discussion. The effect is often to trigger new lines of thought, and escape from dominating mind sets.

Buzan diagram (CPST): A visual method of structuring ideas, in which the core idea is written at the centre of a page, with related ideas branching off like spokes of a wheel.

CPST: creative problem-solving technique. Although large numbers of CPSTs are known, many are marginal modifications of earlier methods. Only a handful of techniques satisfy the criteria of having well-described stages or operational mechanisms, and a rationale that is consistent with what we know about creativity, and means of stimulating it.

Close ended problem: Problems with well-defined boundaries which are treated as 'givens'. Creativity occurs within these fixed constraints. (NB: in many work contexts problems are assumed to be close ended, but when the assumptions are recognized and challenged, shifts in perception occur.)

Closing down techniques: CPSTs often result in large numbers of ideas. They are essentially opening up techniques. But each sequence of opening up options requires a closing down technique to reduce the options to manageable proportions.

Cognitive mapping (CPST): A method of representing in graphic form a model of a belief system or mental 'map'. **Buzan diagrams** are examples of the outputs of cognitive mapping.

Comfort zone (psychological, in acceptance seeking): If a person's interest in an idea is low for very low-risk ideas, and low for very high-risk ideas, he or she may be said to have a comfort zone which admits medium-risk ideas. Different people will have different comfort zones, and in presenting ideas it helps to assess the likely comfort zones of key members of the audience.

Creative analysis: A conscious attempt to understand and analyse creative behaviours, particularly those associated with some deliberate strategy for being creative (e.g. during use of a CPST). Creative analysis helps preserve the power of a CPST in generating fresh insights for its regular users.

Creative climate: A rather loosely used term referring to an environment in which new ideas are encouraged (or at least, not discouraged).

Creativity: Hundreds of definitions have been suggested. In this book we have taken the simple one of 'escape from mental stuckness'. Many of the more formal definitions imply a process which leads to a sudden and significant discovery. Novelty and usefulness of the product are emphasized.

Critical examination (CE; CPST): A method for studying and understanding systems, combining idea-spurring checklists, brainstorming and critical evaluation of the ideas produced. It has been extensively used in ICI for engineering projects, including hazard and operability studies, and plant design.

Cube crawling (CPST): A picturesque term to describe the process of systematically exploring the cells or cubes within a three-dimensional matrix in search of new ideas. I would attribute the term to John Carson in the 1970s during his development of the Scimitar method for inventing and commercializing new products for the chemicals industry.

Deferred judgement: The state of mind which is required to permit generation of new and unusual ideas (because censor mechanisms have been weakened). It is a central concept in the brainstorming family of CPSTs.

Eureka moment: The instant of creative discovery, from the story of Archimedes and his bathtime insight, popularized by Arthur Koestler (who also called it the aha! moment).

Excursion (metaphorical): The process of getting away from a problem in order to return with fresh insights. Excursions are practised as an important part of the CPST Synectics during which ideas about a problem are considered in terms of metaphors, and then force fitted back to the original problem.

Fallback strategy: Many behaviours appear to be strongly influenced by dominant mind sets, although there are other approaches or strategies which could be followed. If the automatic choice fails we may switch to a different one, called our fallback strategy. For example, a person with a strong bias for analysis and logic may have a highly intuitive fallback strategy.

Fishbone technique (CPST): A technique often mentioned in Japanese accounts of creativity meetings. Ideas are collected and represented as items linked to a core issue. The result looks like a fishbone.

Force field analysis (**FFA**; CPST): A method for making clear the dynamics of a system to suggest ways of influencing it. Sets of forces assisting a change are represented in equilibrium with forces resisting the change. Implementation efforts should seek to reduce the restraining forces, which otherwise increase as change processes are introduced.

Force-fit (**Forced relationships**; CPST): The process of creating a new idea synthesized out of two partially connected ones, or two unconnected ones. **Building on an idea**, and **'yes anding'**, are specific kinds of force fits. The **lateral thinking** approaches and **excursions** also require the user to combine ideas in this way.

Goal Orientation (**GO**; CPST): A technique which helps focus attention on the central goal or desired achievement during problem solving. The suggested operational mechanism is to describe the problem as a 'how to' statement, including a verb which should trigger off images or 'visions' of what needs to be done.

Gut Feel: Anglo-Saxon version of *intuition*. Sometimes we have a general feeling that we should act in a certain way, without being able to justify it in words. Our senses may be picking up messages which we become conscious of at first through our bodily reactions. Rather than ignore gut feel, or rely slavishly on its messages, we should develop our abilities to treat it as a starting point for decision-making in the absence of other information.

Human Information Processing (**HIP**): A recent (1970s) term adopted by a group of workers interested in the workings of the brain, the essential human information processor.

Idea: In this book we have defined an idea as the conceptual product of someone interpreting or making sense of observed facts or feelings.

Idea killers: Automatic negative responses to ideas by individuals who have strong initial reactions against change. These signals of negative mind sets include habitual 'yes but' and 'it will never work' replies. In bringing about change we have to treat the mind sets as well as the idea-killing statements, which are simply symptoms of the problem.

Incubation: The period between consciously struggling with a problem, and consciously becoming aware of a new idea. Many creative insights follow a period of incubation, when the conscious mind attends to other issues. It is unclear whether the incubation period operates to facilitate memory, or reformulation of data.

Innovation: The process of solving needs in new ways. 'To invent is to find a new thing; to innovate is to get the new thing done'. An invention has to be 'new to the world'; an innovation has only to have some element of novelty in the context in which it is being introduced. (The transistor was an invention; the Sony Walkman was an innovation.)

Insight: The sudden realization of the key principle or relationship of a task – e.g. an elegant solution to a problem. In problem-solving studies, insight learning is taken as evidence of creativity.

Intuition: The ability to reach important conclusions in the absence of hard facts. Psychological tests suggest there are some people who rely strongly on impressions and feelings, and who have a generally intuitive approach to problem-solving. However, it is possible that intuition, like creativity, can be stimulated through training and practice.

Knight's move (KM; CPST): A recent technique for discovering unexpected but valuable ideas – e.g. in competitive situations, or when problems are leading to stuckness. One simple mechanism is to convert either/or thinking into more open-ended thinking, through a reframing of the problem.

Lateral thinking (CPST): Edward de Bono's famous development for escaping from excessive logical ('vertical') thinking, and for discovering new insights. He lists a range of approaches including the deliberate introduction of random stimuli, and seeking after ideas perceived as impossible from a conventional veiwpoint.

Left Brain Thinking: A term found in studies of left/right hemisphere differences to suggest thinking which is dominated by logic and verbal reasoning. The term is mainly used as a contrast with right brain thinking, which has a greater visual and non-verbal content.

Metaphoric thinking: A recurring theme in creativity research is the importance of metaphoric thinking which triggers images of a non-verbal, often highly visual, kind. A metaphor 'works' by linking an evocative symbol with a second item of significance – e.g. a personal problem. Dreams can be interpreted as metaphors.

Mind set: Highly personalized ways of selecting information and interpreting it according to past experience. Mind sets can help us deal with complexities, and speed up problem-solving. They can also lead to stuckness if the world changes, but we persist in interpretations based on our old mind sets.

Morphological analysis (MA; CPSTs): A range of methods of structuring information, and for modelling systems as a starting point to understanding and for idea generation of a systematic kind (e.g. through 'cube crawling' in a three-dimensional MA).

Nominal groups (CPSTs): Versions of brainstorming in which the group members work for some of the time in isolation, to reduce social pressures on vulnerable individuals or groups involved (e.g. shopfloor representatives in the presence of senior managers).

Open-ended problems: Problems whose boundaries are treated as starting points which may be challenged to suggest new possibilities. Thus there are no 'correct answers', only a range of possible solutions.

Opening up techniques: The assorted CPSTs for opening up options in problem-solving and opportunity searching. Best-known families of techniques are versions of **brainstorming**, **lateral thinking**, and structuring techniques like **morphological analysis.**

Operational mechanisms (of a CPST): The describable steps that are put into practice during the execution of a CPST. There are frequently a large number of possible operational mechanisms, with scope for experimentation, taking into account the presumed theoretical precepts of the technique, and the circumstances in use.

Paradigm. A broad framework of knowledge and beliefs, usually shared by a body of people, for example, the scientific management paradigm. Paradigms will contain mind sets which are rarely challenged. Sometimes there is a sudden change ('a paradigm shift') and a different set of beliefs emerge (e.g. when Einstein challenged the Newtonian paradigm).

Process skills (in group leadership): Those skills which are concerned with the general structure and flow of the meeting, and the well-being of the group. In ideas meetings the group leader concentrates entirely on process skills, leaving the task component to appointed experts or owners of the problem.

Quality Circles: Groups of industrial workers assembled to consider ways of achieving improved quality in their work. Members might use the various CPSTs for cost reduction, process improvements, innovations in work practices, even more general quality of working life topics.

Reformulation (**redefinition**, especially in creative problem-solving): The process of seeking new perspectives on problems. The redefinition stage of CPSTs involves generating a range of possible reformulations to increase the chances of discovering more significant and actionable ones. (See **reframing**).

Reframing: The process whereby an individual takes up a substantially new perspective on an important issue. The result is a switch of attention, often with accompanying challenges to beliefs. Reframing can be seen as a kind of personal paradigm shift.

Right-brain thinking: A useful description for a mode of thinking identified with activity in the right cerebral hemisphere, and contrasted with left-brain thinking (located in the left hemisphere). Right-brain thinking is more visual, and concerned with relationships. Left-brain thinking is more verbal and logical. Research continues apace; the terms are at best over-simplifications, and should be treated as metaphors, not physiologically accurate descriptions.

SCAMPER (CPST): A simplified version of an idea-spurring checklist: substitute, combine, adapt, modify, put to other uses, eliminate, reverse. Of use in engineering and design ideas sessions, and Quality Circles.

Structuring techniques: Methods of structuring complex systems so that relationships can be investigated. **Morphological analyses**, **Buzan diagrams**, **checklists**, are examples of them. They are sometimes, but not always, linked to creative efforts and innovation seeking.

Stuckness (mental): A shorthand for the state of being unable to find satisfactory ways to resolve a problem. The stuckness may require the challenging of a deeply-held assumption or mind set. Escaping from stuckness produces the moment of insight (although this new perception will itself involve its own assumptions and mind sets).

SWOT analysis: A way of understanding a business situation by examining the strengths and weakness of the business, and the threats and opportunities in its environment. The technique offers scope for creative thinking, especially in turning threats into opportunities, and weaknesses into strengths.

Synectics (CPST): A well-researched approach to creative problem-solving. It provides a supportive environment for individuals and ideas, through skilful process leadership, and opening up and closing down techniques at problem, and idea searching, stages. The technique has contributed to our understanding of **excursions** as ways of operationalizing metaphors in problem-solving.

Trigger sessions (CPST): A version of **nominal group** brainstorming. Individuals use small cards to write ideas on. Each idea card is subsequently examined and further ideas triggered off.

Vicious problems: Problems in which the obvious 'solutions' create bigger problems. Industrial and political problems are often tackled so that they become vicious.

Visioning/visualizations (in CPSTs): Several CPSTs (e.g. Synectics) encourage the discovery of goals in visual terms. A visualized goal can be communicated and shared in a motivating way which assists commitment and action.

Wicked problems: Situations in which important problem-solving decisions commit those involved irrevocably to the exclusion of other possibilities. The design of the traditional production-line is an example. The decision to build multistorey flats was another. There are usually opportunities for reducing the dangers of wicked problem-solving when you are sensitive to the dangers of premature design descisions.

'Yes and' (CPST): A simple but powerful way of dealing with negativity, setting a positive climate, and strengthening emerging ideas. The operational mechanism is to respond to perceived weaknesses in a genuine attempt to overcome them. ('yes and . . . we could reduce the cost by subcontracting'. not 'yes but . . . it would cost too much for us to make it.')

Recommended reading

A manager once told me that he was suspicious of people who gave hundreds of references at the back of books they had written. 'They must be doing it to impress somebody', he went on, 'but all I want is a very short list of books for me to go more deeply into the subject.'

'How short a list?' I asked, ignoring his scurrilous remark about the motives of academic authors.

'Six would do nicely,' he replied, 'if you couldn't get it any shorter. And it would help if you could say something about each of the books to help me decide if I wanted to read it or not.'

Well, that was the challenge. To offer a follow-up course of self-study for those who have gone round the creative problem-solving golf course and would like to dig more deeply into the subjects presented. In the traditions of creative search I first made a list of all the books that had influenced my thinking and writings over the last twenty years. Then I culled the list by eliminating those that were written primarily for academics, or highly specialized research workers. Also out went books that are now difficult to obtain, and important earlier books if they have been summarized elsewhere.

This process cut me down from several hundred references to about thirty, and then to fifteen. The final list includes some important texts dealing with creativity, and also some with broader themes such as organizational psychology and general business practices. Together they provide a practical set of starting points for anyone interested in a deeper understanding of creativity at work.

Adams, J.L. (1980), *Conceptual Blockbusting: A Guide to Better Ideas*, (2nd ed), Norton, USA. An easy-to-read book introducing the general principles of creative problem-solving, originally intended for engineers and students. You will find a lot of Adams 'borrowed' in later popular paperbacks on creativity.

Belbin, M. (1981), *Management Teams: why they Succeed or Fail*, Heinemann. One of the few research-based explanations of the roles people take up in teams, and why we need a mix of different types of people to make up a good team. Can make an excellent diagnostic tool for team selection and understanding possible weaknesses in teams.

Blanchard, K. and Johnson, S. (1982), *The One Minute Manager*, William Morrow, NY. Brief, elegant, brilliant account of a series of techniques for effective people management. The techniques of goal setting, rewarding effective behaviour, and giving constructive critical feedback, are versions of creative problem-solving techniques.

de Bono, E. (1971), *Lateral Thinking for Management*, McGraw-Hill. Edward de Bono is one of the most fluent and readable writers on stimulating creativity. This early book outlines his conceptual framework, the general philosophy of lateral thinking, and its best-known techniques.

Isaksen, S.G. and Treffinger, D.J. (1988, 2nd ed.), *Creative Problem-Solving: The Basic Course,* Bearly, Buffalo, USA. Authoritative manual on creative problem-solving from the leading creativity research institute at State University Buffalo.

Kanter, R.M. (1983), *The Change Masters*, Counterpoint, London. Classic study of organizations that change, and the people who bring about the change.

Kolb, D.A., Rubin, I.M. and McIntyre, J.M. (1979), *Organizational Psychology: a Book of Readings*, Prentice Hall, NJ. Designed to be used with the text *Organizational Psychology: an Experiential Approach*, by the same authors, these readings equip the manager and student of management alike with current ideas in organizational psychology, with particular strengths in problem-solving, motivation, perception, and group dynamics.

Ornstein, R.E. (1975), *The Psychology of Consciousness*, 2nd ed., J. Cape, London. The pioneering book which drew popular attention to the role of 'right-brain' behaviours in human problem-solving. Authoritative and mind-expanding.

Peters, T.J. and Waterman, R.H. (1982), *In Search of Excellence*, Harper and Row, NY. Managers need to read this book, if only to communicate with the large numbers of other managers who have been influenced by its deceptively simple messages of effective corporate behaviours, such as attention to quality, concern for the customer, building on strengths ('sticking to your knitting') and so on.

Prince, G. (1970), *The Practice of Creativity*, Harper and Row, NY. George Prince describes the early work which led to the Synectics approach for creative problem-solving. Many later workers were strongly influenced by this work, and reading the book gives insights into the deliberate use of metaphor ('excursions'), goal seeking through 'how tos', and ways of setting up meetings to release the creativity of the participants.

Rawlinson, G. (1981), *Creative Thinking and Brainstorming*, Gower. The most readable British book on brainstorming. The author was a pioneer in introducing the technique in Europe, and wrote from great practical experience.

Rickards, T. (1985), *Stimulating Innovation*, Frances Pinter. Yes, well, it does cover all those other books I didn't have room for in this short list. It describes the process of forming a new products group through the recounted experiences of its four members, and through more traditional summaries of central issues such as innovation, organizational structures and strategies, leadership, and teamwork.

Rogers, C.R. (1980), *A Way of Being*, Houghton Mifflin, Boston. Carl Rogers is perhaps the most influential humanistic psychologist of his time. Rogerian psychology emphasizes the capacity of every individual to develop through creative discovery of his or her potential. It also offers a practical and ethical system for working with other people and dealing with personal problems.

Smith, M., Beck, J., Cooper, C.L., Cox, C., Ottaway, R. and Talbot, R. (1982), *Introducing Organisational Behaviour*, Macmillan. A clear and understandable introductory text from a leading British Department of Management Sciences. Includes a good chapter on creativity.

Vernon, P. (1970), *Creativity*, Penguin. This (paperback) book of readings covers a wealth of material from introspective studies by great inventors and artists, to important psychological experiments into the nature of creativity. With one or two exceptions the articles are very readable, and give a good summary of the main ideas on the nature of the creative process.

Index

active listening 98
Adams, J. 232
'Aha' effect, see eureka
alcohol (creativity myth) 171
attribute listing 223

Bath, University of 159
Battelle Institute 95
Beckhard (change equation) 198
Belbin, M. 232
deBono, E. 74, 232
Blanchard, K. 232
Blake's grid 121, 125
blockbusting 73ff, 223, 232
blocks (to creativity) 16ff
   tricking your way out of thinking blocks, 16
'blowing a whistle', in group work 105, 107ff, 157, 223
Boston Consulting Group (grid) 121
BRAIN computer program 220
brainstorming 21, 31, 45 62ff, 91ff, 161, 166, 171, 181ff, 224, 225
   benefits from 94ff
   case examples 152ff 166ff
   definition 93
   leading 104ff

nominal group version 31
   planning 101ff
   structured 112ff
   visual 112
   when to use 110
Buijs, J. 207ff, 211
'bunch of bananas' technique 80ff, 122, 190
building (on an idea) 224 (see also, 'yes and' technique),
Buzan, A. 116
   diagrams 116ff, 162, 224

Carson, J. 122, 203ff, 211, 225
case examples
   breakaway lamp standards 32ff
   changing corporate culture 192ff
   diversification 160
   engineering problems 147ff, 166
   force field analysis 140
   introducing new technology 179ff
   lasers 78ff
   penicillin 78
   pilferage 77ff
   strategy formulation using metaphor 37
   unreproductive result 78

INDEX

unsuccessful problem-solving 151ff
chess
  intuition in 44–5
  and the horse's head symbol 6
checklists 115ff, 123ff, 210, 225
Churchill W. 38
climate 81, 109, 111, 165, 174, 194ff, 209
  creative 18ff, 225
  setting 20
closing down techniques 43ff
  clustering 44, 47, 54
  decision tree 53ff
  gut feel 44ff, 54
  hurdles 48ff, 54
  voting 46ff, 51, 54
  weighting systems 49, 54
comfort zones 141
cognitive mapping 160, 224
comfort zone (psychological) 224
concept challenge 76ff
creative
  analysis vii, 58ff, 66, 101, 177, 225
  problem solving 26ff
    techniques (CPSTs) 17, 62ff, 224
  process 10
creativity ix, 9, 17, 21, 133, 225, 232ff
  computer aided 219ff
  stimulation 35ff, 73ff, 123ff, 159
critical examination 124, 225
'cube crawling' technique 122, 225
culture (corporate) 168
  changing 192ff

DBMs (Do By Monday actions) 113, 176
Delbecq and Van de Ven 99ff
Delphi techniques 51
defer judgement principle 26ff, 225
diverge/converge couple 26ff, 27, 62
Duggan, R. 203

either/or thinking 40, 84ff
Eliza (computer programme) 219
Elliott, P. 83
empathy 135ff
ETHICS system 209ff
eureka (moment of insight) 10, 13, 17, 225
excursions in problem-solving 65, 225

'the eye buys' 132

fall back strategy 40ff, 83, 225
  decisions, 45ff
fishbone technique 121, 225
Fleming, A. 78
force field analysis 138ff, 198ff, 226
force-fit 226
  problem-solving 66, 87
forced relationships 226
frameworks for thinking 115ff
Freud, S. 34ff

General Motors 132
Germany, creativity techniques in use 100
Glossary 223ff
goal orientation (GO) 28ff, 42, 172ff, 184, 226, 233
  right brain technique 134ff
  metaphor production 37
Gordon, W.J. 96
gut feel 44ff, 51, 226

Hatton, R. 213
how to (*see* goal orientation)
human information processing, (HIP) 226
hurdles, (screening technique) 48–9

IBM 179ff
ICI 124, 181
idea, (definition) 59, 226
  killers 226
  screening 206ff
implementation 127ff
  strategies 128ff
  of new technology training 188ff
incubation 35, 47, 226
innovation 13, 132ff, 226, 233
  structured approaches 166ff, 202ff, 210
  teams 144ff, 179, 193ff, 202ff, 233
insight 10ff, 26, 35, 73ff, 87, 227
inspiration, misguided 45
instant winner decisions 45, 175
intermediate impossible 74ff
intrapreneurs 147ff
intuition, (see also gut feel) 13, 44ff, 227
Isaksen, S.G. 232

Japan, creativity technique 48

INDEX

Jones, C. 213
Jones, L. 192ff
Jones, S. 159

Kanter, R.B. 232
Kekule, insight into structure of benzene 35
Kepner-Tregoe, decision-making system 49
Kettering, C. 132ff
killer phrases 28
King, Martin Luther 38
Kipling, checklist 124
Kolb, D. 232
KJ technique 48
knight's move thinking 83ff, 227
Kroyer, K. 95

lateral thinking 73ff 87, 227
leadership
  creative 20ff
  facilitating 20
  process-oriented 20
left brain thinking viii, 14, 16ff, 28, 40ff, 44ff, 80, 99, 210
Lever Brothers 203
Little, A.D. 96
Loose-tight, organizational structures 40

Management Development, Journal of 159
Manchester Business School 83, 179, 209, 213, 220
mapping, technique 159ff
  cognitive 160
memory hooks 116
metaphor 24ff, 36, 227
  blockbusting 34ff
  ideas sessions 65, 122, 148ff, 152ff, 233
MICO 210ff
mind maps 115ff
mind set(s) 15ff, 19, 21, 39, 221, 227
  and goal orientation 30
  and implementation 127ff, 141ff, 177
  dominant 46
  'set to break' 15
minibrainstorming 65, 183
monopoly 131
morphological methods 115ff
  analysis 119ff, 227
Mumford, E. 209

nominal group techniques 99ff, 227

Oech, R., von 18
operational mechanisms (of techniques) 61ff
opportunities 39ff
ORACLE, computer programme 220
Ornstein, R. 17
Osborn, A. 62, 93, 202
  checklist 123

paradigm 228
Parnes, S. 93
Peters and Waterman 40, 232
PII project (Holland), 207ff
PIS system 26, 97
precepts 67
Prince G. 96, 99, 232
problems
  challenge 79
  fuzzy 14, 44
  insight 13
  one right answer 12
  open-ended/close ended 228
  solving 12
  swotting 79
  types 12ff
  vicious 13, 137ff
  wicked 13
process consultancy 207ff
  skills 228
Proctor, A. 220
PROFS networking system 187ff
puxxles 22ff

quality Circles 95, 96, 228, 229

random juxtaposition technique 75ff
Rawlinson, G. 95, 233
redefinition, in problem-solving 28ff, 37, 42, 228
relaxed attention 36
relevance systems 118ff
reframing 228
reversals 77ff
Rickards, T. 233
right brain 14, 28, 30, 41ff, 44ff, 157, 228
  creativity myth as 14
ripeness, in ideas 39
risk 19
Rogers, C. 233

SCAMPER technique 124, 229
scimitar system 203ff, 211, 225
set to break set 6, 15
sex (Freudian symbolism of sexual problems) 35
Sims, D. 159
6-3-5 method 99
Smith, M. 233
split-page problem-solving 65
Steetley organisation 122
strategies
   fall back 40ff
   dominant 40ff
   implementation 127ff
stress, and mind sets 15
structures for creativity 125ff
structuring techniques 229, *see also* 115ff
stuckness 16, 26, 182, 229
   escape from 24ff, 59, 82ff
   option deficiency 24ff
   option surfeit 24, 27, 43
   signs of ('SOS' signals) 80
   technique 62ff
SWOT technique 79, 229
synectics 18, 96ff, 148ff, 202, 206, 229, 233

systems thinking 131ff

Taylor, R. 211
tramlines, mental 160, 164
trigger sessions 99, 154, 229

value engineering 94
vision getting and giving 38ff, 133ff, 186, 229
voting, in decision making 46ff, 100

WGAI, reminder for positive behaviour 20
Wallis, B. 36
warm-up (before creative group work) 100, 108ff, 153ff, 192, 221
weighting techniques 49ff
whole brain ix, 14, 18, 82, 159
   storming 112
wishful thinking 82

'yes and' 31, 42, 87, 99, 190, 230

zero defect objectives 110